Skipping Through the Graveyard
in My Puke-Stained Suit:
Growing up in 1970s Rural Pennsylvania

by William S. Repsher

D1413767

Skipping Through the Graveyard in My Puke-Stained Suit: Growing Up in 1970s Rural Pennsylvania

Credits

The chapter "Sympathy for the Devil" originally appeared in *NYPress*.

The chapters "Little League," "My First Drunk," "The Blue Shirt" and elements of "Fore!" originally appeared on *Leisuresuit.net*.

Many of the other chapters, or elements thereof, have appeared on my blog, *Positively Catherine Street*.

The photographs are from my family collection. Erica Schwamlein took my current photo that appears in a strange way in the "About the Author" section.

Cover design by Scott Sullivan.

Blame this fiasco on my English teachers, all of them, but in particular:

At North Schuylkill School District:

Patricia Brennan, nee Murphy

Robert Judd

Thomas Smeltzer

At Penn State University:

Charles Cantalupo

Robert C.S. Downs

I also want to include the late J. Keith Christian, aka John Orzechowski, who inspired me with his DIY, country/punk spirit and would have loved this.

Table of Contents

2017: Introduction

Last year, it occurred to me that I've spent more time living in New York City than I have in rural Pennsylvania. I was born and raised there, left when I was 23. This year marks my 30th anniversary of living in the city. I arrived at a time when the stock market had crashed only weeks earlier, and the crack epidemic was in full bloom. The city was at a low point, but it made perfect sense to me. My rent at Eddie Cornier's boarding house in the Bronx was $180.00/month. I came with a suitcase full of clothes, my stereo and maybe $500.00 to my name.

Am I a New Yorker? You tell me, but I can tell you that I don't feel like one. I know this place has seeped into my being over time and strongly influences how I see the world. Deep down, beneath whatever layers of street smarts, worldly experience and painstaking lessons on human nature this city imparts, I am from a small town in northeast Pennsylvania: Fountain Springs. That will always be how I see myself. Not a good or bad thing, not some declaration of independence, or any disrespect towards New York City. I'm sure there are native New Yorkers living in rural America who understand they're New Yorkers, through and through.

More recently, it occurred to me that after decades of writing, whether it was the failed novel of my 20s, my time at *NYPress* (working for the great John Strausbaugh), running concurrently with my time at *Leisuresuit.net* (kudos to Jordan Hoffman and Kerry Douglas Dye), and over the past decade on my blog, *Positively Catherine Street*, I now have enough material to construct a road map to my childhood in Pennsylvania, starting roughly in 1972 and ending in 1984 when I went away to college. I'm not sure if I can do this for any other part of my life. It feels like that distance, of time and space, has allowed me to see those days as clearly as I ever will. It's not enough to have a memory; it takes years to place it in context and see how it fits in with the rest of your life.

This book is only a beginning. There is no middle or end. There is no moral to the story. I'm hoping to convey how it was for me growing up in a small town in the 70s, into the early 80s. Much like Billy Pilgrim in Kurt Vonnegut's *The Slaughterhouse Five*, I will become unstuck in time. I'll position a story in 1978, but it may have roots in 1969, and end in 1983. That may not be how narratives work, but that's how memories work. This is a book of memories, which never play by the rules. Sometimes I will use real names for people in the book, other times initials or fake names. This is based on my comfort level as a writer; names have been changed to protect the guilty.

Back in the 90s while rooting through a work desk in a midtown Manhattan office, I came across a religious pamphlet called "This Was Your Life." I liked the story line: a middle-aged man is driving to work when his car goes over the high side and bursts into a ball of flames. This is only the beginning. The man meets up with St. Peter, who guides him to a celestial theater. This is where the man will watch a movie encompassing every second of his life -- filmed, I take it, from God's omniscient camera angles. In this case, it was a sad ending, as the man was given a Siskel and Ebert-style thumbs down and sent to his eternal damnation.

The last frame of the comic is the man's face surrounded by flames, emblazoned with that great comic-book exclamation, "AAAIIIIEEEEEE" with four exclamation points. That pamphlet got me thinking. Wouldn't hell itself already be watching a movie of every second of your life? The pamphlet boiled it down to key moments, but our lives contain vast seas of drudgery and routine.

Drama and deeper meaning are not every-day parts of our lives. Most of it is working, sleeping, eating, traveling, relaxing. Thankfully, I will be glossing over these topics, although I've noticed a propensity for bodily functions that won't win me any Pulitzers. I'm not searching for meaning here. The memories that stay in our heads often don't appear to have any connection to a larger theme. Sometimes the most important events in our lives become vague over time, while some passing moment from 1977 stays with us forever. I try to capture a little of both here. This is not the movie of my life. My ass gets sore spending over two hours in a theatre, much less the decades it would take to watch the movie of my life in that celestial cinema house. I can't guarantee you won't have the same reaction as the man in the last frame of "This Was Your Life" after reading this, but if you're still with me, let's go back to 1972.

1972: Easter Sunday

There's a picture of me from Easter Sunday 1972, smiling broadly, surrounded by my family. My family members are dressed in their Sunday finest, fresh from church, even Mom, the filthy Protestant who was always on the outside of the Catholic stranglehold my grandmother (who lived with us) enforced with an iron hand.

The simple fact that I'm wearing a grey USA t-shirt in the picture while the rest of the family is dressed up is a tip-off that something here is askew. That t-shirt says a lot to me. As some of you may recall, 1972 was a Summer Olympics year, this one encompassing the infamous Munich terrorist incident. Easter was long before the start of these Olympics. All the kids in the neighborhood had caught Olympic fever early. We spent a lot of time that spring staging our own Olympics: runs around the cemetery, throwing home-made javelins and shot-puts, wrestling. No organization. A bunch of kids getting together and staging their own Olympics. The long run winner was determined by the last kid standing, as kids have no concept of distance and would conk out after a few hundred yards.

I was wearing that t-shirt because my Sunday's finest were soiled. Why were my clothes soiled?

The story starts early Easter morning, which began as it always did for us as kids. Easter was behind only Christmas and Halloween in terms of childhood excitement. That's because we knew we'd wake up to find the Easter Bunny had visited overnight and left us with baskets filled with goodies: all sorts of chocolate, jelly beans, our painted eggs, etc. Tons of candy. All to celebrate Christ rising from dead. We never made the connection between chocolate Easter rabbits and Jesus. Shouldn't we have been eating chocolate crucifixes and such? We gathered that Easter also represented a type of spring/renewal ritual. The major joy wasn't Christ's resurrection; it was gorging ourselves on candy.

That's exactly what we did. Every year, we made pigs of ourselves. One of the few things my parents did wrong was inundate us with sugar products. Our childhood was riddled with junk food. We normally had bad diets and as a result were chubby kids. I think it was two things: junk food was cheaper and within budget, and our Depression-era parents knew how to eat only small portions of junk, whereas we didn't.

Easter was an all-out chocolate frenzy. Our parents would warn us not to eat too much, but that was fruitless. We'd go crazy on the Hershey's and other candy bars thrown in haphazardly with the more Easter-styled chocolate products: rabbits and flowers that came in special boxes made for the holiday.

My undoing that morning was a gigantic chocolate rabbit's head. This thing was the size of a doberman's skull, solid milk chocolate and must have weighed a pound. The whole thing went in my belly, along with half a jar of peanut butter I kept dipping chunks of the rabbit head in. I'm sure I ate other junk on top of that, but that big head sticks in my memory. I was waddling around like the child version of Orson Welles after that.

That was the first part of the morning. The next was to go to Easter mass, which meant getting dressed up in our best clothes and walking across the cemetery to our Catholic church for a long, special mass. Dad would always attend mass with us on Christmas but often not Easter. (Dad was a different kind of Catholic: the kind who would get dressed up in a suit and tie, tell us all he was going to mass the next town over, then he'd drive off, and no doubt cruise around for 45 minutes, listening to a Big Band station on the radio, over-joyed to have that much time to himself, his only "alone" time aside from driving to and from work. He'd then come back with Sunday papers, and treats like Tastycakes and such.)

We had the same pew in church: the first one on the right. It was ours. I don't know how this happened. I think it was our grandmother was so fanatical about church attendance that we'd get there early and stake out the pew. Not just that. Fountain Springs was and is a small town of a few hundred people, and it was mostly the same people attending each week. Most of them had their prime spots staked out, the smart ones in the back, near Sharon M, wearing her huge peace-sign necklace as she pumped out religious numbers on her Wurlitzer. It was a rare session that we didn't get that front right pew.

You better believe we got it Easter Sunday, which was no small feat, as Easter, along with Christmas, was that mass where all the part-time Catholics made sure to put in a cameo appearance, an SRO performance. I stopped going to church all together in my mid-teens and don't regret it. I never liked church, wasn't particularly enthused by the mass itself, and had a boat-load of issues related to Grandma forcing us to go constantly. It felt like not so much a chore, but a punishment we had to endure. I certainly don't fault anyone who attends mass and feels a sense of spiritual enlightenment and duty from it. I respect the fact that they have this thing in their lives that serves as a rock of stability. But it wasn't for me.

Nor Mom. In that picture she's dressed for church, so I'm guessing she went to visit her Brother Bob in Pottsville and attended Protestant mass with his family. She usually didn't go to church at all. I envied her.

So, we got to Mass. Father B was the new priest in town, replacing old standby Father M, who had been the well-loved parish priest for decades. I remember him once grabbing me by the shoulders and wailing, "Sing, child, sing" when he noticed none of us kids was going along with the hymn – "Faith of Our Fathers" or something. He was a good old guy. Father B seemed all right, too. Years later, while he was serving in another parish near Allentown, a break-in at his rectory lead police investigators to uncover a photo album with pictures of underage boys in various states of undress. Despite my grandmother's burning desire to make all us kids altar boys, my parents put the ix-nay on that, possibly sensing that Father B was chicken-hawking his way through life. We came to call him "Father Bendover" – a ghoulish play on his surname. It really wasn't all that funny to learn this about him years later.

That revelation was years in the future, and all was well that Easter Sunday morning in 1972. Save for one thing. I was starting to feel nauseous. Feverish. Dizzy. Not good. Not good in a way that suggested I should get out of there. Now. It came over me in a hurry. No doubt, I was white as a sheet and sweating profusely. Easter Sundays were weird in that one year we'd have a blizzard, the next it could be 70 degrees. This one was a moderate spring day. I knew I had an upset stomach from eating all that candy.

I had to communicate this to Grandma, who was sitting a few people down. I was on the end of the pew, near the stained-glass window, Sister K was next to Grandma, Brothers J and M were next to me. They let Grandma know I wasn't doing well, and her response was to pass me her hanky. Under no circumstances was I to leave. Just couldn't happen on Easter Sunday. Probably wouldn't happen on any

Sunday, but certainly not this one. I was told to tough it out, that this spell would pass, and I'd feel fine in a few minutes.

My stomach had other plans. I don't know how I did this, but I somehow managed to choke up a sample puke into that hanky. A little stream of dark-brown bile. I held it out in front of me, like an offering, and quietly pleaded with Grandma to let me get out of there. She still shook her head no. I could see J and M getting queasy, like a pair of inmates in a cell with a lunatic who was about to have a psychotic episode.

I'm sure I did everything I could to stop it. There was no stopping it. Moments later, I vomited.

When I say "vomited," I don't mean some tasteful little ralph into my lap. I exploded, a gushing, brown fountain of stomach bile. Projectile vomiting of all the chocolate I had gorged myself on that morning, along with whatever I had stored up from the night before. Nose and mouth. It nearly came out of my eyes. Some went straight into the pew, some onto my navy blazer and grey corduroy pants, but most flew over the dark mahogany railing.

Until you're doing it, you tend to forget how traumatic vomiting is. It's an awful experience under any circumstance: frightening, painful and jarring. To do so in the front pew of Easter Mass was mind-blowing. If a naked savage had burst into the church and heaved a spear into a statue of the Virgin Mary, it would have been less shocking. This was during a quiet part of the Mass. Father B was singing some lines in Latin. Parishioners were silently praying, so the full effect of my groaning, sobbing and splashing was seen, heard and smelled by all.

I recall looking up, a chocolaty mulch oozing from my nose and mouth, and seeing the altar boy Joey C doubled over in laughter. He was laughing so hard that he screwed up that part of the mass where one of the altar boys rings a small xylophone. He got it backwards, the tones descending rather than ascending. I knelt there grasping the rail with my

Sunday's finest stained with dark brown vomit, which had the appearance of shit and blood mixed together. I turned to see brother J in absolute shock, his eyes about to roll back up in his head, and trying hard not to vomit himself. Brother M was much like Joey C – in total, crying hysterics and trying to push J into my massive pool of vomit, in which one could still decipher partially-digested chunks of that rabbit's head, an ear here, an eye there, a half-digested marshmallow chick also in the mix.

Well, I finally got out of there. No one stopped me! The strange thing was, aside from Brother J and Grandma rushing out the front door with me, nobody moved. Father B didn't skip a beat; he'd seen stuff like this many times before. Those were some hard-core Catholics. That church smelled like a dead dog's asshole. I had unloaded the contents of my stomach, and it's unbelievable how much strange, unidentifiable substance that entails. Not one of those parishioners left, although I recall making eye contact with a few who had hankies and tissues pressed over their noses and mouths. The look wasn't so much outrage or pity as "you little bastard." If I were them, I would have fled that church as if it was on fire. Anyone with half an ounce of common sense would have bolted. But not on Easter Sunday! The mass went on, and people maneuvered around the brown, stinking puddle after receiving holy communion. A real statement would have been blowing chunks directly after receiving communion, but I couldn't hold out that long.

I can't recall exactly what happened next. Grandma probably yelled at me, not realizing that I had given her full warning, pleaded with her to let me go, and all I gave her was payback for not recognizing the gravity of the situation. (She was the one who would later clean up the unholy mess with mop and bucket.) J was still too freaked out to do anything. Grandma simply asked if I could walk home. I could. I felt great, as does anyone who has one of those life-affirming regurgitations where it feels like every negative thing in your life has just been expelled from your body. I skipped through the graveyard in my puke-stained suit, feeling pretty good about life.

There was no punishment afterwards. I got sick – I surely hadn't intended to, one of those freaky kid things. Went back to church the next week, and all was forgiven. This act took on legendary proportions in my childhood. I was the kid who puked in church on Easter Sunday which had a large cartel of coolness attached to it. I recall playing this up as some grand statement of how I felt about church. When movies like *The Exorcist* and *The Omen* came out, I would tie in this act with Regan and Damien's brazen anti-religious acts in both movies. It could have been easily avoided if Grandma hadn't been so adamant about making me stay the course that day. Otherwise, it would have been a kid blowing chunks into a bush by the side of the road and coming back into church. A combination of events turned it into one of those mythical childhood exploits.

1972: Butch

Mom found him in a cardboard box by the loading dock on the right side of the Acme parking lot in Ashland. It wasn't the first time she found abandoned, often beaten, dogs dumped there. She wouldn't admit it, but she parked over there on purpose to make sure this hadn't happened again, although it happened routinely.

Butch was our second dog. (Smokey was the first: a large, black collie who could get nippy if his tail got yanked hard enough, but in general was good with kids.) Butch was truly a mutt, hard to tell what breed he was. Surely part terrier. Maybe a little beagle. A nondescript hound with no clear lineage, who had been beaten and left for dead in a cardboard coffin by a supermarket.

Usually Mom would take these animals in for a week or two, feed and nurse them back to health, then take them to the animal shelter, albeit the one with the no-kill policy, which was a dealbreaker with her and the SPCA-sanctioned shelter. She couldn't bear the thought of an animal she had cared for being put down months later because no one wanted it. If it wasn't for people like Mom, the animals more than likely would have wandered off into nearby woods to die. What was the point in killing them after saving them?

Butch was different. Smokey had died a year earlier, and we were at a rare loss for a family dog. He was a strangely wise and serene dog from the first time we met him, like an elderly friend. He developed the habit of picking up his empty food bowl, walking it over to the nearest human with a sad look in his eye, and somehow understanding this routine would get him more dog food. He became a plump, happy mutt as a result, after being found so gaunt his rib cage was visible through his fur.

My childhood was spent watching Mom rehabilitate lost dogs. She became an expert at it, especially with strays who wandered the neighborhood back then. Lost or abandoned dogs were left to fend for themselves, feeding off garbage cans and the occasional meals put out by kindly people who didn't want or need another dog in the house. Nor did we, but we often would as Mom worked her magic any time a strange dog was spotted traipsing through our neighborhood. It started with soft, reassuring words, an extended hand that was shied away from. The next day, leaving some food out, which the dog would devour – this, of course, being the key to winning over the starving animal. Third day, more food, the extended hand and calm, reassuring words. By the fifth or sixth day, there was the moment, when the dog's head bashfully rose to meet Mom's extended hand, and the war was over. She'd try to wash the dog a few days later then take it down to the animal shelter to hopefully find a better owner than the one he had.

She surely didn't know it, but she was teaching us by example. How to live. How to see the world. How to change things, if change was at all possible. It rarely happened with dramatic strokes and bold declarations. It happened quietly, in small increments, over time, one good turn leading to another, and eventually a door that seemed impassible would slowly swing open. Lost dogs were a great way to grasp this as they were so smart and forced into mercenary conditions the way she found them, underneath simply wanting to belong, somewhere. Of course, we learned the flipside, too: there were evil pricks in our midst.

That was the interesting thing about Butch. He was fully approachable from the first moment Mom laid eyes on him in his rain-soaked, forsaken box. Most dogs in those boxes were distrusting and snarling, made painfully aware of what humans were capable of. Butch was an open book, despite whatever harm had been perpetrated on him.

He also had the shortest lifespan of any dog we ever had, given that he already must have been middle-aged by the time Mom found him. He developed health problems almost immediately, gas being one of them. Farting was generally cause for laughter in our house, at least among the boys, like cavemen marveling at the obtuse sounds bursting from their bottoms. Not when Butch left one. Those farts were brutal. We would always try to blame each other, but generally farting was a team sport with prepubescent males, each trying to gross out the other with how loud and foul he could crank one out. When we got hit by a silent-but deadly-wave of methane, it was often a sign that Butch, gently dozing in a bar of sunlight cast on a throw rug, was cracking rats in his sleep.

I went with Mom and Dad to see what could be done. The vet produced a six-inch long charcoal stick and didn't say anything. "Which end do we put in?" Dad asked. I couldn't stop laughing. Of course, Butch would have to chew on these sticks to decrease his gaseous emissions. Unfortunately for Butch, he did experience some rectal discomfort as the vet then took his temperature the most accurate, and uncomfortable, way. I'd never seen his eyes grow so wide and expressive. It was one of those childhood things: the most I've ever laughed in any medical office.

I wouldn't be laughing for long. He was eventually diagnosed with heart problems that required liquid medication to be fed to him orally, with an eye dropper. These feedings were awful. Butch knew what was coming and grew agitated, always choking horribly on the dropper in his mouth. Two people had to do it, one to hold him down and the other to guide in the dropper without getting nipped on the hand.

That's how he died early one spring morning in 1972. Brother J and I were in the living room, just up and getting ready for school. We could hear Mom and Dad in the kitchen. J said that Butch had been hacking earlier and that Mom and Dad could see something was way off about him. They were in the kitchen trying to administer the medication. The last thing we heard was that awful hacking sound, followed by stunned silence, then Mom eventually gasping, "He's gone."

I surely wept a few times after that, but that morning I wept openly, my first brush with death where I was old enough to have some idea of what it meant. Mom tried to comfort me, but I was inconsolable, in my pajamas long after it was time for school. I eventually got dressed, and Mom walked me up to school, explaining to my second-grade teacher what had happened that morning. She was so kind to me that day. A day later, I snuck down into the basement to see Butch one last time. He was in a cardboard box again, wrapped in an old blanket. At least this time the box meant he had spent the past few years of his life being treated like royalty instead of getting his ass kicked by a redneck. I unfolded the top of the box, and there was Butch, his head poking out of the blanket. His eyes were blank, nothing there. It hit me directly that he was gone. I started crying again, shut the flaps and ran out of there. Dad would later bury him in a corner of the backyard where all our dogs went when their time came.

1972: The Sunoco Football Stamp Book

Our parents claimed we fought like cats and dogs as kids. Years later, I can barely remember any of these blowouts but am certain they happened. Usually on Saturday mornings. Even with adults, that seems like a tentative, emotional time. In early adulthood that often implied massive hangovers. I still get that sense with people now, ostensibly the best time to have a senseless emotional brawl with a family member.

Brothers M and J had a simmering competitive streak that usually involved M establishing himself as alpha dog in the pack, with J brooding in the shadows, especially academically. As time went on, and Brother M found himself having creative differences with authority, the tide would turn in J's favor. M would find himself on the receiving end of the scolding high-school secretary's inquiry: "Why can't you be more like your Brother J?"

Sister K could be a holy terror, the only girl in the family, with her own room. (It was actually her and Mom's room, but Mom preferred sleeping downstairs on a sofa for reasons I'll never understand. Yes, our parents didn't sleep in the same bed, at least not after kids came into the picture. I didn't find it peculiar, much as I thought everyone bought their house from a grandparent for $1.00. Now that I'm an adult? The precise positioning of a pillow between my knees and necessary angles I need to have with my arms and legs to avoid waking up feeling as if I've been beaten … it's perfectly acceptable to have your own bed.)

Sister K rarely picked fights with Brother M, recognizing him as an authority figure. Save for that time she accidentally heaved one of the cats on his face while he was reading the newspaper on a sofa. She was trying to play a prank on him by gently heaving the cat on his belly, something we did all the time, but she missed, and M got a face full of claws. That was as close to physical violence I ever saw them get. Sister K was much more content getting into senseless verbal sparring matches with Brother J and me.

I can see now that she felt cornered and alone as the only girl. We felt she got special treatment as the only kid with her own room (while three boys were jammed into a tiny bedroom with no privacy). A perfect storm of childhood misunderstanding, with none of us wise enough yet to untangle the wires and figure out why this was happening. I can never recall what we argued about, save that it seemed like the end of the world. That went on through our teenage years, when Sister K would have half a dozen friends call her every night at home and rarely pick up the phone herself. She'd have to tolerate Mom and the rest of us watching endless hours of football each fall weekend. (Mom was that rare, wonderful woman who genuinely loved football.) Situations like this caused simmering resentments, but as time went on and each of us matured, these things fell away.

I was beset on all sides. Being the youngest, not just of immediate family but of the extended family's Baby Boom Generation, I was doted upon by parents and relatives, the last of my kind. It automatically put me at a disadvantage with older siblings and cousins, and I learned early how to fend for myself with stinging words. Brother M loved to torture me. By the same token, he loved to torture everybody. Sister K and I were known for having the loudest, most asinine screaming matches, again, over what, I haven't a clue, other than territorial pissing.

Brother J and I rarely fought. I can count the times on one hand as an adult. We were both imbued with Dad's quiet nature. To avoid conflict? No, it was deeper than that. To recognize most conflicts were a waste of time and live accordingly. That more accurately described our nature, then and now. Go along to get along. Brother M was trying to set the world on fire (and the rest of us, too). Sister K had her dramatic outbursts. Brother J and I spent a lot of our time on the defensive.

There was that one major blowout over my 1972 Sunoco Football Stamp Book. We collected baseball cards as kids, trading them and playing our knockdown games where we'd lean a dozen cards against a kitchen counter and then flick a card at them. Whatever cards we knocked down, we could keep for ourselves. The cards were a wonderful bartering system among the boys in the neighborhood, always a topic of interest every summer, with Philadelphia Phillies cards, of course, being our gold standard. We also loved the dusty stick of bubblegum that came with each pack.

Cards for other sports never quite held the same allure. Thus in 1972, the National Football League and Sunoco gas stations came up with the brilliant concept of passing out massive blank stamp books to customers that contained spaces for every player on every team, along with an introductory envelope of stamps to get started. The promotion took off like wildfire. As with baseball cards, after a month or two of collecting, we'd find ourselves with duplicates that we'd trade with each other. The gold standard here was the Miami Dolphins, their team red hot at the time. And the player names: Mercury Morris, Larry Csonka, Jim Kiick. This was what football was all about!

There was a Sunoco gas station down the hill from Fountain Springs on the way into Ashland. Dad normally didn't go there, but he had to during this months-long promotion. We quickly learned the attendants working there loved to give away these stamps, even to people who walked in and didn't buy gas. Many of us kids routinely made the dangerous journey down that hill, along the death-defying, shoulder-less part of Route 61, past the Coulihans' crooked house on the hill, past Danny's Drive-In (with its highly-touted mystery hot sauce) and the shit creek, just to get extra sets of these stamps.

By bombing the station and assiduously trading with friends, I found myself with a complete book by late December. A huge achievement, no other kid in the neighborhood had mastered this. Some would come by the house to marvel at it. At that point in my childhood, I had so few things that were genuinely mine. My clothes were handed down, with hem lines in the pants and faded stains in the shirts. I didn't yet have any hobbies that required money, nor the money to buy anything. The only other things I had were toys from Christmas and Scholastic books my parents bought for me at school. (Given that the family library was copies of *Readers Digest* on the upstairs bathroom radiator, I cherished those books.) I loved having that stamp book in my possession.

So, there was that cold, slushy morning a few days after Christmas where Brother J and I got into it over some forgotten issue. J was a few years older and twice my size. We never got into physical confrontations, due to our natures and this size differential. After a few minutes yelling at each other, something snapped in J's mind. He ran into the living room, grabbed my stamp book, stormed into the kitchen where we were fighting, went straight past me, opened the back door and heaved my stamp book into a thick layer of slush on the back porch.

It was one of the most shocking things I'd ever seen, deeply uncharacteristic of J and an extreme act of disrespect. Brother M had been drawn into the kitchen by our yelling and saw what had happened. For once, some innate sense of frontier justice kicked in with him. J was bigger than M, but since M was older and so competitive, we still answered to him in an undefined, but unquestioned, sense. M jumped on J, wrestled him to the floor and pulled him up with his arms behind his back. It was clear that he was inviting me to start punching J.

So I did. I cut loose on him with all the rage that came boiling up. It was frightening. I was really kicking his ass hard, with the unanticipated help of Brother M. I was crying, not enjoying what I was doing, but feeling some primal need to punish my brother for doing something so unbelievably callous. I punched myself out after a minute or two. J was crying too, although Brother M seemed OK with what was happening in that semi-demonic way he had as a child.

Just then, Mom rushed in, alerted by the screaming, sobbing and sound of blows being landed. She lost it, in total disbelief that her boys were beating up on each other. Even greater disbelief when she realized I had been pounding on J. Mom rarely got mad, but when she did, we got more scared than when Dad did as we knew she wouldn't tolerate violence. She was angry at all of us. Before anything else, she ran onto the porch to retrieve my water-logged stamp book which still was intact, but severely damaged after resting in slush for a minute or two.

Brother J took the brunt of the punishment from Mom, which always held more sting than Dad playing the usual role of enforcer. I recall Brother M and me getting a stern warning from Dad later, that this sort of thing was never going to happen again. It didn't.

Honestly? That's one situation from when I was a kid, burned into my mind because it was such a behavioral aberration. The reality of our childhood, at home, was more peaceful than that; we were hardly a brawling family. Dad's quiet nature and Mom's open sense of humanity prevented us from indulging in anything more than temporary sibling skirmishes, although they were legion.

Most nights, we were in bed around 10:00, in that insufferably small bedroom that we shared for well over a decade. When the lights went out, we were whispering to each other about local gossip, favorite TV shows and movies, or plans for the weekend. J and M had the advantage of their beds being perpendicular to mine, so they could fart under their sheets, kick their sheets up and bomb me with the dreadful odor.

The best nights were when we would make fake farts by blowing into the palms of our cupped hands, unbelievably loud and funny. We would collapse into hysterics on nights like this, until Dad would crack the door open and quietly say, knock it off, guys, we need to get some sleep.

When's the last time you laughed yourself to sleep?

1972: Muriah, Muriah

Aunt Bess was a brassy, brick shithouse of a woman, leader of the Port Carbon spinsters. She would out-live all her sisters in their crooked rowhouse in the rain. I still can't even recall the exact number of sisters living in that house – four or five. That specter of aging Irish-Catholic sisters living together in an old house created a gray force-field that could replicate an elderly woman at the drop of a memory. Dampness. Clouds. Cigarette smoke. Bing Crosby records playing on the hi-fi. The unidentifiable hard candies in trays next to ash. The nasty chihuahua and friendly Irish setter, napping behind the coal stove for warmth. Faded flower wallpaper, dark drapes, heavy wood furniture, lamps, their shades all faded and brown. Minutes passing like hours, hours passing like days. The ragged, rock-faced hill in front of the house. The forlorn park between the shit creek and power plant. Instant Belfast.

One mystery about their house in Port Carbon was the man who was always there with the aging sisters. I can't even remember his name, an old man perpetually planted in a ragged easy chair, unfiltered Camel in one hand, a Rob Roy in the other. He rarely said anything. Their brother? A suitor? It was never made clear, or I've forgotten. He owned that chair, wouldn't move an inch, with Crosby's mellifluous voice and cigarette smoke wafting around him. Never seemed happy or sad. Just there. I half-expected him to transform into a butterfly as the Crosby song ended on the hi-fi.

And there was Bess, in her perpetual pillbox hat. She must have slept and bathed wearing it. Cigarette planted firmly in the corner of her mouth. Cat-eye glasses. Faded dress covering her boxy frame. I recall her hiking up her dress to tie some kind of strange knot in her stocking garters. This was in no way erotic: it was frightening. Along with her booming, raspy voice. If she didn't like you, she'd tell you so. Didn't give a damn if you didn't like her.

I didn't know what happened that all these aging sisters would end up living in a house together. Being the Coal Region, maybe their husbands were miners and passed in their 50s? This was never made clear to me what lead up to the circumstances of that house. They never married? People think that's strange now. In a small town in the middle of the 20th century? Even stranger.

Going upstairs there was like visiting a vampire's den. We had to go up there to use the bathroom as that was the only one in the house. Of course, we'd take the opportunity to wander around their rooms. Littered with old lady things. Black-and-white photographs from the first half of the century. Moth-eaten sweaters. Jewelry not worn in decades, gathering dust on those elegant, plaster mannequin heads. That cigarette smell saturated in every fabric. I didn't believe in ghosts, but there were times up there when I was certain I'd turn around to see one gazing out the window at the falling rain.

Brother M would later tell me the story of going up there to use the bathroom. Like the rest of us, he would tip-toe around the rooms. He found a hatch to what looked like an attic crawl space. He creaked open the door and crept up the short stair case, only to realize it must have been the bedroom for the mystery man normally crashed out in his favorite living-room chair. The elderly man raised himself from a musty bed and fixed a jaundiced eye on my brother. He nearly screamed but had the presence of mind to blurt out "sorry" and bolt from there as if he had wandered into Satan's hidden palace.

This all seemed alien from my child's point of view. Now that I'm older, I can see, you do whatever comes along to get by in life. You have a house? You live in it. You get along with these people? (They all seemed to get along in a deep, abiding way.) Then go on doing so. It occurs to me that the person I am now, and how I live, would seem strange and alien to me as a child. Why aren't I married? With kids? Living in a house? With a car? Most kids have such expectation of adults because those are the adults they deal with in their immediate vicinity.

Aunt Bess in her Port Carbon homestead was a unified whole: a perfect blending of human being to her physical environment, as if she materialized from the ancient, browning wallpaper in a haze of Camel smoke every time we visited.

Out of her environment? I'll describe a typical situation in our house in the 70s. Family is at home, at various places in the house, going about their routines. I'm on the living room floor, reading the sports section of the local newspaper, eating a bowl of ice cream.

We suddenly hear the back door in the kitchen slam open against a chair. Someone's breaking in! Stomping flat feet. Creaking floors. Then the unmistakable, growling, gravel voice:

"Muriah .... Muriah ... Muriah ..."

It's Aunt Bess, on one of her unannounced visits (her only kind) to see her sister/my grandmother, Marie. She'd pile into her badass 1973 Chrysler Newport, floor it up the Broad Mountain, pop out and slam through our back door like the house was hers. Seconds after croaking out her take on "Marie" ... there she was, standing in our living room, cigarette smoke trail in her wake, looking at everyone as if we were the ones out of place and intruding on her. She came barging into a house with a family of seven and calling out one person's name, as if the rest of us weren't there. The usual greeting most people have: "Hello, everyone!" Not Bess.

We goofed on her use of "Muriah" as there was a 70s hard rock band called Uriah Heep, and the act of associating this tough old broad with a band like that tickled us no end. We pictured her jamming to "Easy Living." If we wanted a good laugh, all we had to do was start burping the words, "Muriah, Muriah, Muriah" at each other.

The visits were on the long side, hours, and often meant her and our grandmother camped out in the kitchen, drinking tea, Bess chain smoking, and bantering about local priests, bingo, dogs and dead men. It was easy enough to avoid her. I find now, all these years later, I was perfectly in my right to be annoyed over these sneak attacks. It wasn't her house. Every time we went to Port Carbon, the visit had been set days in advance, often associated with other relatives visiting and making the usual pilgrimage. Her visits to our house felt like a mild form of harassment, to remind us that our grandmother was her sister, and that relationship trumped whatever we had going on with her. It didn't bother me that much, and I knew my grandmother loved spending time with any of her sisters. I took issue with the mild disrespect she was showing the family, which was simply her way. She would not have seen it this way, but it surely was. I was in no position as a small child to take a stand or even mention it. I'm sure Mom and Dad thought, correctly, "Getting into this will be far more trouble than it's worth."

Adding insult to injury was the time she made me eat a bar of Irish Spring. Yes, that old wives' tale about kids with fresh mouths eating bars of soap is, or was, true, once upon a time. (I'm not sure why Irish Americans gravitated towards Irish Spring soap, save for the name. Ditto, Lucky Charms cereal. I often imagined the Lucky Charms leprechaun heaving a Molotov cocktail at a British troop carrier.) As with most adverse forms of punishment, I can't recall the circumstance of what I did wrong, but I can surely recall the punishment. I'm certain that she was ordering me around in a fairly bad, disrespectful, "I own you so do as I say" tone, as she always did. I could handle this coming from my parents in rare bad moods. But from her? I remember barking out, "Go to hell!"

You ... just ... didn't ... say ... that ... to ... an ... elderly ... female ... relative ... in ... rural ... Pennsylvania ... in ... 1972.

Yes, society had gone mad in the 60s, but not there. Not in that house either. I elongated that sentence to underline the sense of shock and impending doom when I uttered that fateful phrase. I knew when I said it, this was going to be some heavy shit. I remember her swatting me once or twice on the bottom, with the ensuing drama, and then Grandma rushing out to the bathroom to get a bar of soap. I recall she opened a fresh box for this purpose. I'm not sure what Mom or Dad were doing while all this was going on. It would have been nice if one or both of them had said, "Wait a minute, that's our son, and we'll discipline him accordingly. You're in our house, and you don't do this here."

That fantastical morality did not occur in this scenario. That crabby old maid made me sit in the kitchen with a bar of soap in my mouth. Couldn't have been much fun for her and my grandmother, with me staring daggers at both of them in between mild bouts of weeping and moaning. I remember her asking me, "Well, have your learned your lesson now?" I sure did, which was don't ever let me catch you in a situation where I hold the power over you, because I'll return the favor!

Of course, that would never happen, and she would start declining in the coming years. All the ill feeling generated in this one situation would slowly blow over. I can't recall which was worse – having the bar of soap in my mouth for that long, or having to listen to old-lady talk and inhale her foul cigarette exhaust for two hours, an eternity in hell for a small child. Besides, I got the vibe she respected me more after that for standing up to her, which rarely happened with anyone.

This wasn't my first brush with disrespect towards elders either. While I can't remember the specifics, I once went upside Grandma's head with a plastic hammer. I was in my high chair, eating. I would say "baby food" but given Dad's culinary tastes, I'm willing to bet I was eating meat. Like a tiger cub with a dead rabbit, using my hands instead of utensils. Mom would tell us we'd sometimes make growling sounds when eating meat. Inject Grandma ordering me around into this situation. You don't mess with a guy when he's eating meat, especially when he has his favorite plastic hammer on his high-chair tray. I surely didn't do her any harm, but the disrespect of lashing out like this was cause for a good spanking. I had all this stuff out of my system before I was 10.

I can barely recall when Aunt Bess passed on in the late 80s. All her sisters had passed on before her, and for the life of me, I can only recall their passings vaguely, which troubles me now, as anyone dying in my childhood tended to leave an indelible mark on me. With them, it was like ghosts fading back into the wallpaper, one after another, and I do feel shame that their passings aren't burned on my memory. Not even hers.

What I do remember is that 1973 Chrysler Newport, mainly because Brother J inherited the car when she passed on. This was no ordinary car: it was a road beast. We could have taken that car into battle and come out victorious. It was the size of a small boat, got about six miles to the gallon and had a back seat that could easily fit a coffin. J would hit the gas on that thing and be doing 75 mph seconds later. Had he floored it, he might have broken the sound barrier. The car growled, even when cruising under 30 mph. Much like the house in Port Carbon, there was something foreboding about that car, the same Catholic brown-ness to everything inside it. The coup de grace was the crucifix glued to the dashboard and St. Christopher medallion on the glove compartment. We felt like were riding with Christ every time we got in that car. And Christ had a pair of Wayfarer shades and a screaming eagle forearm tattoo.

That car was another manifestation of Bess, the act of things in her life taking on her character and living on after she was gone. Much like that house. When she passed on, the house was sold for some humble price, and new people moved in. When I go back there, I have very little cause to visit Port Carbon, as it's not along my normal routes. To get to their house, you have to be leaving town, headed towards Tamaqua, which is a trip I rarely take.

Every now and then, with time on my hands, I'll head over that way and purposely drive by the house. It still looks the same. The dumpy bar on the corner with the Pabst sign in the dirty window is gone, but I suspect that forlorn park may still be there on the other side of the shit creek. And that craggy, rock-faced hill will surely be there forever, with the meadow and a nicer park on top of the hill. I can't even recall how to officially get up there, but I'd guess there must be a way back there on the other side of town, marked paths leading up the other side of the hill. I'd like to go up there, one more time, on a clear day and take a good, last look down on the town, especially that house, and remember all those old women who were my only connection to a long-lost past.

1973: T. Rex

On a recent visit back home, as I was heading down an alley a few blocks from the house, I heard a man's voice yell out, "Bill or J?" He meant was it me or Brother J he was seeing. I turned to look, and it was a middle-aged guy in a baseball hat, a little burly, but not huge, standing in the middle of a backyard vegetable patch. It's Bill, I said, slowing down to try to figure out who was talking to me. This happens every now and then back there with people I haven't seen in decades.

"It's me, Joe H," he said. I should have known as he was standing in his mother's backyard. All I knew of him in adult life was that he was a postman for years, still was to judge by his tan. I told him I was back for a few days, and he said he was taking care of his Mom. Might have to move back into the house as things weren't going so well.

I hadn't seen Joe since at least the early 1980s. He was a good six years older than I was, a great high-school athlete, known for his speed. There's probably still a picture of him hanging in the awards case at the high school with the four-man relay team he ran anchor on. Back then, he was a sleek, naturally-muscled kid with shaggy black hair and clunky horn rims. The guy I saw in his mother's vegetable patch had a small belly going on, looked like either closely-cropped or shaved head under his baseball hat. When I looked him in the face, yeah, that was Joe.

That really wasn't what he was known for back then. Every waking hour of every day, every time Joe came walking up the street to the heart of the neighborhood, the schoolyard, he would have Rex with him. Rex was a big black collie/labrador mix. They were inseparable. I'm not even sure where Joe would walk Rex when they came around. Usually when you walk a dog, there's a certain, long route you follow to give the dog a good workout. It seemed like Joe and Rex weren't going anywhere in particular and walking towards infinity.

Heading up to the schoolyard, at least in daylight hours, didn't imply hanging out. It implied x number of kids gathering, almost every day, to indulge in a game or two of whatever sport was in season. If there were six kids, it would be a small game. If there were 12, a bigger game. If everyone showed up, upwards of 20 kids, we would head over to the open field by the hospital and play a big, official game on grass. We'd also do that sometimes in the cemetery, although that was a bit of a pain in the ass as the open field there was on a hill. It didn't seem incongruous to us to play football in a cemetery: any open field in our hometown was fair game. Despite being a rural area, there weren't a lot of open public spaces like that. Plenty of woods, but not so many fields.

For better or worse, Joe served as a guide as he was older, a real baby boomer, as opposed to the bulk of us who represented the tail end of his larger baby-boom generation. There were plenty of kids Joe's age in the neighborhood, the issue being most of them, like him, were in the middle of their teenage years and heavily into drugs and partying. Joe wasn't, and because of that, and his clunky glasses, and his constant companion, Rex, he was considered a little odd by the other kids his age. It didn't help that he shared his food with Rex, including ice-cream cones.

Joe would never come by the schoolyard at night. The older neighborhood kids would come by the schoolyard to hang out at night. Druggy/stoner teenagers for the most part, doing nothing. Not necessarily looking for trouble, but by the same token, they were smoking cigarettes, taking drugs, making noise. I don't know how the adults around there put up with this, including my own parents.

In the summer there were nights we would all hang out, but that would be to play hide-and-seek, and later Jailbreak, a hide-and-seek derivative our relatives from Point Pleasant taught us when they visited. Even that must have been pretty harrowing for adults, a dozen kids screaming "jailbreak" at the top of their lungs every 20 minutes as a kid who hadn't been caught by "the jailer" would steal back to "the jail" (usually the cement steps at the entrance of the elementary school) and set them free with that joyous yell, allowing the kids to hide again. It was an impossible game for the unfortunate kid picked as jailer for the night. (The choosing process was usually all of us gathered in a circle, fists out, while one kid tapped each fist, chanting "one potato, two potato, three potato, four" with the last potato stuck as the jailer. I suspect kids good at math could do a rhythmic count of the potatoes and determine where to stand in the circle.) At least the adults grasped it was an all-age event that would break up no later than 9:00 pm. As opposed to the harder-edged kids hanging out year-round, later than that, and playing different, darker games.

Joe would come around during the day, and that meant starting whatever game we were going to play that day. He would tie Rex's leash to a shady spot in the chain-link fence and get into it. Like most of us, he was a good athlete. Our social lives at the time were built on sports, with the schoolyard serving as the hub of that activity. I would later find this smothering and annoying, especially with our house right next to all the action, but it was good up through the age of 12, after which time, man, how many pick-up games did I have to play? While I don't look back fondly on the druggie kids in the neighborhood, I can also see they went through their sporting days, and at the age of 12 or 13, like me, wanted to spend their time doing other things. In my case, it was reading Stephen King books. In theirs, it was smoking joints or dropping acid. Although I suspect the greater reality was drinking alcohol and smoking cigarettes, more so out of economics than desire.

We never paid much attention to Joe as an authority figure, but he was, by sheer dint of his age. It also helped that he was fair-minded, not an asshole, and a stickler for rules. (We would later learn that his father had developed and patented a football board game that we never could find in stores.) Unlike some of the older kids, he would never pick on a younger kid, never threaten anyone, never take that upper hand that an older teenager with less character would assume was his birthright. I point this out to underline what a positive influence he had on all of us at a crucial time in our lives. He wasn't the only one. The brothers Mark and Dave T had the same love of sports and were roughly the same age, as was Brother J. They were hardly at war with the druggy kids, but there was a clear delineation, often drawn by the quality of a kid's family life.

Turning 16 for a boy was like Cinderella putting on her magic slippers: it signaled the real end of his neighborhood sporting days, assuming he hadn't thrown in the towel sooner. The ability to go out driving with your gang of friends opened a whole new way of life. By that point, a kid who was genuinely into athletics would be fully integrated into high-school sports and no longer have the time or inclination for neighborhood pick-up games. Not to worry though: through the mid-80s there always seemed to be a batch of kids coming along who fell into that under-15 age bracket. The batch after me, in the early 1980's, could be a bunch of insufferable little pricks as they had no older guides like we did with Joe. Even when Joe and the other older kids started getting into high-school sports and not being around as much, I can recall some of us being abusive and weird with each other in ways that wouldn't have happened with Joe around.

The main difference between Joe and a lot of those wayward kids, aside from a stable home life, was drugs. The stoners had rough home lives, with troubled or abusive parents, so it was in their best interests to stay out of the house as much as possible. It only made sense for them to group together with other like-minded kids, their defense against the world outside and inside. Drugs helped them get out of their heads, out of those inescapable problems, not realizing they were already mirroring their parents at that age, fruitlessly trying to escape their asshole parents in a never-ending chain of abuse. At that age, it seemed like we had a thousand choices, but we were already starting to imitate our parents in ways that suggested we would be just like they were. In some cases, that was a nightmare, in others, good news.

If there had been no buffers like Joe, the wave of drugginess and bad behavior that ran so deep in the first half of the decade might have overtaken the whole gang of kids through the 70s, as opposed to petering out the way it did as time wore on. It made me feel some sense of delayed gratitude and recognize that most of our time as kids back then, it was older kids who guided us in those endless hours we spent outside of parental and all other adult boundaries. We were like animals in the wild, but even animals in the wild have their own rules.

My last 70s memory of Joe was him and Rex coming down the street on a summer afternoon. One of those unbearably humid days, around dinner time. A thunderstorm was going to explode any minute. I could feel a few raindrops as I sat on the steps in front of our house and was thinking, "Man, we're going to get hammered." Just then I saw Joe and Rex, tearing down the street. He yelled out, "We're running through the raindrops!" It seemed like they did for a few dozen yards as he and Rex sprinted down the block. Then a wall of hard rain came along and soaked them before they even crossed Route 61.

1973: Waiting for Charlie

There's a picture of Brother J and me on the back porch, still little kids in the late 60s, dressed up in military duds, me in an empty metal drum, with our toy rifles. Waiting for Charlie.

"Charlie" was the Vietnam-era euphemism for the Viet Cong who came in the night to wreak havoc on the American soldiers in their outposts. This meant we were playing war, something we did constantly in our early childhood. Television was awash with all those heroic World War II movies in black-and-white, and there were cool shows like *Rat Patrol* to constantly remind us of that era, although we hadn't lived in it.

Since we lived just north of Fort Indiantown Gap, and our neighbor Bubba's Dad worked there, we had an inside line to all sorts of cool military swag: shirts with name tags and sergeant stripes, jackets, helmets (inner lining and hard metal shell), even gas masks and C rations (which tasted awful). The gas masks were of questionable value, too. I recall the time we had a farting contest to see if they worked, and the hapless kid wearing the mask whom we bombarded with methane blasts started crying and retching.

Decades later, I don't see it as much in New York City, save fashion designers mimicking those military styles. The 70s and 80s found all of us wearing military gear well into our teens and 20s. Real military clothing, found in Army/Navy stores that were much more prevalent back then. I hid inside my treasured Navy peacoat through high school, Jimi Hendrix, Kinks and Beatles buttons pinned to the lapels. Army fatigue jackets were standard-issue for the stoner crowd in high-school parking lots, the fabric permeated with nicotine and pot odors.

Playing army tapped into senses of imagination and adventure that peak around the age of eight, lasting maybe another two years before easing into the pragmatism of early adolescence. We had woods all around us, so we could either have the Tet Offensive around the schoolyard in summer, or recreate the Battle of the Bulge in the woods by the cemetery on a cold winter's day. Our language and way of communicating had far more to do with those dated World War II movies, the clipped, masculine way of addressing each other.

Shooting someone was designated by pointing a gun at the enemy soldier, making a piercing sound ("pier-pier-pier"), then calling out, "You're dead!" The kid being shot gathered he had been shot, followed by a faithful request, tell Ma I love her, then the fake coughing spell, seconds before dropping the toy rifle, falling to the ground and playing dead until the game ended. What did we think about after we died? Usually the next episode of *The Partridge Family*, or what Mom was making for dinner. I wonder if real death will be the same.

World War II cast such a shadow over us. That's a good way of describing it: not something physical and solid, a shade that fell on us from our parents' generation. I remember Dad taking us to see *Patton* at the local drive-in.

The drive-in out the road was normally a chore for Dad, figuring on some kid-based double feature of *The Computer Wore Tennis Shoes* with *Where Angels Go, Trouble Follows*. Mom was there, too, and we kids were fidgeting in the back of the station wagon in our pajamas (inevitably falling asleep before the movie's end) with a bucket full of ice-cold A-Treat sodas and other snacks. (The drive-in closed in the mid-70s, once showing *Deep Throat* in their waning days when attendance was almost negligible. Brother J and I drove by that night, hoping to see the screen beyond the tall pine trees. No such luck.)

Patton begins with that wonderful speech, George C. Scott strolling out in front of a massive American flag as General Patton, and delivering his hard-assed sermon to the Third Army in 1944: *"No bastard ever won a war by dying for his country. You won it by making the other poor dumb bastard die for his country ..."*

And so on. Dad was laughing his ass off and muttering to himself, god damn right, say it, like a Southern Baptist testifying, pounding the side of car occasionally. Mom tried to get him to stop, mainly because of the bad language. Dad wasn't particularly gung-ho about the military, although he had volunteered a year early to fight in World War II, then spent a decade after the war working as a mechanic at numerous air bases around the world. He was glad to get out. I think the *Patton* incident had more to do with pressure at work, and the normal stresses of having four kids, but finally getting a moment in a movie where someone lays it all out. We kids were giggling over the occasional curse words and sleeping like lambs within the hour.

Considering that there were guys from our town in Vietnam, it was strange that there was such a gulf between the war they were fighting and the lives we were living. Of course, we watched it all on TV, saw the horrifying pictures of the naked girl being napalmed in the paper, but this was a small town, where everything seemed to run a few years behind cities and college campuses. David, Bubba's older brother, and Lee, son of Soytz (whom I'll describe later) were two kids on our street who went to Vietnam, but I gather there were a few more. And more went to college, whether to avoid the draft or get an education was a contentious topic with Dad's generation.

Every Memorial Day back then found us waking up before sunrise so we could get to the Protestant cemetery for the American Legion's ceremony. It was tradition for them to line up a gun salute and fire off a round of shots before a bugler, recruited from the high-school marching band, blew Taps in the still morning air. It was a dramatic ceremony, made cool for us by the firing of guns in public. The real attraction for us kids was scooping up the metal shell casings after the ceremony as mementos. Even after I grew out of this phase, I always smiled while dozing in bed those Memorial Day Mondays, hearing the gunshots, followed faintly by the bugler.

There was a wave of older kids, older than the "bad" kids but narrowly missing Vietnam, who seemed wise and benevolent. Janey O and her cool boyfriend, Phil, would often tease me in my military fatigues, calling me Sergeant Sacto (a character from a kids' show on a Philadelphia TV station from before my time), sensing I was still a kid and relating to me on that level. Phil was a star on the high-school basketball team, and I would wager slightly too young to be drafted, i.e., graduating high school after 1972. There was always Sharon M in church, rocking her massive peace-sign necklace noted earlier. That thing was made of vinyl and seemed more like a steering wheel removed from a rock star's limo. I often wondered if she snuck into church and played songs like "A Whiter Shade of Pale" on the organ when no one was around. These kids weren't hippies by any means. The closest we got was the Protestant minister's wayward son Albert, who was caught naked and stoned one glorious spring day under a tree in the cemetery, enjoying the company of his equally stoned-and-naked lady friend.

Years later, in high school, we had a general come to the auditorium to give us a speech. This was not normal for my generation. In the 60s and earlier, it wasn't unusual for the military to come into high schools in working-class areas and encourage young guys to enlist. This was during the Iran Hostage Crisis in 1980.

His speech that day was stern and blustery. "The winds of war are blowing," he thundered at one point while we slouched there in our flannel shirts and jeans. I wasn't sure what all this meant. There was no draft. His speech seemed to be gearing us up for the prospect of war breaking out, and kids like us fighting it. I can't recall who it was, but one of the parking-lot stoners muttered "the winds of war can blow me" loud enough for a flurry of snickers and a patrolling teacher to lose his cool. I was outside the auditorium when the general and the principal came barreling through the front door, as if we were on a military base, and all us kids were supposed to stand at attention and salute. I can surmise the general's thoughts in moments like that in similar high schools: "If our future depends on these clowns, we're doomed."

Ironically, a few months later, there was another presentation featuring an Army rock band, a bunch of enlisted guys who toured high schools, no speeches, just pure entertainment for the kids. Although they had short hair and played in their uniforms, they rocked, and I knew rock. Stones. Aerosmith. Bad Company. They were great. Of course, the cool kids wouldn't acknowledge that a bunch of short-haired guys in the army could play rock and roll. They nearly lost the crowd when they broke into "Pump It Up" by Elvis Costello, which probably went over like gangbusters in suburban schools, but was a kiss of death in rural areas. (I'll describe this phenomenon later.) They were smart enough to win the crowd back with stomping versions of

Foghat's "Slow Ride," Grand Funk Railroad's "We're an American Band" and, of course, Led Zep's "Stairway to Heaven." This is where my exposure to the military ended, on a good note. Much like Godot, Charlie never came.

1973: Cabbage Head Malarkey

Cabbage Head Malarkey was the smartest kid I knew: a genius. Why his parents didn't push him forward a few grades, I have no idea. He had the brains to be one of those kids who graduates Harvard at 16. We called him Cabbage Head because he had an oblong-shaped head, and since he was so smart, we thought the shape of his head was necessary to hold all those brains.

His parents used to live out the road on Route 61. Last I heard Cabbage Head was a lawyer working for the U.S. government in Germany (which, as I'll illustrate later, makes perfect sense). His parents freaked out many people back home when they planted "Bush/Cheney" signs in their front yard. The Malarkeys had been staunch Democrats for decades, but they clearly changed their minds somewhere along the road. Conservative/Republican signs and bumperstickers were not unusual back there, but the Malarkeys swinging their allegiance so far that they'd willingly put signs up in their yard was.

Back in the 70s, I can't recall how Cabbage Head and I became friends. It must have been that we went to the same grade school (right next to my house, which is now a day-care center), and since we were both recognized as smart kids, we usually sat next to each other and got put into the same groups.

This explains my most vivid memory of him: vomiting all over Joy R in our first-grade reading class. We were in that upper-echelon reading group, sitting in a circle. I'd imagine that month's package of Scholastic books had come through. I loved that function in grade school, the teacher passing out the circular, filled with books for us to choose for our reading assignments. Some kids loathed that stuff, but I'd have my parents buy me books on top of the assignments. Since they were cheap paperbacks and often less than a buck, it wasn't that big a deal. I loved seeing that huge Scholastic box being delivered and knowing that my books were coming in.

Kids were always puking in grade school. Why is that? I'd guess it has more to do with wacky diets, kids eating anything they can get their hands on, junk on top of good stuff. It seemed like kids were forever blowing chunks at school, usually in the lunch room or halls. This was often hilarious, provided you weren't directly involved.

I'll never forget Cabbage Head looking woozy as we all sat in a circle in our "enlightened" group, reading a biography about Roberto Clemente or something. He casually stood up and gushed out a stream of vomit that absolutely coated Joy R, who was sitting next to him, from head to toe. I'd never seen anything like it.

Another grade-school hallmark: chain vomiting. One kid vomits, the sight and smell of it freaks out kids in the immediate vicinity, and they start vomiting, too. This started happening. Three other kids started blowing chunks, albeit with far less shock and awe than Cabbage Head's original fountain. I remember laughing hysterically, although when Cabbage Head got Joy R, he also tagged some on the corner of my red, plaid, polyester bell-bottoms. (I was a fat kid – I looked like a mental patient in those pants.) It looked like clam chowder and had that awful stomach-acid smell. The teacher freaked out, heaving kids away as if Cabbage Head had spontaneously human combusted. It was a disaster zone, complete with weeping, hysterical children, that took half an hour to calm down. When Louie Balls ("Balls" being a playful shortening of his much longer and hard-to-pronounce Slavic surname), the janitor, showed up with his mop and bucket, things slowly got back to normal. All throughout this, Cabbage Head stood there with a maniacal gleam in his eye, while Joy R wept in disbelief. I can't remember how she got cleaned up.

The problem with Cabbage Head was that while he was clearly the smartest kid in the entire school, including kids a few grades ahead of him, he was also diabolical. In that same first-grade class, I also remember him getting Melissa M to show us her tits in the back row of class. Please, no judgments here. This was all very much in the "playing doctor" category of kids innocently finding out about each other's private parts.

Besides, as a chubby kid, I had bigger tits than Melissa M, who had a crush on Cabbage Head because of his huge brain. Still, I can recall the slow process of Cabbage Head convincing Melissa it would be advantageous of her to show us her tits, bribing her with cartons of milk and orange juice, to the point where one day she turned around at her desk and flashed us. Both of us probably had erections like those science-book bananas frozen to 100 degrees Kelvin used to hammer nails. It became a regular thing, until someone squealed on us, and our parents were called in for a stern talk which didn't really amount to much.

Worse, by far, was Cabbage Head's fascination with Adolph Hitler. In the fourth grade, he kept a picture of Adolph in his locker and would give it a "Heil" salute every morning.

What do you do when the smartest kid in grade school appears to be a Nazi sympathizer? For a long time, nothing was done, because it was a well-kept secret among all of us. His parents were staunch, working-class Irish Democrats. His father may have been a World War II vet, although I suspect he was a bit younger than Dad, and a Korean War vet.

Cabbage Head's fascination was based more so on the documentary *The World at War*, which we all watched religiously Saturday nights on the local PBS station. (Grandma forced our family to sit through *The Lawrence Welk Show* before this, which frightened me more than the Nazis. Later, we'd also watch *Monty Python's Flying*

Circus. Saturday night was a wild time on PBS back in the 70s.)

I have *The World at War* series on DVD. It's a well-done, comprehensive documentary on World War II, from the causes in the 1930s to the aftermath in the mid-1940s. It's what documentaries should be and no longer are: a fair-minded, historical look at an event without shades of personal politics thrown into the mix. Much of it was horrifying: the episode on concentration camps in particular, which gave all us kids nightmares for months afterwards.

For whatever reason, Cabbage Head took a real shine to Hitler. I don't ever recall him espousing anti-Semitism or such. He was enamored of the war process and how Hitler came to power. I think in his nutty, advanced mind, he saw that Hitler pulling his country out of a deep Depression and then moving forward to near domination of Europe was an amazing transformation, and he was also fascinated, in that little boy's way, with the darker side of how this transpired. He threw in the "Heil" salutes as a show of black humor.

By the way, none of us followed him on this endeavor! I knew that the Nazis were bad news and couldn't quite wrap my mind around putting a picture of Hitler in my locker, much as I wouldn't put a picture of Charles Manson up there either.

Cabbage Head's undoing was writing an essay about Hitler for our fourth-grade teacher, Mr. D, whom we called Wedge Head because he was a big guy with a giant forehead. Wedge Head thought the essay was brilliant, but was a little freaked out by its thoroughness and scholarly intent. He knew Cabbage Head was a genius, but he thought that either he must have cribbed some of the material, or if he hadn't, needed a serious talking to about Hitler. This coincided with Wedge Head seeing the Hitler picture in the locker, and that called for a parent-teacher sit-down. After which point, Cabbage Head got over his Hitler fixation in a hurry.

The nicest thing Cabbage Head did for me was let me win the class spelling bee in the third grade. I knew he was miles ahead of me in terms of intelligence and could easily out-spell me. He knew it, too, but must have also sensed that I was tired of always coming in second to him in these contests. The spelling bee came down to him and me, and I can clearly recall him purposely blowing a word I knew he knew how to spell. Then me pulling in for the glory and getting some kind of paper crown with the word "champ" scrawled on it in blue crayon. I went along with it, and felt fine, but I knew he had let me win. He was basically a friendly, well-adjusted kid beyond his intelligence.

Cabbage Head eventually went to Cardinal Brennan, the Catholic school, which was where we started losing contact with each other. I played basketball on the CYO team in the 5th/6th grades, but felt like an outcast because I was one of the few public-school kids in the program. That was the last real contact I had with him, although we'd see each other occasionally in our teen years.

1973: The Birthday Party

The last time I had anything approximating a birthday party was when my landlady at Penn State, Olgie, staged an impromptu gathering at the end of my junior year, near my 21st birthday. Even then, it felt odd, a bit long in the tooth. I did appreciate her corralling my newspaper and German Department friends and making a cake. It isn't all downhill after 21, more of a blur, with occasional road signs like "30" and "40" passing through the fog.

Birthday parties were part of our landscape as kids, although I have a hard time picking any from the dozens I attended. I do remember celebrating classmate Eugene M's eighth birthday in his house, out the road across from Cabbage Head Malarkey's. Cake, ice cream, and since it was a Friday night, a TV party, watching ABC's spectacular line up of *The Brady Bunch*, *The Partridge Family*, and the late show of *Room 222*. Between Marsha Brady, Laurie Partridge and Karen Valentine, I expertly concealed a near two-hour erection behind a throw pillow. (Years later, I would inadvertently screw over Eugene by forgetting to vote in an election at our Penn State branch campus that cost him the class presidency.)

There are a few pictures in family albums of me at what must have been a third- or fourth-birthday party circa 1968. I'm perched in a high chair at the head of the dining-room table, my face smeared with chocolate cake as if I had picked it up and mashed it all over my cheeks. I gather that's why bibs were invented. A gold-painted, plastic crown wouldn't have been out of place at this event.

Brother J recently reminded me of the one we had for neighbor Bubba in 1973. His brother David was home from Vietnam, trying to process a bunch of howling, American kids after the brutal carnage he had witnessed in-country. Bubba's Dad was a gruff World War II vet, cigar stump planted in the corner of his mouth, a twinkle in his eye. He seemed like an older version of Popeye. His mother had a lot of patience … and patients, as she was a registered nurse over at the hospital.

Bubba's Dad loved to tease him, one of those guys who flashed a wink to let us know we were in on the joke. His favorite was to crank out a fart then gruffly state, "Hey, butt, yah done left a rosy, didn't yah?" "Left a rosy" was his slang for flatulence. This would drive Bubba out of his mind, being accused of cranking one out when he hadn't. I could see his Dad's eyes in the rear-view mirror, throwing me a playful wink. There was a subtle give-and-take in the teasing that was impossible for outsiders to fathom.

While Bubba wasn't an only child, it sometimes felt that way because David was in Vietnam for most of the late 60s and early 70s, and then got married and moved out when he came home. As a result, we played army quite a bit before neighborhood sports set in. I didn't see this at all back then, but I can look back now and see faint lines drawn along religion. This was surely the influence of parents and whatever issues they had. It didn't occur to us to treat each other differently, yet there were times the division materialized. Once, a bunch of us had gone into the Protestant church, right next door to our Catholic church, to help one of the kids stack chairs in the basement, an assignment his father had given him. Pat Hanlon and I sat down at the piano and tunelessly pounded away for about a minute, probably wailing "The Night Chicago Died." That weekend, there was a minor crisis as the woman who ran Sunday School noticed the piano was out of tune. Those meddling Catholic kids, rumor had it, broke in earlier that week and did this on purpose, why, they'll pay for this, etc.

Stuff like that happened every so often. You would figure with the implicit divide that all the Catholic kids would get along, but this didn't explain why Bubba couldn't stand the Hanlon brothers. We would play together, but sooner or later Bubba would drop a caustic remark about Kevin's speech impediment, and all hell would break loose. After awhile, the Hanlon brothers and Bubba kept their distance, which became much easier when the brothers went to Cardinal Brennan.

Maybe Bubba felt they were infringing on the informal, family-style relationship he had with Brother J and me? The Hanlon's were late-arrivers to Fountain Springs, whereas our families had been there for years. I got along very well with Pat, almost like brothers, and I suspect that closeness threatened Bubba. Or maybe there's an incident that helped create the divide?

Bubba's birthday party was like any other: cake, ice cream, pointed hats, party horns, K Tel "blockbuster hits" album on the record player. I must have played Pin the Tail on the Donkey dozens of times, but that's the one instance that stays with me. I can't remember what I bought him as a present, but I would guess it was a plastic model of a World War II airplane, probably a Messerschmitt or Stuka as the Germans made such cool planes. For the hours we spent gluing these things together, it would only take minutes to light them on fire and pretend they were shot down over Normandy.

While a shy kid in public, Bubba in his house was the wild man from Borneo. He blew out the candles to his cake with a plastic harmonica, pulling a big chunk off for himself and diving right in. He disappeared for a few minutes after we had our cake and ice cream. We were all milling around, energized by the massive sugar intake. Suddenly, the lights in the dining room went off. What the hell we thought, a power outage?

When the lights came back on, there was a ghost among us, i.e., Bubba with a white sheet over his head making those windy "wooh" ghost sounds and waving his arms.

We all started kicking his ass.

It's not like we thought it was an actual ghost; we knew it was him. It was one of those spontaneous "boy" moments where the light bulb over our heads flashed the message "ass-kicking time." Everyone pounced and started landing soft kicks and punches, not wanting to get too crazy, more a playful hazing. It seemed like part of the show? Innocent horsing around? After a few seconds, Bubba started howling for real. When the sheet came off, we could see he was in tears and enraged.

"Hanlon, I know this was your idea!" he raged while pointing a finger at Pat. If that was true, Pat hadn't enlightened the rest of us. Maybe he did land the first punch? If so, it was by chance as we all bum-rushed the ghost. It was one of many *Lord of the Flies* moments from our childhood. All the usual kids were there: me, Brother J, Pat and Kevin, George B, Joey C, Jimmy S, Jerry E, etc.

Bubba pounced on Pat, swinging wildly. By this time, the adults knew something was way off and separated everyone.

"Get out of my house, you donkey Irish prick!" Bubba tearfully thundered. We usually didn't break it down ethnically. All of us were various mixes of German, Pennsylvania Dutch, Irish, Scottish, Polish, Lithuanian, Italian: mutts, a melting pot of various white ethnic groups that settled America in the early 20th century. No one group held sway in our town, in numbers or money. The Hanlon's probably were Irish on both sides.

Bubba's Mom stepped in and quieted everyone down, making sure Pat wasn't ejected from the party, but there was a pall cast over the event. None of this appeared to rub off on the parents, who could see it was some indefinable childhood beef that had come to a head. I can't remember how it ended, save that the Bubba/Hanlon rift grew wider. As usual with such childhood skirmishes, they evaporated in our teenage years, leaving only faded scars as reminders. I suspect every birthday party back then had at least one moment of similar high drama.

1974: Sympathy for the Devil

We called Joey Flanagan Satan because he drove a beat-up Harley with a busted tailpipe down our quiet childhood streets, frightening all us kids and annoying the adults. Satan was 17 and trouble. His father was never around, and he had dropped out of high school.

He was heading for a showdown with my Dad. I thought Dad was a little nuts. True, he had seen the tail end of World War II and certainly didn't need this shit, but this was Satan! You don't confront Satan! You hear his noise coming, tolerate that horrible grind for a few seconds, then hear him fade into the distance. In those few seconds you feel afraid and insulted, spit on, in a sense. You don't confront Satan! Dad certainly wasn't legendary. No one called him by any avenging angel's name. But he did have a way about him. Once, I had done something very bad. (I can't even remember what it was.) Instead of taking my spanking, I took off running. He came after me. I was running uphill toward the cemetery and the woods beyond, and I knew he had a bad back. Rather than losing ground, I was rapidly losing him. I could escape.

Right then it hit me that there was no escape. Whatever I had done was wrong, I had it coming. How far could I run? Forever, I guess, but I lost my urge to run away, realizing you can't run away from yourself. I could say something dramatic like I became a man that day, but I wasn't even 10 and would cry a few more times after that. I stopped running. Instead of letting him catch me, I ran back towards him, tears running down my face.

Did he hit me? No. He shook my arm hard and gave me a speech, and we walked back to the house. At that point, the whole neighborhood had been alerted that a scene was taking place, and they stood on their porches watching us walk back to our house. I felt like Billy Jack at the end of his movie, coming out of that farmhouse.

It felt like High Noon when Dad went after Satan. He came out of our house in a hurry, going straight for Satan, who was sitting on his bike in front of the school, revving the engine. We had all been playing kickball, but everything stopped for this. I became very afraid, in that nerve-shattering when physical violence is about to happen. I was more afraid for Satan.

Dad took Satan's arm, not like he took mine that time, but in a more friendly manner. He wasn't smiling. He leaned close and whispered a few lines to him. Satan whispered back. This went on for a few minutes. Old faces stared out of windows. The birds stopped singing in the trees. After all this, Satan simply drove away. He came back again after that day, but not nearly as much. We could hear him sometimes in the distance, driving down Route 61, as opposed to taking the longer route through our streets. I never asked my father what they had said to each other, and I don't doubt a verbatim transcript would be straightforward and uncryptic. It worked.

As noted earlier, Dad never went to church with us. That was partially why Satan occasionally sat in our pew. Grandma was perched in her permanent part of the pew on the far end and couldn't stand the sight of Satan. Everyone knew it was our pew, we always sat in the front pew, and we didn't like strangers, much less Satan, sitting there.

I got the stained-glass window seat when Satan wasn't around, watching the sunlight flow through the blood of Christ. Satan, strangely enough, was the churchgoing sort. He was usually standing in the back, like everyone else who came too late. Every now and then, he got there early and sat at the end of our pew. Walking in before Mass and seeing him there was like seeing a dead groundhog by the side of the road. I'd feel frightened and revolted for a second, but then I realized we were in church and nothing horrible was going to happen.

We minded our own business, but there was that part of Mass where we had to turn to our neighbors and offer peace, which generally meant a handshake. My brothers and I often gave each other the peace sign instead. I had to shake Satan's hand, and it was only right to look him in the eye as I did so. He smiled at me, and I smiled back. His hand was limp, and it felt good to shake Satan's hand.

Our only other contact was for me to pass him the money basket during collection. I was shocked to find that Satan had a parish collection envelope with his name on it, just like I did.

At some point Satan must have moved away from our town, and we never heard his beat-up Harley again.

I got lucky the summer after my freshman year at college. Money was going to be a problem, and no matter what, I was going to have to take out loans to continue my education. That was when Dad came through with a summer job at the plastics factory he worked at. It would pay about $7.00 an hour, which was more than I could hope to make at any other job. A large part of the job was painting the factory's roof, which meant getting a tan with no one else around.

I felt great about it, especially because I was the youngest, and this opportunity hadn't been offered to my brothers or sister before me. I had to wear a uniform, a hard hat and goggles for the job. The uniform was a jumpsuit, and it made me feel like I was in the band, Devo. I was in heaven, even though it could be hard work some days.

One day I went into the lunch room for my morning break, and there was a man in jeans and a t-shirt smoking a cigarette. This was unusual as all the workers, save a few managers, had uniforms, and they rarely came into the lunch room as it was sanctuary for the workers. He looked to be in his late 20s, short hair, a trimmed beard, thin. Only his hard hat suggested that he worked there. I nodded at him when I came in and took a seat at an empty table.

This man came over to my table and sat directly across from me. He was looking straight at me, but not saying anything. I nodded at him again. This happened all the time. Everyone knew who I was. Dad had worked there for over 20 years, and I found people looking at me as If they knew me from somewhere before.

"You don't remember me, do you?" he finally asked in an even voice. He was smiling now. I looked at his face, and I didn't remember him.

"You used to call me Satan," he said, the grin growing, "I'm Satan, Bill, Joey Flanagan."

My eyes must have rolled back in my head. Satan looked like any average Joe, a factory worker. Not the tall, bearded, lanky-haired biker I had remembered. When he came over to sit with me, I noticed that I was bigger than he was. I remembered him being gigantic and menacing.

"I know your face, but everything else about you has changed."

His voice was friendly; there was no bitterness at all. Our conversation was easy from there. Satan had a wife and kids, and he lived a few miles away. He had done a bad turn in biker bars and found himself in a rehab program a few years ago.

The tail end of the program was to find work via a sanitation agency which hired out people from the program. Satan started work in the factory the year before. In that time, he had worked hard and become the leader of the sanitation program in the factory, managing a team of workers, all much like him, guys who had crashed and burned early on and needed a new start. They always looked the same. They weren't allowed to wear uniforms, which was a blessing and a curse, because the color of one's uniform gave one a sense of identity in the factory, and not to wear one was to be in the front office or upper management, which was frowned upon by the general populace of workers.

Not to wear one was also to be a sanitation engineer, and depending on how one felt about drug rehab workers in the factory, it could be good or bad. The older workers seemed to frown on them, but the younger ones were more sympathetic; a few of them probably not too far from enrolling themselves in the program, too.

The sanitation people all looked the same: a little wild-eyed and eager to please. Most of them had longer hair and beards, but Satan had purposely cut his hair short and trimmed his beard to look more presentable. I could see why he had succeeded. He was friendly to everyone and never turned down any job, no matter how dirty or time consuming it was. Satan, it seemed, had truly turned over a new leaf. He drove a pickup truck to work.

That night on our way home, I had mentioned meeting Satan to Dad. He didn't really want to talk about it. But he had to feel strange about it. Satan had been there over a year, and this was the first time I had heard about it. If he mentioned it to Mom, she had kept it to herself. I could say he found it so insignificant so as not to mention it, but anyone who's done time in a factory or small town knows that a subject like this is a hot topic. Satan had a yellow hard hat and a mortgage. He must have longed for a white jump suit, the most popular uniform in the factory.

That summer, there were more than a few instances where Satan, Dad and I had lunch at the same table. We never mentioned the old Harley, or the confrontation. We did talk about church, something which Satan had never truly given up on, even in his darkest nights. He didn't claim to be Born Again, but he had that way about him. Our lunches were quiet and pleasant, talking about work and sports.

My father retired about 15 years after that summer we ran into Satan again. At the time, I asked him whatever happened to Satan. Dad smiled and informed me that Satan had a relapse a few years after that, and it became clear that he was losing his grip, turning up late for work, if at all, and spending a lot of time in the break room with his head resting face down on his arms, like an errant school boy. Satan got laid off when things got tight, and that was the last Dad had heard of him.

I often wonder if I'll ever meet Satan again, even though I no longer live back there. It certainly wouldn't surprise me, and in the back of my heart, I would love nothing more.

1974: The Drill

I spent close to a decade of my adult life not going to the dentist, then getting a ton of work done to make up for my absence. Why so long? Not having medical insurance for years was a large part of that. I'd been working freelance/temp gigs for years. I realized it makes sense to keep up with the dentist, because there's just so much you can do with toothpaste, mouthwash and floss. The deep cleaning I received on my first visit was revelatory, like I had a new set of teeth afterwards, the spitting of blood into the rinse basin was worth the pain.

Flashback to my childhood, and it's another story. There's a deeper reason I'd been more than fine with letting the dentist go by the wayside. Being a kid in rural Pennsylvania in the 70s, I was used to the concept of a no-frills way of life. Everything Mom and Dad bought in the store was cheap and made to be re-used. Pants were hemmed so one kid could pass them on to another. Gallons of soda were bought instead of healthier, more expensive drinks. The idea was "bang for the buck" more than subscribing to some type of "American Way" of raising kids where everything they had done for them was undeniably right.

I won't bust my parents for much, but something I surely will was that crazy, sugar-pounding diet we had, and their lack of enforcement on sound dental habits. I mean to the point of watching us brush, gargle and floss ever morning and night. I would have chafed like hell at this, but would have been thankful for that sort of discipline today. You know kids: they hate to do stuff like take baths and brush teeth. I wish they would have enforced the teeth thing. It would have saved all of us money in the long run, and many mouthfuls of pain, then and now.

Going to the dentist back there at that time, I *know* Novocain existed and was in popular use back in the 70s. We never got it! We went to Dr. Morrison, an aged dentist a few towns over in Mount Carmel. Can't recall his first name, so we thought it was Jim. A ride over there would have my brothers chanting, "Mr. Mojo Rising ... Mojo Rising ... Rising, Rising ... Got to keep on rising!" Or crooning, "This is the end ... beautiful friend, the end." Because it was a Doors-like experience of darkness and doubt to make that long station-wagon ride to the dentist's office, like we were riding into hell.

Even the door on that office, with the pebbled glass and wire-crossed window, scared the shit out of me. It was like an office out of a 1940s private detective movie: dark, foreboding, always twilight, shadows everywhere. I expected to open the door and see Humphrey Bogart sitting there with his fedora and cigarette. Instead, I found copies of *Highlights* magazine for kids, the sight of which still scares the shit out of me. And the tense sound of drills whining in the background.

I can't even recall if Dr. Morrison was a nice guy or not. I suspect he was a crotchety old man, as I seem to recall him being in his 60s or 70s at the time. I can't even remember what he looked like, save for the white smock and ever-present surgeon's light he wore on a headband.

What I do remember, to this day, is getting drilled repeatedly without the benefit of Novocain or any other anesthetic. It's laughable today to envision that scene, a kid undergoing a medical procedure like this without having his mouth numbed, but Dr. Morrison was of the era where Novocain was for pussies. World War II, longshoremen swinging hooks, why, all I ate was a baked-bean sandwich all day Depression era shit. I had a bellyful of it from Dad, but Dr. Morrison lived it.

It was agonizing. There were two types of drills: the high-pitched, keening drill that was used for the fine-styling along the edge of a tooth. Which sounded horrific, but really wasn't that bad. And the low-rumbling, deep drill that took out the bulk of the cavity.

That was the pain machine. Tear-inducing pain. White-knuckled, seat-rail clutching pain. Smoke coming out of my mouth. Afraid to move despite numerous alarms firing off in my synapses. Shaking in the chair like a dog dreaming. All I could do was stare at the light and try to put my mind somewhere else. The dental assistant at a recent trip commented that I was the most relaxed patient she'd ever seen. Another dentist years ago called me "stoic." No. I go back to those horrifying visits to Dr. Morrison's office when I realized the only way out was to disassociate my mind from the situation. Feel the pain, but put my mind somewhere else. Torture victims have described the same mental exercise.

You would think, having that done to me once, I would have said, forget Mom and Dad, I'm going to brush and floss twice a day, maybe more, now that I know what will happen when I don't. But kids are stupid: I use myself as a prime example. I have a mouthful of fillings and missing back molars now as a result. The stint with Dr. Morrison must have ended by the early 80s, because I remember a series of dentists in my teens and early 20s. Dr. Hale in Frackville? He seemed like a good guy – can't recall why we stopped using him, unless he retired. A few quacks along the way apparently, as one of them did a number on Sister K in terms of faulty work that she still pays for today. Those few I saw in my teens and early twenties are a blur. I didn't go that much. A habit that, regrettably, stretched into my 40s.

What's odd now is that when I visit back there, and Brother J and I drive through Mount Carmel, we can't even remember exactly where Dr. Morrison's office was. A dark place that was drilled into our memories.

1974: Stop Spreading the News

After 30 years in New York, I often wonder how I chose to move here. There was that one strange night in 1987, sometime after graduating Penn State, a failed, weeks-long stab at adulthood in Venice, California under my belt, where I lay in my childhood bed listening to "I'll Take New York" by Tom Waits on my Sony Walkman. It's a wavering, ironic shamble of a song about a guy falling down an elevator shaft, a perverse answer song to Sinatra's "New York, New York." For some reason, listening to that song filled me with the spirit and desire to be there.

The roots of that desire stretch all the way back to the 70s, to the least likely of places: *The Waltons* TV show, set in Depression-era Virginia. Our parents loved that show for taking them back to their own rural childhoods in the same era. Of course, we loved it, too. All kids mimicked the finale to every show, where the members of the family bid each other good night in the darkness of their humble-but-happy home. It was inevitable that Brother J or M would emphatically punctuate their less sincere good nights with a fart blast. Always good for a major laugh. We loved the show for different reasons than our parents. It made perfect sense that the two older sisters in the show would one day pose nude for *Playboy* in real life. Our adolescent fantasies willed this so years before it happened.

In *The Waltons*, John Boy was the eldest son, an aspiring writer who longed to move to New York, a near-impossible dream given where he lived and how poor his family was. Naturally, once I started showing writing talent in middle school, kids would jokingly call me John Boy, and I related to his character. As with all TV shows, and the writer of the show who was John Boy's real-life counterpart, his impossible dream came true. My possible dream came out more like the Tom Waits song.

New York seemed like another planet to us in the 70s, as did Philadelphia. Neighbor Bubba had relatives there and would sometimes visit. Philly may as well have been Paris as far as we were concerned. We thought major cities meant Scranton/Wilkes Barre, Harrisburg, Reading and Allentown. Downtown Pottsville, our county seat, felt a little like a city, although it was on the cusp of the Fairlane Village and Schuylkill Malls ripping its retail heart out. I once wrote a story about getting an erection the first time I saw the hazy New York City skyline on the swampy New Jersey horizon, approaching in a car on Route 78. It was no lie. I was intimidated by buildings over three stories high. That city looked like Oz in the distance to a kid who had no real grasp of city life.

But we weren't raised in a vacuum. When cable TV came into vogue sometime in the early 70s, we immediately picked up channels from New York and Philadelphia, the New York channels being 5, 9 and 11. We were watching the same TV as people in New York! These people seemed harder than we were. Their news shows, in the pit of the 70s New York financial collapse, often featured reporters in gloomy night-time urban scenes describing multiple murders, the inevitable black or Hispanic kids hovering behind the reporter and waving cheerfully at the camera.

To this day I have a penchant for movies set in 1970s New York. I should have known even then that movies like *Dog Day Afternoon, Law and Disorder* and *Looking for Mr. Goodbar* held some special allure for me. I was drawn to the grittiness and the hard-edged but friendly vibe the city seemed to impart. It was aggressive, but it had heart, too. So unlike the mannered, respectable way of life we aspired to in rural Pennsylvania.

We even got to spend time with a city kid through the Fresh Air program. One day in 1974, I was hanging around the schoolyard by myself, bouncing a rubber ball off the schoolyard wall, when three hippy teenagers approached me.

I should have been wary. This was the age of the Manson Family and Patty Heart. (Hearst, as it turned out, was spending time hidden away on a farm just north of us near Scranton.) They seemed more like Janey O and Phil: older, smart and friendly. This should have made me even more leery. But the first thing they asked me was if I could take them to my parents, which was about 50 feet away. Dad was at work, but Mom was usually home.

They explained to her that they were part of a state-funded program to provide guidance to working-class children in rural Pennsylvania, a sort of "summer camp" program to kids who really had no need of one as our lives were one big summer camp. (Most of us skipped the Boy Scouts, too, although those kids had an amazing skillset far beyond our basic rural knowledge.) Mom seemed a little suspicious, but the next day there was a picture of me in the newspaper on the schoolyard wall with these hippies, two girls and a guy.

I can't remember their names, or how long the program lasted. It might have been just that summer and the next. I'm not even sure where they lived, but I would guess they were college students from nearby towns working on a summer project for their social-science degrees. All they seemed to do was play along with us, provide occasional equipment like baseballs and bats, and sometimes sponsor field trips to the swimming pool in Hegins or Knoebels Amusement Park. I call them hippies now because of the hair and clear liberal bent of their program, but my memory is hazy as to exactly what they were. No matter, they were smart and kind, and we liked them.

The second summer, they brought around a Fresh Air kid whom one of the parents had agreed to put up for a few weeks: Curtis from Newark, New Jersey. Curtis was an excitable little black kid, my age. I should note here that part of Pennsylvania was (and is) overwhelmingly white. There were only white people in our town. Later in high school, the only black family was The Gregory's from Ringtown.

We took to Curtis like a long-lost brother. He had the same rough-and-tumble vibe we were raised with as working-class kids. There were strange differences, too. He grew frightened after dark and refused to walk down alleys at night, even when there were a few of us with him. It made us recognize he was being exposed to dangers that were not present in our lives. Curtis was living one of those Channel 11 news scenes where crime was an every-day reality.

There's one Curtis memory burned in my mind. When we played schoolyard baseball in summer, the game went on for hours. Inevitably, we'd get thirsty. While it would have been easy for any of us to walk the few hundred feet or yards to our houses to get water or Kool Aid, it made more kid sense to run up to the cemetery and drink from the rusty pipe and spigot by the road. Like dogs lapping from a toilet bowl, we were forever drinking water from questionable sources like that, garden hoses running a close second. It seemed like a betrayal to go home and spend time among adults to drink water; we'd rather do it with each other.

I remember racing Curtis to the spigot after one of those games. The kid loved to run, although he wasn't any better an athlete than we were. Gorging on water after a hard, sweaty game was such a sweet reward. I remember taking turns with Curtis, cupping our hands underneath the rusty water gushing from the pipe, both of us laughing at the patty-cake style rhythm we had going, then sitting back on the immaculate cemetery grass, listening to the locusts buzzing in the trees and taking in the summer twilight. It must have been heaven for him to go to a place like this. I'm sure I sat there thinking, "There's no way on earth I could live some place where you'd be afraid to walk down an alley at night with a group of friends."

Flash forward, and I've spent the past 30 years doing just that. Shit happens. I sometimes think it was a mistake to come to New York. The gritty, hard-edged, sprawling mass of contradictions I moved to in 1987 has faded. The nature of the city, especially in the last decade, has grown uncomfortably materialistic, even for New York. Gentrification is frighteningly out of control; middle-class people like me are being forced out. So much of the city is the antithesis of the working-class values my parents instilled in me. I live here for those moments of humanity, much like Curtis and I had, the quiet, persistent reminders that there are a lot of us in the same boat, struggling to get by. Everyone in my hometown knows how it feels to not want to be erased. We're here, too.

1974: Dropping In

Grandma's favorite mythical definition of hell was of a man standing up to his neck in a pool of cool, clean water, dying of thirst, but unable to drink any of it. Uncle Bob got to do his take on this parable at a high-school football game.

Uncle Bob was Mom's big brother who lived in their hometown, Pottsville, with his wife and two daughters. He was "big" literally and figuratively, around 6' 4" and solid, made his living as a well-respected carpenter. He reminded me of Lennie from John Steinbeck's *Of Mice and Men*, this gentle giant with a cheerful demeanor, who could most likely strangle a man with one hand.

There's surely truth in construing that Dad, and as a result his sons, weren't too hot on Uncle Bob visiting the house. This was for a number of reasons, not all of them to do with Bob. The largest was that Fountain Springs was home base for all Dad's siblings with multiple, insane visits yearly. Mom went out of her mind before relatives visited, cleaning every object in sight, raising everything up a notch so that we felt like an eager-to-please hotel staff waiting on our arriving guests. She ran a tight ship anyway, so this was some strange insecurity Mom had that Dad's relatives might look down on her if the place was "a mess."

And we had the Port Carbon spinsters to deal with, another layer of pressure with relatives. These weren't Mom's "people" – not her blood relatives. Both her parents had passed away by the time I came of age; that generation on her side of the family remained a mystery to me. She got along with everybody, relative or not, so she had nothing to worry about. It was her nature to worry. As kids, we picked up on that low-level tension and didn't like it.

The largest factor was Dad, who didn't like any non-blood relative in the house. I would imagine anyone who got the cold shoulder from him over the years must have thought, "Why is that prick freezing me out?" No. He was quiet to begin with, but put him around relatives who weren't his siblings or us, and he shut down. Brother M and I mimicked his behavior, but grew out of it and developed our own personalities around relatives. Brother J mimicked Dad exactly, and does so to this day! Sister K took Mom's side and went out of her way to please visiting relatives.

Uncle Bob and Dad had a personal history I knew nothing about, too. Bob had employed Dad in his carpentry business after he came out of the service in the mid-50s. I have no idea what happened there, guessing it fell somewhere between "not my bag" and catastrophic. All I knew was Dad worked in the factory from the early 60s on. I'm assuming he was either dating or married to Mom to receive the job offer, so I should factor in the concept of a big brother looking out for his sister, too. (These were things that did not occur to me as a child.)

The one large positive was that Dad came away with enough carpentry skills from working with Bob that he had the ability to build a much-needed bathroom extension onto our house by himself. Before that, it was seven people sharing one bathroom, with the outhouse at the far end of the yard. I see these things portrayed in old western movies. Rest assured, they were still around in the 70s. Going up there to use the bathroom in an emergency was a horrible experience. Dumping into a wooden hole that covered nothing more than a sewage pit? Flies? Splinters? Brother M sneaking up and banging on the door while I was pinching one out? All this and more. The worst was gazing into that dark, stinking pool beneath the seat and waiting for a deformed feces monster to spring up from the depths.

As always, Dad built the extension with the help of the boys, Brother J in particular, Dad's workhorse. It took close to two years to complete during Dad's vacations. There were a few instances where Grandma flushed the upstairs toilet while J and I were in the plumbing pit on the back patio working on open pipes. "Look out, she's gonna' blow," J would cry out, as if we were oil-well workers. Instead of black gold, we got brown trouts if we didn't scramble out of the hole in time.)

When Uncle Bob visited, he and Dad got along fine. Bob had the same warm, inviting personality that Mom had, and he'd easily draw Dad into conversations. But Bob came with the whole family: Aunt Carol and cousins Suzie and Sandy. In the early 70s, this was bedlam. Our cousins fought as much as we did, if not more. I recall a few screaming matches and brawls in the living room, not just with each other, but with us, too. The same petty bullshit we put each other through as kids. Dad already had a bellyful of this dealing with us alone … and our legion of cousins on his side of the family … and the Port Carbon spinsters.

I rarely brought friends into the house because I knew it made Dad uncomfortable. Many times, whoever answered the door would let them in, and they'd wait right there by the door in the dining room. If they came in to sit down, it was like pulling teeth for Dad to connect with them, and he wasn't particularly worried about it. I can see the way I am now and how it draws back to him on that sofa, but I've also been imbued with Mom's nature. Dad blew everyone off, Mom befriended everyone, and I landed somewhere in between. (Rest assured, if people think I'm quiet, the real reason is they either make me uncomfortable or my instincts tell me to shut down.)

The deal breaker for Dad was Uncle Bob's unannounced visits. Dad knew when his relatives were coming. They had to drive many miles to get there, so the trip was planned days or weeks in advance. Like German soldiers on the beach at Normandy on June 5, 1944, we were ready and waiting for the inevitable onslaught. Uncle Bob, much like Aunt Bess, was like a wild Indian in comparison who pulled up in his station wagon and walked right in.

We joked that we needed a fire alarm that went off every time Bob's car pulled up, and perhaps a sliding pole allowing us to drop down to the basement. I pondered making a prison-style rope of my bed sheets to escape from my bedroom window. Once, I do recall maneuvering over the slanted roof outside my window, the theme from *Mission Impossible* playing in my head, and jumping the 10 feet to the back porch where I took off like a shot for the schoolyard. After a certain age, I was normally in my room anyway, reading or listening to music. One of those days sticks in my mind, Uncle Bob visiting during a freak snow squall in early April. I sat on the corner of my bed near my open window, watching silver-dollar sized snowflakes fall while Bob Seger sang "Still the Same" on my stereo.

These were low-level tensions. Uncle Bob and Mom got along fine as adult siblings, and it's to our discredit that this became such a sore topic in our childhood. I can see now that while a lot changes between siblings as they age and mature, hopefully for the better, the structure of how they relate to each other doesn't. We could all see that Bob and Mom got along with little to no friction.

One fall night in the mid-70s, we got an emergency phone call. It was Aunt Carol calling from a hospital, trying to explain what had happened. The one thing Bob shared with Mom was a passion for high-school football. We always went to our high school's games back then; I still go now when I visit in the fall. Pottsville in the 70s was a perennial powerhouse, a much larger school than most of the surrounding rural districts. Like Mom, Bob tried to attend every game and loved to go on the road to different stadiums in those small towns. You didn't need a map back then to find the stadium. You could drive around a town on a Friday night and sooner or later see a large bank of lights 100 feet in the air. All you had to do was drive towards the lights, the only game in town.

It might have been Shamokin, but I can't recall. Bob had gone to see Pottsville play on the road. At half time, like a lot of fans, he needed to use the men's room. So, he went, finding the squat, cement pillbox near the concession stand. No doubt there were metal troughs lining the walls.

Who knows how this happened, but the floor to the men's room collapsed, plunging over a dozen men and boys into a pit of raw sewage. There was no plumbing at outdoor stadiums like this back then, only a large latrine pool under the wooden floor boards. I can't recall if anyone was hurt in the floor collapse, but the next immediate danger was being cast into deeply-fouled water. Bob recalled the water being up to his chest, so I could guess any small men or boys in there were treading in the raw sewage. One by one, the men crawled or were fished out of the entrance. I could picture Uncle Bob, like Ernest Borgnine in *The Poseidon Adventure*, heaving shit-covered bodies through the doorway.

I don't know the exact treatment, but spending time in raw sewage surely requires tetanus shots and an extreme body cleansing. We weren't sure what had happened, whether men had died in the collapse or were drowned. As it turned out, it was just a harrowing personal experience that could have been much worse. It seemed like something that could happen only to Uncle Bob!

The only connection I had to Mom and Uncle Bob's parents was the graveyard, this one in Pottsville. I still drive by there now sometimes when visiting. I have a hard time remembering which hilly side street to turn down. Mom would usually take Sister K and me down to plant flowers and spend time, the same way our visiting relatives did for their father in our cemetery. We'd visit Uncle Bob on the tail end of these trips, and they would share stories and memories about their parents.

Unlike our cemetery, this one was walled off from the public. There were no kids playing football in an open field of the grounds, or dog walkers, or kids playing Jailbreak at night. As kids, we made the cemetery part of our living environment. We did the same as teenagers: roads along cemeteries were outlaw territories to under-age drink or have sex at night. (I recall one winter's night having to jump start friend Mike T's car on the Catholic side, his girlfriend too embarrassed to make eye contact.)

As I got older, it occurred to me that my body is going to end up in the ground, and I have no urge to hang out there. I'll be hanging out there for a *long* time soon enough! Brother J used to dump leaves by the township grounds next to the cemetery, something I help with when visiting for Thanksgiving. In the last few years, he simply drives into Ashland and dumps into their official mulch pile. The last time we dumped next to our cemetery, there was an elderly, bearded man with long, flowing hair and a headband sitting lotus-style in front of a tombstone. Sometimes he'd raise his hands to the gray, November skies. He wasn't weeping; it seemed more like meditation. We felt like we were in our own early 70s cult movie even though it was 2010. We opened and closed the pick-up truck tailgate gingerly when dumping the leaves so as not to disturb his reverie. Both of us had spent decades around that cemetery, and I can't speak for Brother J, but it didn't register with me until that day what this place meant to most people who didn't live next to one. An hour later, it was a relief when a middle-aged man in an SUV who bore a physical resemblance to the old man picked him up and drove off.

Mom was uncharacteristically moody and sad in her parents' cemetery. She had to be in her 30s by the time both had passed on, far too young, but probably not out of the ordinary in the Coal Region back then. It helps explain the strange distance I feel from her side of the family history.

1975: Soytz

As kids growing up in our neighborhood, we did some pretty stupid, mean-spirited things that should have gotten our asses kicked. Even if it was by association. I can't recall raising my voice in dissent in a lot of situations that were clearly wrong.

What comes to mind most is Soytz. There were three grown brothers in my neighborhood, all with houses on my block. Frank, Joe and Eddie. Frank was the lawn-mowing king of the neighborhood: a good guy. He also had an infamous eye for junk, which he'd store in this cavernous two-story concrete bunker in his backyard. If he was out driving and saw a pile of dirt by the side of the road with a few bricks in it, he'd pull over, retrieve the bricks, throw them in the back of his pick-up, drive home and put them in the bunker. By the time he passed on, he had a two-story junkyard. None of it made any sense.

Joe lived down the block. He was famous for being a war hero in World War II. The local paper once re-ran his story. Somewhere in the South Pacific, he and a severely wounded buddy had been isolated in the jungle. So, he heaved the guy over his shoulder and walked him through miles of enemy territory before re-connecting with the troop. An amazing feat – can't recall the medal he won, but it was impressive. He was also known as "Hammer Man" in the neighborhood, for once going off his nut and attacking another guy at the polling office (i.e., the firehouse) with a hammer during a particularly heated election. Despite this, I can't recall him ever being rude or unkind to me.

Across from the schoolyard, Eddie lived with his wife and son, Lee. Picture the father in the animated series *King of the Hill*. This was a lot like Eddie, with his burr-head haircut. As with Frank and Joe, I don't recall anything particularly mean-spirited or wrong about Eddie. Baseballs would constantly be hit into his yard when we played in summer, so I imagine there might have been a few altercations, probably over kids dawdling or messing with his property rather than just retrieving the ball. Since our family's house was on the other side of the schoolyard, this happened with our yard, too, and was much worse as we had a dog called Duffy, a mutt whom we unfortunately trained halfway in terms of fetching balls. He'd fetch them, but never give them back. You had to chase after him for minutes on end, and at that point, usually have no luck prying the ball from his jaws as he snarled. He wasn't a mean dog. We simply made the error of not training him properly on this.

The difference between Eddie's and our family? We were kids in the neighborhood, thus a connection to the other kids, so we were spared any sort of antagonism, since were one of them. Eddie's son went to Vietnam, was older, and out of the loop age-wise with the kids of the 70s. I've noticed with kids that they can't comprehend adults who don't have kids, or kids their age. That seems like a very important connection. Without it, adults seem vaguely menacing, strange, not worthy of respect, to be watched. I can sense the same vibe living in this neighborhood in Queens. It says a lot more about how dumb and tribal kids are than it does about the childless adult.

That's the key difference, because kids, wherever they live, form their own little insular world, with its own rules, completely divorced from the adult world, and it usually holds sway in places like playgrounds. In this way, kids think they "rule" a certain neighborhood: it's theirs because they live there. Of course, they don't quite grasp that they're children, not able to support themselves, totally dependent on their parents to survive. I suspect there's a hard-to-classify resentment in that, so when some kids see a free shot to take at adults, whether it's something as mild as cocking off or vandalizing property, they'll take it. As kids often wander around in groups, that gravitation towards bad behavior is reinforced.

I mention all this because I think it gives good background towards the ongoing negative treatment that was meted out towards Eddie, who didn't deserve one ounce of it. As noted, Eddie would often be brusque with kids who dawdled in his yard when a ball was hit into it. As an adult now, I can see it's very easy to be brusque with kids, because they'll often have openly antagonistic stances with adults who aren't their parents.

Eddie got the nickname Soytz in a strange way. One summer day, while Eddie was doing something like washing his car in a pair of shorts, a mildly retarded kid in the neighborhood with a speech impediment said: "Look, there goes Eddie in his soytz." He meant "Eddie in his shorts." For some reason, the word "soytz" blew everybody's mind. At the time, the Elton John song "Bennie and the Jets" was a huge hit. "Eddie and his Soytz" fit the rhyming scheme. So, all summer, kids were singing, "E-e-e-e-e-ddie in his soytzzzzzz." The name stuck, although it was senseless and indicative of nothing but a kid with a speech impediment making a stray comment, and how well the mispronounced word fit in with a hit song of the day.

I'm not sure if this is a national trend, but back there we had a thing called Mischief Night: the night before Halloween. The concept was for kids to go around raising mischief, before receiving goodies on Halloween night. In actuality, Mischief Night would unofficially begin in mid-October and culminate in one night of insanity on October 30th. Our two big things to do were to apply bar and shaving soap to the side windows of cars (if you did the front and/or back, you were a real asshole), and to pelt the windows of houses with corn. Since we grew up around farms, and corn was hitting its stride in late September, we'd make clandestine forays into farmers' fields to steal ears of corn for mischief night, often resulting in us getting shot at by farmers with shotguns, using buckshot shells. This was tremendously exciting to us kids, gave us a real sense of danger. Once we had the corn, we then had to shuck the kernels from the cob and store them in paper bags for Mischief Night. Generally, we'd soap windows up to that point, not wanting to deplete our corn supply by the 30th.

I realize how strange all this sounds, but I wouldn't be surprised if it still goes on some places (although no longer back home, simply less kids around, and some thread was lost in the 90s with customs like this). Everybody got soaped and corned back then – even our own families' houses. It was tradition. I guess in the grand scheme of vandalism, it wasn't that horrendous either: hit the windows with a few sprays from a garden hose and a sponge, and the soap was gone.

For whatever reason, probably associated with him constantly chasing assholic kids from his yard, Soytz got pounded every October. By Mischief Night, he'd simply leave town with his wife and son so that his trailer would be empty. We all knew not to hit his house for Halloween, because he wasn't in the mood and wouldn't have answered the door at that point. In the weeks leading up to it, every night there would be kids soaping his windows and corning his house. With his trailer, the roof and sides were metal, so the corn must have sounded like machine-gun fire. I remember some of the wackier troublemakers in the neighborhood openly taunting him and his wife on the street. I also remember his wife coming out and pleading, "Why are you doing this to us?" And all us little assholes laughing at her. I can't believe neighbors didn't phone the police more often on this. It would be literally a dozen kids openly screaming in front of a house, pelting it with corn, and doing silly shit like running up to the trailer and pounding on the windows. It was open harassment, awful shit that shouldn't have been tolerated by the community in any way.

This went on for a few years. It's to Eddie's credit that he never went off his nut and shot a kid, or even beat one up, as it would have been well-deserved. Why Eddie? I guess because he had the audacity to yell at a few kids who were in dire need of life-threatening ass-kickings, never got them, and went on to patchy lives of drug abuse and low-level crime. It was also simple geography: his trailer was right across from the front of the school, where the bad kids hung out at night.

How much did I go along with this? Enough to feel guilty and embarrassed all these years later for playing any part in it. I got as far as being a part of the mob and throwing corn a handful of times, but I wouldn't go on his property or soap his windows. My parents warned me not to be part of the mob stuff in mid-October; they understood we were going to go out on Mischief Night and do the usual stuff. They also understood that harassing Eddie wasn't cool and made no sense. If I'd had a real set of balls, I'd have told the kids they were wrong for singling out this person for such rotten, abusive behavior, but such is peer pressure, and I quietly assented to this.

Soytz wasn't the only one; there were other old people who got the same sort of abuse. The pattern was always the same: if you in any way reprimanded a kid publicly, it was open season on you. Granted, some of those people were loony old cranks, but some weren't. I remember the paper boy who walked through the neighborhood being physically attacked a few times by various nuts in our gang. Why? Because it was cool to yell out "paper boy" in a loud, sarcastic drawl, and watch him get pissed off in return when he knew he was being made fun of.

When you leave kids to their own devices, it's the law of the jungle; there is no higher authority at work, no innate desire to be good and righteous. Kids have to be taught those sort of things. When not being taught that, and amongst themselves, they sometimes resort to the worst possible behavior. Some people might classify that as rebellion, but I view it more clearly as an acceptable form of mental illness that doesn't serve as any sort of healthy outlet, or do anyone any recognizable good. How much a kid chooses to indulge in that insanity is going to be a mark of what kind of person he turns out to be.

Eddie's gone now, as are his brothers, even his wife recently, his son now well into his 60s. It's strange for me to go back there and physically see these people and places, realizing all is relatively normal now, as opposed to the sort of insanity that went on far too many times back then. I'm still wondering what's happened in our world, as true in the 70s as it is now, that kids are given such free reign to get away with behavior that would land your average adult in jail and make him the pariah of a community.

1975: Mowing Lawns

I'm never quite sure why people carp about mowing lawns. I love doing it and do it every chance I get. The sound of the mower, the physical exertion, time spent in the sun, the visible sight of a finite job being completed: all these things make me enjoy the experience.

Mowing a lawn is a direct connection to nature. The grass grows, with or without you. If you want a nice, clean ground to walk on, you have to make it that way. With snow or leaves, you have to clean up after nature. Doing these seemingly minute things reminds you of the constant motion of the world and your small place in it, and that you have to do something to exert control over it. My true pleasure with mowing lawns is tied into the fact that I made money as a kid doing this.

I can't remember how we got roped into mowing other people's lawns, but I'm glad my brothers and I did. The first big client came with Dr. Heber, who lived out the road on a few acres of land, a humungous front and back lawn. Brother M started doing this, but soon realized he was on an eight-hour slog every time he mowed. Thus Brother J and I were enlisted to help with old lawn mowers Dad had tinkered back into (sporadically) working order.

It would take the three of us three hours to do the whole lawn, with Brother M stuck with the shit job of mowing over the septic tank. The 70s were a weird time for septic tanks. When I go back home now, everyone has a septic tank, as the township switched over to this system a few years ago.

The only way you'd know everyone has a septic tank now is that you can see the pipe tops jutting a few inches out from the grass in each yard. Back in the 70s, the few people who had septic tanks all had the desperately cheap habit of letting the tank overflow, thus creating small shit swamps in their yards, and toxic run-off into near-by gutters. Mr.

Hanlon got on everybody's bad side by pumping their septic tank one summer night. We were all sitting around watching TV, probably *Chico and the Man*, when the most overpowering stench of fresh shit filled the air. This was like Dad, who took the most astoundingly "my god, what did he eat" dumps, taking 10 in a row and lighting them on fire.

We ran out in the streets – everyone on the block did – to realize that Mr. Hanlon had run a hose into his septic tank and was pumping into the street. A few of the neighbors, Dad included, called the cops, and that was the end of that. Mr. Hanlon alienated a lot of people with that stunt, as well he should have. After that, he still left the tank overflow on the lawn. Their house was next to the schoolyard. Many of us had sneakers suctioned off our feet when we had to romp through their lawn to retrieve a rubber ball.

With the Heber's lawn, Brother M would find himself ankle-deep in sewage sludge and clods of floating grass. It was virtually impossible to mow. All you could do was hack it down a few inches with scythe and sickle. (This was before weed eaters came into vogue.) He'd find dead or dying copperhead snakes stuck in the sewage, craning their heads while the rest of their bodies baked in shit. He'd usually put them out of their misery with a whack of the scythe. If that sounds harsh, try picking up an agitated, shit-covered, poisonous snake by the tail and walking it a hundred yards to the nearest woods without getting bit.

I'd do this, too, eventually. In fact, I remember Brother J and I taking over the business and doing the Heber lawn ourselves, five-hour mowing marathons that would find us drinking a gallon jug of water a piece and still dying of thirst by the end. The lawn was an easy mow, but doing a few acres with a push mower was a time-consuming ordeal. I looked at it as strenuous, vertical sun-bathing that I got paid to do. The worst aspect, beyond the horrible metallic sound of a blade violently scraping on an unseen rock, was the mowers running out of gas, which would entail at least 15 minutes of fruitless chord-pulling in extreme heat. Once those mowers got that hot, restarting them was a bitch. We learned the trick of unscrewing the carburetor cover and jamming a screwdriver into the gas-flow valve.

Many times, I'd be there in my skimpy 70s shorts, my balls nearly hanging out, white tube socks pulled up to my knees, pair of chlorophyll-stained sneakers, tan as any surfer, cursing over a dead mower that wouldn't start. To get through that, drive back home, unload the mowers, sit in the backyard in the cool of the evening, sipping Kool Aid, with $10 in my pocket (the job went for $20, which seemed like a lot of money to kids back then), and the knowledge that I'd be driving to the local mall in an hour or two to buy an album: a nice feeling. (A perfect summer memory, a little later, was mowing a particularly onerous lawn for one of Dad's coworkers in Primrose, covered in dirt and sweat, taking my $20, driving straight to Listening Booth and buying Ian Hunter's *You're Never Alone with a Schizophrenic*. Every time I hear "Cleveland Rocks," I can almost smell the freshly-cut grass.)

There were other lawns. The next worst was a woman up the road from the Heber's who had a non-descript, shady lawn, save that it had a "rock garden." This meant a bunch of decoratively-painted stones placed into a ridge on her lawn, about 15 feet long, four feet wide. The problem with the rock garden was that we had to get down on our hands and knees to pick out grass and weeds from between the rocks, making sure to leave any colorful flowers or heather untouched. What a pain in this ass this was. It would take an hour to mow the lawn, then three more hours to clean out the rock garden. On our hands and knees, or leaning on rocks for leverage. Couldn't use gloves either as they'd make our fingers too clumsy to grab the small weeds. Thus, we'd leave the place with sore knees and backs, small scrapes and cuts on our fingers. The rock garden only happened once a month, but we dreaded it.

Even our own lawn had its problems, namely dogshit. Running over it with a lawnmower is not a pleasant proposition. The turds are cut and flung over the lawn, leaving the mower, and maybe you, smelling like dogshit. So, before every mowing session at home, I'd have to shovel the numerous mounds from the lawn. We kept the stuff in an old tar bucket, then once it was full, bury the contents in the backyard. It was sort of a dogshit stew in that tar bucket; the contents liquefied over time. A real nightmare would have been one of my older brothers chasing me down with that bucket and dumping it on me.

What I remember most about lawn mowing was that deep-summer zen, the same feeling I'd get distance running. The heat would add to it. Anyone who's done any prolonged cardio workout knows the feeling: body under duress, but also working at peak form, pumping out sweat to cool down, the repetitive action, lulling the mind into a sense of calm. People would never believe me when I'd tell them how relaxing it was to run six miles in 85-degree heat, but it was. The same went for lawn-mowing, along with that sense of isolation the sound of the motor would bring. The outside world existed only in passing, a wave to a friend passing by on a 10-speed bike. Even now, if someone starts up a piece of equipment like a lawn mower, I can sleep straight through it, so long as the sound remains steady. You couldn't hear anything outside it. You had to concern yourself only with what was directly in front of you, a visible square that shrunk with every passing lap, until there was nothing but a freshly-mown lawn, the smell of it mingled with hints of gasoline. A perfect little world.

And a pocket-full of dough afterwards. I can trace back my relationship to money and work to allowances (believe it or not, a quarter a week ... how in the hell I did anything with that amount of money is beyond me now), but it wasn't until lawn mowing that I got the first taste of comparatively big money. A strange thing about me, work and money. I've found that so long as I feel productive and useful, money's not a burning issue in my life. Sure, I could use more -- most of us could. I'm not driven by money; I'm driven by the concept of work. It's surely a detriment to me that I don't insist on climbing a money ladder to ensure my self-worth. That may not seem like much of a distinction, but from what I've seen, it's a huge in terms of the difference between ambition and work itself. This all goes back to mowing lawns, and the simple pleasure I got from being able to take stock in a job well done, and knowing the whole process would need to be done again, and again, and again.

1975: The Cheerleader

Connie W was the first girl I kissed. It must have been 1969, right around kindergarten age. We were always doing that, under the apple tree in the backyard or in the schoolyard. I felt like Bobby Sherman wearing his patent-leather, dog-collar necklace. Her older sister Annie wasn't too thrilled about this and ended up scraping the smallpox vaccination lumps on my right shoulder with a toy Tonka truck. Things cooled down after that.

It seemed a strange anomaly that a majority of the kids in the neighborhood through the 70s were boys. Or maybe I remember it that way because we were so engaged in seasonal sports? There were girls around, but rarely playing along with us. Annie W did at first, but we kept growing, the games grew more competitive, and she developed other interests. It seemed like school meant girls, and neighborhood meant boys. This Peter Pan world evaporated when we grew old enough to drive.

Towards the mid-70s, some of the girls in the neighborhood were practicing to join their cheerleading squads for organizations like Pee Wee football and Catholic Youth Organization sports. The boys gathered in the schoolyard to play our seasonal sports. When the girls needed a place to practice their cheerleading, they would do so in that patch of schoolyard right by the school's main entrance, while we played our games on the adjacent side lot.

The amount of activity and peculiar social patterns going on any given day were astonishing. Most days there would be eight to 20 boys playing a game, usually with at least one fight or verbal sparring match, six to 10 girls practicing cheerleading, and as the sun set, about half a dozen scumbags, those dreaded older teenagers, whose presence felt like an unhinged relative showing up unannounced at a wedding. Sometimes they'd play along.

Sometimes they'd dangle one of us by our ankles from the school's second-story fire escape.

While the cheerleading portion wasn't so much odd as unexpected, something really odd happened concurrently. I mentioned Joey C in the earlier story about Easter Sunday. He was the altar boy doubled over in laughter as I blew out the contents of my stomach in the front pew that fateful day.

Joey came from a troubled family who lived down on Route 61. None of us outside the family knew what was going on. Their father, while nice to people in the neighborhood, was a large, powerful man, and gave off the impression that getting physical wasn't out of the question. Oldest brother Jimmy was a great athlete who walked away from an invitation to play in the minor leagues. Middle brother Larry was the leader of the bad kids, a very hard character with an intense stare who scared the shit out of all the younger kids. He could usually be found in the company of his malicious valet, Monk, similarly troubled and hard-edged, but nowhere near as intimidating. (One of my finer 70s memories was Brother J kicking Monk's ass after he started an impromptu snowball fight in front of our house, assuming J was too timid take a swing at him. Wrong assumption!) These guys did drugs and made no bones about it. They would hold a dark sway over that slightly older group of kids and drag them in a bad direction.

Joey C was the youngest brother, and I would guess his mother's son. Being raised in that house, it was impossible for him not to possess that volatile edge, the sense that he could turn violent at any second. He was also kind and gregarious, which everyone surmised had little to do with his father and more with his mother's influence. I could picture his parents offering him up to the church as an altar boy, in hopes that one of their boys would lighten the darker path the older brothers were walking down.

Well, it happened, and it didn't happen. Because of that dual nature, Joey came off as a flamboyant kid: loud, aggressive, like a teenage Mick Jagger. When the priest offered me a communion wafer at the altar railing, I half expected Joey to give me a Three Stooges-style slap on the head immediately thereafter.

Something else he was famous for was blanket dancing. In summer, we would often gather in our backyard, or any other yard that had a clothes line strung up between poles. Just after night fall, instead of trading ghost stories, we would hang a thin sheet or blanket over the clothes line, break out a series of flash lights, and hopefully someone would produce a Panasonic portable eight-track tape player (the one with the hand pump to change tracks). While two kids would take the flash lights and shake them behind the blanket, another kid would dance in front of them. Everyone else on the other side of blanket would see that gyrating silhouette with a strobe-light effect. In tandem with the music, our favorite tracks for this were "Do You Know What I Mean" by Lee Michaels and Grand Funk Railroad's cover version of "The Loco-Motion," the results were often hilarious, especially when Joey C got his turn. The night would then devolve into chasing down fireflies and capturing them in mason jars, their glowing tails illuminating the summer night.

One summer day during a high-stakes baseball game in the schoolyard, Joey, while halfheartedly waiting his turn at the plate, dropped his aluminum bat, walked over and started doing cheers with Annie and Connie W and their girlfriends. There wasn't a trace of awkwardness in him doing so, suggesting to us that they had done this before in private, and Joey was simply gravitating towards what he preferred doing.

I can't recall who it was, but one of the kids inevitably bellowed out, "Fag!"

Mistake. Whatever Joey's orientation, it had nothing to do with his ability, and family pedigree, to kick serious ass. Joey dropped the set of shredded newspaper pom-poms he had been swinging, tore across the schoolyard and tackled that kid, who was fleeing in fear, like an antelope from a charging lion. It was one of the legendary public beatings of our childhood, made all the more notable because Joey was crying far more than the kid he was pummeling. He was also delivering a very loud soliloquy:

"You idiot, son of a bitch, jack ass, jerk off, prick, why are you making me do this to you, why are you making me hurt you, I am not this person, I am *not* this person, I am a good person, I hate you for making me do this, I hate you, I hate you, I hate you!"

The kid was almost out cold, too stunned to cry, thinking these were the last few moments of his short, miserable life. When Joey started slowing down his punches, he could see that he was seriously hurting the kid and started crying even harder.

"Oh, no, what have I done. I'm so sorry. You shouldn't have said what you did. I am sorry. Please forgive me. Never say that to me again. Never make me hurt you again. Never!"

Everyone stood there in shock. Violence from Larry was expected; it felt strange and unnatural when he wasn't putting out an aggressive vibe. Until that point, we had only been aware of Joey's hardened attitude, not really knowing he was as formidable as his brothers in terms of physical confrontations.

Joey helped the kid up, walked him home with a few of the other kids, explained what had happened, then went home for what had to be a rough night. Then again, every night was probably rough in that house. He didn't seem any worse for wear after that. From that day forward, he veered away from team sports and would spend more of his time gossiping and laughing with the girls, occasionally joining in whatever nascent cheerleading routine they were practicing.

No one ever called him "fag" again, at least not to his face. Save for Larry. Larry could lay into Joey with the most cutting homophobic comments imaginable, and all it would do was create a seething, angry space between them that luckily never boiled over into public violence. Dark undercurrents flowed through that family that none of us would ever understand.

1975: Bowie in the Basement

When it came to Bowie, Brother M was the first fanatic in our family. It didn't take me long to catch up to him later in the 70's, but by sheer dint of age he was there first.

I don't know exactly when Brother M's teenage rough patch began. 1975? Surely before he could drive in 1976, his stormy teenage rebellion was already brewing. A lot of factors, I guess. As noted, the older kids in our neighborhood were a surly bunch. Drug addled, often not very smart, some really screwed-up kids who would have pissed me off terribly had I been a parent at the time. One of their more notorious episodes was the lawn party at Tangie S's house, a bright girl raised in that time of strangeness. Her parents were unpredictable in a way that suggested they could handle kids getting stoned on their property, within reason. They even made a huge pot of bean soup, much like the kind served at block parties. The highlight of the party was someone vomiting, and Joel Y, a reprobate in the making but not one of the harder kids, calmly walking over with a spoon, getting down on his hands and knees, and eating chunks of it off the lawn, bringing the party to a screaming conclusion. Brother M came in on the tail end of that crew and went from that industrious straight-A kid to a surly pain in the ass in the span of a year or two.

The basement was his domain, the only place our parents allowed him to smoke in the house. (The other smoker, Mom, would do so in the kitchen and in her favorite chair in the living room.) It wasn't a "rec room" basement either with finished walls and carpeting. The walls had the stony look of a dungeon. The coal bin and furnace were down there, as were Dad's massive piles of tools. The washer and dryer often hummed away while he smoked. There was a refrigerator for cans of A-Treat soda and extra milk, and a freezer for meat and Mom's array of frozen-dinner sides. (I still have uncharitable memories of salisbury steak.) The floor was concrete and puddled when it rained. (I would later spend a lot of time with him down there, the basement serving as my gym in terms of lifting vinyl-and-cement weights. And hanging upside down like a bat with my gravity boots after seeing Richard Gere use them in *American Gigolo*.)

Starting around 1974, most nights would find him down there relishing his "alone" time in a house full of seven people. Sometimes his good friend Barb D would be down there, younger sister of Lorraine, basically good girls from out the road playing bad for awhile due to their strict disciplinarian father. (They would have a dramatic falling out later in high school, over what I'm not sure, but it felt like *Phantom of the Opera* at the time.)

This was also where he had his massive console stereo: turntable, eight-track tape player, AM/FM receiver (tapped into the house's TV cable to get the best FM rock stations), all encased in fake-mahogany plywood. The stereo was like an altar, with a cardboard drum next to it filled with all our 45's, and a scattering of vinyl albums that were pretty much ruined after he got hold of them. This is part of the reason that I got into Queen, ELO and ABBA as I knew he had zero interest in more pop/rock bands like that. He was a hard-rock kid. Foghat's "Slow Ride." Nazareth's "Hair of the Dog." One troubled and stormy night in summer, I had gone downstairs to sleep on a sofa. I could hear Brother M in the basement, the rumble of bass seeping through the floor. After a few moments awake, it occurred to me that he was repeatedly listening to "Mamma Mia" by ABBA. He must have been really high.

We could both agree on *ChangesOneBowie*, that ubiquitous greatest hits album we both owned in various formats in the 70s. I'm not sure if *Diamond Dogs* or *Young Americans* was the first non-greatest hits Bowie album he bought. I'd guess not *Diamond Dogs* as I bought it myself a few years later and recall him borrowing it for his basement domain. Thus, I had dibs on discovering "Chant of the Ever Circling Skeletal Family."

That summer of 1975, Brother M found himself on the wrong side of the fence. Breaking bad, but not totally broke. He was wearing goofy clothes, too, like Depression-era hats, bib overalls with no shirts, maybe even platform shoes. I guess the sort of things a rock star would wear, but looked strange on a teenage kid in a small town. Some gear had shifted in his head, and he was hanging out with all the wrong kids. Although doing so in our town at that point simply implied walking out the front door.

He made one last valiant stab at purity, hanging around with some Christian-based youth group in Hegins, the farm town in a valley synonymous to us with the public swimming pool. (A few years earlier he had tried to drown me in the shallow end of the pool while "Cisco Kid" by War played on the outdoor jukebox. Just another rite of passage. Like the time he pinned me on the living-room floor and blurted out, "There are two kinds of people in the world: me and everybody else!" Before blasting me with an exclamatory fart. Or the few times he pinned me to the basement floor

and blew smoke in my face. Little did he know he was turning me off cigarettes forever, although I'm certain that wasn't his intention.)

Farm kids, I could never trust; they got strange ideas in their heads surrounded by corn rows and barnyard animals. A whole gang of them found Christ in those corn fields and, for a few weeks at least, Brother M was along for the ride. Prayer meetings where the kids could "rap" about "reality" and "where their heads were at." Guitar masses. All that *Billy Jack*-type shit.

How did I know this? Simultaneously, he was freaking out over Bowie's *Young Americans* album. I'm sure this album is his sentimental favorite, if nothing else, for the time it represented in his life. My real-time Bowie memory would be "Heroes" and foolishly trying to emulate the album cover in a Polaroid photo. (Nobody told me Bowie was at least 30 lbs. underweight. I looked like a linebacker with a bouffant hairdo, although I only weighed 155 lbs. and was as thin as I'd ever be in my life.)

The key song for him on that album was "Somebody Up There Likes Me." Any fool knew "Fame" and the title track were way beyond everything else on the album, but I gather the religious undertones of the song really spoke to him that spring and summer.

How much? There was Brother M, in the kitchen with Mom's ironing board and his newly purchased iron-on letters, carefully laying them out on a white t-shirt, to spell out "Somebody Up There Likes Me," with the "u" in "Up" sporting an arrow extending upwards. The hot iron, the summer heat, his determination to make this t-shirt perfect, to show his new-found faith in the Lord. We were tie-dying shirts routinely at the time, stirring up these psychedelic aberrations in coal buckets in the basement, like teenage warlocks gathered around a cauldron. He didn't tie-dye this shirt as he wanted the message to come through, loud and clear.

He also joined the wrestling team around the time, Brother J and he being groomed for this by Coach C since middle school. He tried to get me, too, but I had a natural aversion to guys touching me like that. Coach C's program was far-reaching and successful, creating state-champion caliber teams and wrestlers during his long tenure. Brother M was good enough to start at some medium weight he'd probably pay a fortune to have now. His first official junior-varsity match, he got rammed into the mat face first and suffered a nose bleed. The blood flowing from his nose seemed to signify time running out on his good-boy status. I don't believe he lasted the season and completed his fade into the loose crowd of disenfranchised stoners and parking-lot partiers.

It was almost a relief when he decided to throw down with the bad kids; it turned out somebody down there liked him, too. For me at least, he was more likable in this condition, whether or not it coincided with him maturing out of that "torturing little brother" phase or was a matter of him being stoned and thus more docile. The strange intensity he felt towards Bowie, that album, that song, at the time. That was rock and roll in the 70s, and for us a demarcation point from a more pure past.

1976: Psychotic Norman Rockwell Mutations

For years, my brothers and I were Dad's unwilling Saturday morning mechanic's helpers. It deeply chagrined Brother M to get nailed some time on Saturday morning, usually right after sitting down with a bowl of cereal or maybe a book. All us kids read a lot, and our father used to say, "How about leaving that book for awhile and helping me with the car?"

It wasn't really a question, more of a healthy suggestion. This was a year-round thing, and it could be a huge pain in the ass to trudge out in the snow to hold a screwdriver in the carburetor while our father fiddled endlessly with the intake valve. As noted earlier, he purposely bought crappy used AMC cars as he knew local junkyards were filled with parts from earlier models of this affordably-priced auto line. There was a perverse sense of anti-cool later driving a yellow AMC Hornet station wagon at college, but it was balanced by the explosion of flame from the tailpipe every time Dad's home-made choke popped out.

In the age pecking order, Brother M was first choice, Brother J second and I was last. On extremely rare occasions, Dad would tag Sister K with a Saturday-morning mechanical assignment, although she superseded me in age. As Brother M eased into a lifestyle untenable with early Saturday morning risings, Brother J became Dad's go-to mechanic's assistant. Years later, he's still pretty good with cars, enough to fix most problems on his own.

Brother M profoundly resented it, mainly because he didn't feel comfortable rebelling in this situation. We were great fans of paperback celebrity biographies, especially for rock stars. Invariably, one of us would be laid out on the sofa, nice and cozy, reading a book about The Beatles or The Stones, maybe wrapped in a blanket or a comforter, when our father would trudge in, shake the snow from his boots and make one of us an offer he couldn't refuse. No one would ever answer. Our father assumed our silence meant "no problem, Dad" and walked right out, certain that one of us would be out in a few minutes. We would mutter "asshole" in our heads, but never to his face.

"Asshole, doesn't he know I'm getting to the best part of the book?" I recall Brother M asking once.

"What part is that?" I said, acknowledging one of his pet names for me.

"That part in the middle right before the picture section, where they're starting to get famous and turn into creeps."

"I guess if you get famous, you can skip right to the middle and make that page one of your story," I replied.

The funny part was I knew exactly what he was talking about. Those damn books were all the same, with the recording artists at the same point in their careers near the picture section. Mick and Keith's first big drug bust. John crying out for attention in songs like "I'm a Loser" and "Help." Dylan strung out and drifting, weeks before the mysterious, near-fatal motorcycle crash. Despite the constant similarities, we read them cover to cover.

So, Brother M would throw on his clothes to go out and hold a monkey wrench or press his foot on the gas pedal for half an hour. It wasn't so much the work itself as the idea that we had no say in the matter. Through this involuntary labor, Brother M and I grew to despise anything mechanical. We associated it with a redneck mentality, that you had to be a man to fix things, and you were a sissy if you couldn't. The experience itself could have been a lot worse. Our father simply did what he had to do and excused us, whereas some fathers would berate their sons when things didn't go right, as they rarely do with mechanical problems.

The fun part about helping Dad was going to the junkyard for parts. There was something to be said for field after desolate field of briar patches, junked cars, copperhead snakes and hornet's nests, sliced through with craggy dirt roads leading nowhere. The world felt flat, and we were at the edge of it in a junkyard. Dad loved to rummage around abandoned cars to find inexpensive parts. The trouble was getting checked out. These parts had no price tags, so it was up to the owner to determine the cost. Actually, it was up to the owner and his chubby son. He was a strange guy somewhere in his 30's who reminded me of vampire hunters in those cheesy Hammer horror films from England. I can't recall if he wore a cape and a round-brimmed preacher's hat – most likely not – but he had that heavy presence, big bushy sideburns, an Eastern European vibe about him, like a gypsy. I'd later realize he was a dead ringer for Van Morrison. These two would whisper over the price in a very hushed, back-turned-to-customer manner, and inevitably it was too much. I think Dad couldn't stand these guys, but even their inflated price was cheaper than buying the part new.

At least the junkyard had a run-down element of fun about it. Far worse were the hardware and auto parts stores, with their smell of clean metal and rubber. The hardware store smelled more metallic due to the large number of nuts, bolts and screws. The automotive store smelled more of rubber because of the tires and numerous belts and hoses.

Either way, they both attracted the same clientele: mechanics. I would later know engineering students in college who had a mechanical background and used it as a foundation to build more knowledge on the structure of machinery. The guys in these stores had only the foundation. Their whole world seemed to revolve around cars. People who didn't know about cars were worthless. If they were men and didn't know, then surely they took home economics instead of shop in anticipation of their alternative lifestyle.

I hated those places, and I know Brother M felt like a caged animal in hardware stores. The minutes crawled by on those Saturday morning trips. There were two kinds of hardware stores: the chains and the local shops. The chain hardware stores like Ace weren't as bad. The guys who worked there didn't seem to want to help anybody. If Dad made eye contact with one of them, clearly designated by his red smock, the clerk would look down and walk away.

For this reason, Dad preferred the local shops, which was bad news for us, as the men working there had no retail training, mechanics who acquired minimal knowledge of how to run a store, which generally looked like a junkyard with glass windows and a roof. They loved to hang out together, especially on Saturday mornings. It wasn't as bad as the diner scene in *Easy Rider*, but Brother M and I always felt like we were in enemy territory in local hardware stores. "Psychotic Normal Rockwell Mutations" was the phrase I'd dredge from memory later at college.

Some of those guys weren't so bad. One time, I must have been around nine or 10, sitting in the front window of one of these shops in Minersville, looking out at traffic on the main street. Two younger guys, in their 20s were standing next to me, longish hair which was unusual for most customers, clearly guys who loved working on motorcycles, there to pick up some parts. Dad was bantering with the older, crew-cutted store manager. Just then, a red fire truck slowly drove down the street, not on its way to a fire. For some reason, the truck had a big red "F" on a placard in front of the grill.

"Look," one of the guys muttered, "here comes the Fuck Truck."

Normally hearing an adult curse in my presence was memorable and funny in and of itself, but the stoned, slow delivery of the line, coupled with the perfect timing of this fire truck cruising by in the sun, members in hats hanging on the side, a dalmatian gazing out the passenger-side window. I lost it. My laughter became infectious, and those two guys, like potheads caught with a case of the giggles, joined in. The rest of the store had no idea what we were laughing at; I can't recall any other instance in a hardware store where I had that much fun.

It was during one of those trip, Brother J and I wedged into the front seat of Dad's 69 Dodge, when we heard Johnny Cash's "One Piece at a Time" on the AM radio. Dad had listened to country music when he was younger, after Big Band in the 40s, in the 50s before rock took over, so he knew it was Johnny Cash. He loved hearing about a guy in an auto plant stealing one piece of a car at a time and over the years building a Frankensteinian automobile by the song's end. Brother J and I thought it was a pretty cool song, too, although it would take years to admit it.

1976: Little League

Baseball for me, whether played informally in the schoolyard or organized, was a test of boyhood. It was the unfathomable shame of booting an easy grounder and the weightless swing of a perfect hit. It was a kid's game, and I haven't played it since those halcyon days of the Ashland Little League. I loved the game so hard my friends and I would pack bag lunches and water jugs, leave for the local field, a huge lawn in front of the hospital, at nine in the morning, play until dinner, go home for some food, then play again until the late summer darkness fell, and we had to stop because we couldn't see the ball. Riding home on those warm nights, we ruined many lucrative baseball cards between the spokes of our banana-seated, 21-inch Huffy Roadsters. None of us knew any better. I'll describe a few aspects of those Little League days that still resonate with me.

Opening Day. Everyone I knew in Little League slept in his uniform the night before the first game of the season. They looked and felt a lot like pajamas anyway, with the stirrup socks being the coolest feature. If a kid didn't clutch his baseball glove to his heart like a leather teddy bear, he hung it on one of his bed posts, with his hat on another. The following day at school was a marathon test of nerves, all the players seeing each other in the hall and giggling like loons, wearing our hats to class, until the teachers swatted us for having such poor manners. That evening, we had a parade up Center Street. The field sat in a park at the end of a steep, long hill. There were fire trucks blaring their sirens, the American Legion guiding us with their stone-faced, war-veteran flag bearers, the high-school band blasting "Take Me Out to the Ball Game" out of key, and all us kids in our sleep-wrinkled uniforms and stirrup socks, lined up by team, marching in three rows up that hill to our destiny. Some of us whistled the theme from *The Bridge Over the River Kwai* as we marched. The big thing was to give each other "flats." This was done by jamming one's foot down on the back of another kid's sneaker, hopefully pulling his shoe off and causing him great embarrassment. At the field, we assembled along the white-chalk foul lines, pledged allegiance to the flag beyond left field and sang the national anthem. That would be the only time we were equal and together. Team loyalty, personal ability, hostile, vicariously-playing parents and intense childhood feuds would break that bond over the course of every season. The field seemed immense: the longest hit I ever had was a triple off the left field fence. A few years ago, I purposely drove by the field and couldn't believe how small it was.

The Elastic Insert. I'm getting ahead of myself describing Opening Day. I missed the first one bridging the gap from farm system to Little League. An important distinction. The farm system was for the younger age-bracketed kids, with the idea that by age 11, the kids would try out for and then play in the actual Little League. Both fields were next to each other, but the farm-system field was a bit more run down, smaller. The whole area was dug out from the woods and looked like desert scrub. The try-out session for the Little League that March seemed more like a formality: most kids would find themselves playing for an older brother's team or over-joyed to be picked by any team and advanced to the big show.

Not me. I still recall opening up the local newspaper the day of the team announcements, racing to the sports page, only to find my name wasn't listed for any team. This made no sense. I was as good as any kid in the neighborhood, known as a great fielding first baseman. I didn't botch the try out: it went well. There were kids I knew personally who were barely coordinated who had been picked over me.

I played along in the farm system for a week or two, but was miserable. All my friends were happily ensconced on their new teams, making new friends, the young rookies. Was it because I was a chubby kid, and there must have been some peculiar discrimination based on this? Or simply an oversight? In either event, I let Mom know, tearfully, that I was gearing up for early retirement. I wanted out.

Knowing how much it meant to me and how good I was, she was pissed. God bless her for getting on the phone and letting the powers that be have it, as she did routinely whether it was the Little League or the School Board. I was more than fine with not showing up anymore and letting it slide, but she persisted. A spot magically appeared on Brother J's old team, the Phillies. It made no sense how the situation was being handled. No one apologized or admitted to any sort of error, but Mom said, don't look a gift horse in the mouth, just take it.

The league president came by with my uniform. It was geared towards a smaller, not even average-sized player, i.e., the uniform fit more snugly than Elvis' black leather pants in the 68 Comeback Special. I couldn't even get the zipper up and button them. But this was the only set of pants they had! I had uniforms two years running that fit fine with my farm-system team, the Orioles. Being handy with thread and needle, Mom ripped open a side seam and sewed in an elastic patch that added three inches to the waistline. It worked. I look back on pictures of myself from that time: chubby, not enormous. Maybe 10 lbs. heavier than an average kid.

The Phillies coach, Larry, probably thought he was getting a talentless brat. Once he saw what I could do on the field, I started at first base immediately, spending no time on the bench. The Little League, like so many other organized childhood endeavors, served as an early warning system for the perils of adulthood.

The Shoup Brothers, Eddie and Rodney. Eddie was a few years ahead of me, on the Phillies with Brother J and a good kid. I say this because he hung out with straggly-haired tough guys in Black Sabbath t-shirts with yellow teeth and fingers. He would look like that, too, in a few years, as so many kids would, but this was before the fall. I remember him well because on one key play, he chased down a line drive to deep center, only to slam into one of the wood-board advertisements lining the outfield fence -- I think it was for Mrs. T's Pierogies -- cracking it in half, then pinning himself underneath the chain-link fence. There was blood all over the place and a swarm of adults. An ambulance came after 10 endless minutes, the fence was carefully pulled from his wounds, and they took him away, unconscious. He had dropped the ball when he hit the fence. Everyone was crying, and his parents were hysterical as they climbed into the back of the ambulance. After the fence was dragged back in place, the game went on, and the Phillies lost.

All his heroics were lost on his little brother and my team mate, Rodney. Rodney hated baseball. His attitude was such that during a game, he would sit down in right field and sometimes take his shoes off. If a ball came his way, he'd watch it roll by and yell out, "What, you want me to get that?" I don't think he liked his father too much, who worshipped Eddie and couldn't understand why he was such a malcontent. Rodney was famous for eating his glove. I don't mean digesting mouthfuls of leather. I mean gnawing on the lacings. We all did that in those long pauses that are such a part of the game, like poker players sucking on cigars as they mull their options. The leather tasted salty, and the consistency of the laces now reminds me of sesame noodles. Rodney did it so much his baseball glove was like a normal glove, with separate, unconnected fingers. Many times, his hand was too damaged to even put a glove on. He often tried to light his fingers on fire to prove how tough he was.

Taxi Slotnick. Long before I played and long after, Taxi was one of the official league umpires. We didn't know Taxi's real name. We suspected it was simply Taxi. Some thought that was his surname, and "Hey" was his first. He drove a cab for the Red Devil Taxi Service. We lived in small working-class towns in the hills of Pennsylvania. No one used taxis, and I have no idea how they stayed in business. Taxi would show up for each game during batting practice in his red military-style hat and matching shirt, a Karl Malden look-alike with cauliflower ears to match his bulbous nose. After parking his cab, he'd saunter into one of the dugouts, strip down to his T-shirt and boxers and put on his umpire's outfit: gray pants, white socks, black shoes, dark blue chest protector and a tight-fitting navy blue jacket. He wore a dark blue baseball cap turned backwards to put on his catcher's mask. He carried around his huge umpire's protector shield on one arm, like a knight without a sword.

Taxi took guff from no man or boy. "Hey, butt" was how he addressed everyone, even women. He may have been a lowly taxi driver in real life, but he dictated those games, bawling out strikes in his hoarse croak. Taxi couldn't have been more than 5' 4" and had a limp. His only problem was he wanted to be a coach, too, and would occasionally stop games to offer sage advice to wayward players. He once did this to Brother J who was striking out batters left and right and well on his way to a win. Taxi stopped the game, told J his wind-up was all wrong, and came out to the mound to show him how it was done. J took his advice and got shelled for five runs before his coach took him out. He never pitched again.

Larry Clews. Larry was our coach, a hard-luck factory worker in his mid-20's who lived for the game. His assistant coaches were Gene Furman's burly dad, and the father of our catcher, Jimbo, who I later realized looked like one of The Fabulous Furry Freak Brothers from the stoner comic strip.

While most coaches were there because they had a son on their team, Larry's sons were still in diapers. His wife always seemed to be pregnant. She would come to each game and cheer us on from the stands, her babies dozing in a huge stroller. In one game, an opposing coach got into an argument with Larry over a close play at the plate and called his wife a fat bitch. We could all see Larry, a much smaller man than the other coach, tensing his shoulders to attack. A few of us grabbed aluminum bats and gathered at the edge of the dugout. Larry threw his hands up, stared at the other coach for a moment, then silently walked back into the dugout. He took his clipboard and car keys, got his wife and kids and went home with two innings left. We were getting clubbed, as usual, and finished the game while the winning coach vainly tried to avoid the withering stares of everyone in the park.

Against his will and after being badgered for weeks on the issue, Larry even let us try his Elephant Butts once during practice, a few of us pulling plugs of the foul chewing tobacco from his pouch and stuffing a pinch between our cheek and gum, like in the Walt Garrison commercial. We spent the next five minutes projectile vomiting while Larry laughed himself into a stupor.

He was the best coach I ever had. Down to earth, approachable, a real stickler for fundamentals, and more proud of a well-played game than a cheap win. A few times he treated all of us to greasy concession-stand hamburgers and warm sodas in dixie cups after a hard-fought loss. We'd sprawl over the picnic benches with hang-dog faces and watery eyes while he laughed and pointed out each of our improvements and good plays. Sometimes he even went all the way and got us those shoe-lace french fries wrapped in old newspapers. We had losing records year after year, but that was due more to a few well-connected teams having inside lines on all the best prospects, ensuring one or two perennial powerhouses tearing up the rest of the league.

Losing wasn't the worst of it. Being the head coach, Larry was expected to pitch batting practice and offer advice to hitters during the pre-game warm-up. This was always great fun. The announcer in the two-story cement bunker behind home plate would play the Top 40 station over the rickety PA system while everyone took his turn getting easy hits and making unpressured plays on the field. We stood in groups of two or three bantering and waiting our turn at the plate. Larry had to pitch with a glove full of baseballs, throwing one after another to the batter who peppered the slowly-thrown balls all over the field.

It was the summer of '75, my first year with the Phillies, and I was grooving to the sound of my favorite single, Paul McCartney & Wings' "Listen to What the Man Said." "Listen" was one of his many ubiquitous summer hits, ruling AM radio for weeks. I had heard it an hour earlier on the car radio when my mother dropped me off in her Skylark station wagon.

George Charlton, our power hitter, came up to bat. On the third pitch, he hit a screaming liner straight into Larry's balls: the ones on his body, not in his glove. Time stopped. One by one, the baseballs slipped from Larry's glove and hit the dirt of the mound with muffled thuds. His face was frozen between a grimace and a scream: a grotesque, silent howl. His plug of Elephant Butts slipped from his open mouth and dribbled down his white T-shirt. No one moved. Paul sang, "Soldier boy kisses girl, leaves behind a tragic world." George stood at the plate, still holding the bat as if he were reproduced in wax.

Larry started to fart and moan. Oh, no, I thought, he's going to shit his pants. After breaking wind a few more times, Larry fell over. Taxi waddled out to the mound. We converged on the infield to find Larry passed out and clutching his testicles. Before we could panic, the announcer yelled down that he had already called an ambulance. Taxi got us to carry him to the dugout. He was immobile, like a stuffed bear, and his dead weight was hard to heave. It took six of us, carrying him as if we were pallbearers in a baseball-themed funeral. Paul sang, "The wonder of it all baby, yeah, yeah, yeah."

A few minutes later, the ambulance crew carted him off, and we played on. Larry showed up for the end of the game, walking slow and eating vanilla ice cream. His face was beet red, and he wouldn't tell us anything about his condition, although we noticed for the next few weeks he wore a particularly baggy pair of Bermuda shorts and walked bowlegged.

Jimmy Reilly. Jimmy might have been the worst player in the league; naturally, he was on our team. Everyone knew it -- his old man, the coaches, every player on every team, even himself. He never got better. He was a well-mannered kid with a high IQ, but he was gawky and uncoordinated. Jimmy tried everything possible to make himself look like a real player: red-white-and-blue wrist bands, leather batting gloves, his own bat, Adidas turf spikes. Nothing mattered. He took mounds of verbal abuse on a daily basis over his lack of skill. Every year, he smilingly signed up and played on. Unlimited errors. Constant strike outs. Snickers. Evil childhood name calling.

Was it his father? I doubt it. The few times I met the man, he was unfailingly kind and clearly not badgering his son into the sport. It was Jimmy. He was like the rest of us in that he lived for baseball, no matter that he couldn't play for shit. Yet he never cried, or threw his bat in disgust, or pointed fingers after a loss. After one particularly bad at-bat that saw him benignly chop at a pitch that was practically rolled in like a bowling ball, he gently removed his batting helmet, smiled that spacey grin of his and walked back to the dugout. Halfway there, Taxi caught up with him, clutched his arm, and croaked, "Hey, butt. You're too well-adjusted for this sport." Jimmy didn't know if it was praise or an insult. He laughed at Taxi and thanked him for his valuable insight.

Chatter. Spectators of major-league baseball never get a feel for chatter, whether they're too far from the field or watching it on a television. Something tells me the pros aren't into chatter anyway. Chatter is more than words of encouragement, like "strike him out, Bobby" or "come on, Ace, one more out." In the Little League, chatter was a tribal art form. Our official chatter song on the field was, "He's a batter, he's no good, strike him out . . . swing!" The first three lines were elongated and tentative, timed to match the pitcher's stretch, and the word "swing" exploded like a Russian dancer crying "hey" as the pitch crossed the plate. That was the formal version. Most days, it got so damn hot and tiresome that we'd simply chant "he-ba, he-ba, he-ba, he-baaaa .... swing!" We sounded like auctioneers stuck on the same price. If we got lazy or disheartened in a blow-out inning, Larry would yell, "I can't hear anyone singing out there," and, in those half-hearted, bored sopranos, we'd pick it up again. Sometimes we'd deviate and chatter in an English accent, or in Flip Wilson's Geraldine voice. It might not have been true, but we felt that we could will the batter to strike out through our chatter -- this is what happened to kids raised on David Bowie.

Gene Furman. Gene's dad was a huge bear of a man with a crew cut. He looked like Art Carney on steroids. Gene was our best pitcher, not necessarily fast, but great control for a 12-year-old. While his dad rarely raised his voice with

Gene, he stood like a sentinel in the corner of the dugout every time he pitched, cross-armed, gazing at his son. Gene cracked at least once a game. He'd purposely throw pitches in the dirt to get a reaction out of his dad. On a good day, his dad would say, "Enough, Gene, enough," and Gene would get back in his groove. On a bad day, his dad would walk around behind the dugout and have a smoke. Every batter would get walked or hit until Larry stormed from of the dugout and took Gene out. Gene wept sometimes, throwing his hat down and kicking dirt on it, tears streaming down his cheeks. In the Little League, it was rare for a retired pitcher to go straight to the dugout, so Gene would trade positions with his reliever and silently weep until the long inning was over. He'd come into the dugout, throw his glove at the water bucket and sulk in the far corner away from his father.

The Moment. I'm a first baseman by trade, not fast, but good-sized and able to dig it out of the dirt. I had my moment when, with men on first and second with no outs, the batter, a big lefty with the best average in the league, hit a line shot straight at my head. I could hear the ball sizzling as it screamed towards me, as if it were on fire. It was more an act of survival than making the catch, but I snapped my glove in front of my face and fell down from the force -- with the ball. The man on first was halfway to second before he knew what happened, and the man on second was touching third. I could have tagged out the man on first and trotted down to second for an unassisted triple play. When I went to tag the man lunging back to first, I hit his back so hard the ball popped out of my glove. I scampered after the ball and had a play at second, but the man slid back in before my throw. Through all those years of solid play mixed with the expected errors, missed opportunities and occasional flashes of brilliance, what I remember most clearly is the ball rolling away on that pure, green, infield grass, and feeling like it was the world slipping away from me.

That Championship Season. Losing was a way of life for the Phillies. We never lost heart, but we did reach a point where we became too pragmatic for kids, that uncharted adult territory where we came to realize it was only a game and nothing to cry over. Once we hit that point in the first half of my last season, we made a serious run for the championship.

I don't know what happened. Larry said it was perfect timing between our fundamentals and an urge to win. We played no better or worse than usual. All we did was pull out the close ones. It helped that we lucked into the second-best pitcher in the rotation of the teams we played. Winning became easy, one win after another, and we crossed the thin line between victory and defeat. We finished the first half 8-2, tied for first with the Pirates, the league leaders for years.

The previously-mentioned team whose coach belittled Larry's wife was the Pirates. The league's best player, Bobby Evert, was the coach's son. There was a famous photograph of Willie "Poppa" Stargell of the Pittsburgh Pirates holding a sledgehammer like a bat, and Bobby had a picture in the local paper of himself in the same pose. He was a great player who knew it. At the age of 11, he signed autographs for wide-eyed farm-system kids and referred to himself in the third person.

Because of the tie, we had to play the Pirates. They had beaten us 10-0 the first game of the season with Bobby pitching, but three weeks into the summer, Bobby got a bad cut on his leg riding a mini-bike and missed a few games. The Pirates lost both, and we blew them out one of those games. Now that they had Bobby back, it was expected they'd take revenge on the Cinderella-kid Phillies.

It was the greatest game I ever played in. The crowd ringed the fences, putting out lawn chairs and cheering from the hoods of pick-up trucks. It had rained earlier that day, and a hazy rainbow shimmered over the left-field fence. Gene pitched the game of his life, striking out two batters an inning and throwing a lot of easy grounder pitches, low and away in the corner. We had no errors, a first and last.

Bobby was throwing pills that day. We didn't have speed guns back then, but he easily had to be pitching around 70 mph, blazing speed for 12-year-olds. Speed like that was frightening. Bobby piled up strike outs because most batters stood shaking on the far edge of the box. Larry told us to stick our bats out and let the pitch hit it. I got two singles to right center like that, and we managed to nickel-and-dime two runs this way, occasional walks and bloop singles. The Pirates came back, putting across one run in each of the last three innings, and we pulled up short.

Larry wept in happiness after the game. He called it the greatest moment of his life and bought us newspaper fries and pizza to prove it. Taxi came by and said, "Hey, butts, youse got heart, all of youse." We looked at each other and knew something great had happened, but no one wanted to admit it.

The second half of the season, we went 5-5, and watched Bobby and his father hold the league trophy over their heads in the back of a cherry red Sedan driving around the warning track.

Summer's End. In that last year, the Bicentennial, my hair was growing longer, and my record collection was getting larger. I had started earlier that year by buying my first album, Elton John's *Goodbye Yellow Brick Road* for $4.99 at Woolworth's, with my snow shoveling money and smuggling it home under my heavy Woolrich coat. (Sidenote: Joe H's best friend, a hulking giant of a kid named Tom who would squeeze his massive frame into a Volkswagen Rabbit, once shoplifted the bulky, three-record *Woodstock* soundtrack by smuggling it out of the store in his huge parka. An amazing feat.) Dad was down on rock and roll because Brother M was fanatical for it and showing signs of serious teenage rebellion.

I found myself talking about The Beatles with Jimmy Reilly all the time. We were both going through our first adolescent brush with the band and referred to the Red and Blue albums as if they were the Old and New Testaments. Something told me I wasn't going to be gung-ho over high-school athletics.

Late June rolled around in that strange summer of '76, the season's end. All the guys said they felt sick that school was coming around soon, but we all secretly loved the idea of it after long, floating weeks of lawn mowing, Bicentennial Moments, and endless ball games. Our world in the summer was reduced to kids in our immediate neighborhood and fellow Little League players. School meant old friends from other towns and girls, who were making more sense all the time.

We lost our last game, and after the ceremonial hand-shaking ("good game, good game, good game"), we gathered in the dugout for the last time. Larry was strangely subdued, not looking at any of us. We took his cue and treated each other the same way. After a few minutes of idle banter, we took off in separate directions, finding our parents along the right-field fence. Mom said she'd be glad not to have to wash my grass-stained uniform anymore, but she didn't look happy. A few of those kids on the team went to Cardinal Brennan, and I never saw them again. Most of us would end up in the same junior high school, slowly forgetting our bonds and rivalries as baseball's allure faded in our outlaw teenage world.

Two years after that, I bought a new glove a few sizes too big with the idea that it would last the rest of my playing days. With a black magic marker, I scrawled my name on the outer middle and ring fingers. I put a large stone in it, tied it with clothes line and soaked it in linseed oil for two weeks. It broke in nicely in neighborhood ball that summer. I used that glove to play softball into my early 30s, even though the glove was old and decrepit. Line shots would get my hand stinging and raw for minutes afterwards. Of course, this was on Randall's Island in the East River off Manhattan, watching the sun set over the skyline on perfect summer evenings so like my Little League days. Instead of shoe-laced french fries and warm RC Cola in dixie cups, the rewards here were pitchers of beer at a sports bar on 96th and Madison where all the advertising-league teams congregated, and trying to score with all those hot, artistic women employed on the Creative side. Most nights were spent going down on a called third strike, and later urinating on a quiet side street in my Bronx neighborhood, like a lost dog trying to find his way home.

I never bought another glove after that. It's sitting in one of my drawers, and I can't bring myself to throw it out.

1976: Paying Dues at the Legion

My parents made a point of never keeping alcohol in the house, a habit I vaguely follow, too. I have a few bottles of Crabbie's Ginger Beer. It's one of those "thrill of purchase" things to buy a few imports every now and then.

I never saw Mom drunk, but every now and then, I would see Dad drunk: paying dues at the Legion. That's shorthand for Dad going out once a month and paying membership dues at an American Legion hall in Mount Carmel. As anyone in rural America knows, the American Legion in any given town is either a meeting hall with a bar, or an actual bar, often with a sign out front. Back then, it was a place for older World War II and Korean War vets to gather and have drinks together.

By and large, you didn't see Vietnam Vets doing that in the 70s. Those guys were still in their 20s and had a bad taste in their mouths over their largely nonexistent homecomings. It might not have occurred to them to hang out at places like this filled with older guys with similarly harsh war stories. I'm sure Vietnam Vets are hanging out at American Legions now, taking their rightful places as the old guard.

Seeing Dad drunk was like seeing me drunk. It didn't fit the traditional experience of a stumbling idiot making more noise than a cupboard of dishes collapsing. I gather Dad liked to go out drinking in his 20s the same way I did. All I know is he only went out drinking once a month when I was a kid, and that was such an odd ritual that it hardly represented a whiskey-soaked free-for-all.

Dad got dressed up to go to the Legion. His taste in clothes was legendary in its uniformity. When he was relaxing, he'd wear a collared, short-sleeved shirt, but it was rarely clean, always some sort of odd spot on it somewhere. (In later years, he'd wear pocket t-shirts all the time, like we did as kids, when he'd chide us for dressing like slobs.)

When working on the fleet of AMC junkers, he'd wear his gray sweatshirt with sleeves and collars cut out, years before this became a trend with the movie *Flashdance*. The sweatshirt was cruddy with grease and oil stains, his usual weekend wear. For pants, he wore a pair of dark gray corduroys, literally until they fell apart, and he'd buy another pair. He was inordinately fond of the Haband slacks store in the Schuylkill Mall. He never wore shorts.

I can see that I've picked up his fashion sense as I've grown older. I'm a uniformity person, too – white sleeveless t-shirt and khaki shorts, white socks, black sneakers. I wear this all summer long when not at work. In my mind, and the city, it's too hot to wear much more. I've taken ribbings over a grown man wearing shorts, but that's generally from guys with chicken legs. I look fine in a pair of shorts, have worn them for years working out in gyms. This bothers me sometimes, as I think I should be walking around in a fedora, dress shirt, slacks and expensive shoes, but it doesn't suit my lifestyle. I can't help but feel haunted by that specter of adulthood I sensed growing up: even working-class guys dressed well in their leisure time.

Dad would put on a white dress shirt for the Legion, never a tie, but a dark blazer of some sort, dress pants, black socks and leather shoes. I should point out he normally wore black slip-on canvas loafers, the cheap kind you'd find in supermarkets for $2.00 a pair. Basically, black canvas sewed onto a small slab of tan rubber. I would buy these on a lark in my early 20s to mimic Dad. (These got to be trendy in the 80s, especially when the black-and-white checkered version started appearing in movies and videos. I still see them now, especially in clothing stores like Old Navy.)

It was always a "what's wrong with this picture" vibe to see Dad dressed-up like that. You can see when a guy is uncomfortable in more fashionable clothes, and such was the case. Dad claimed to be more fashionable when he was younger, and he probably was, simply by dint of the times, coming of age in the 40s. It was always a major freak-out for us as kids to dig up old military uniforms in the attic and realize that Dad had a 26-inch waist. The last time I had a waist that size was the 5th grade. He must have grown quite a bit after leaving the army, because I later wore some of his old blazers while at college.

We'd all be sitting around, watching *Sanford & Son*, and Dad would come down the staircase like he was headed to the prom. Mom would blurt out something sarcastic like, "Oh, look, here comes prince charming," and they'd laugh. She knew he was off to the Legion to pay his dues, because the only other reason he got dressed up was for church or funerals. I'm sure it would have been nice for him to take her out like that every now and then, but it rarely happened. They went out driving almost nightly anyway. It was more their style to hit a McDonalds, grab a Coke, then keep driving. They'd later add a mutt named Maggie that Mom picked up from the local pound to their nightly drives. (It wiped out Dad emotionally when that gentle, forsaken dog passed on quietly in her sleep one night in the mid-90s.)

I don't know what Dad did while at the Legion, save for have a few beers. I'm sure it was guys in the same boat, World War II and Korean War vets, working in factories, getting dressed up for one night a month to hang out and talk about their days in the armed forces. I'd have loved to hear this stuff, because Dad never discussed his war experiences at home. He'd drop bits here and there. His favorite story being the time he fell asleep on a bus in the midwest while trying to get back to the base, woke up with his head resting on a large black woman's bosom, and they both realized the driver was going around in circles through the rain in East St. Louis.

I'm hazy on the exact story, but supposedly he was injured in a boot camp training drill. A live grenade was accidentally used with a bunch of blanks. There was an explosion, and the guys behind Dad were killed. He would have been, too, had their bodies not blocked the impact of explosion. He took shrapnel in his lower back and legs, laying him up for a few months. In those few months, his platoon was shipped off to Europe, ending up in The Battle of the Bulge, where you were as likely to freeze to death in a foxhole as get shot. When he came back, the war was over, so he spent a few months traveling around immediate post-war Germany, still a dangerous place, and took in a few days at the Nuremberg Trials when Rudolf Hess was on the stand. He then spent a decade afterwards traveling all over Europe and America doing mechanical work at various air fields, bridging into the Korean War, although he never spent time in Korea. That much I know for sure as I've seen the Honorable Discharge papers, which dropped him back in Pennsylvania in the mid-1950s. His rank was some level of Sergeant, might have been Staff.

I would guess that most of the vets gathered in American Legion halls were like him – sergeants, corporals, privates – the guys who did the grunt work. I'd be curious to know how many officers would be found at the Legion bar; it seemed like one of those things the rank-and-file would indulge in far more. There would be Big Band music on the jukebox or radio. The guys would talk, about the insanity of the service, work, families, etc. I didn't know until I actually worked in Dad's factory that he was fairly outgoing and got along well with people; he was quiet around the house. Knowing how he was at work, I could picture him having a blast at the Legion, the relaxing pull of a few beers helping out, too. He'd leave around 7:00 at night and usually get back around 10:00.

I could tell, he was tipsy. Flush in the face, relaxed, holding himself differently ... the way we all do when we're a little drunk. He'd walk in, take his usual place on the sofa next to Mom's chair, and quietly watch some TV. For all I know, he was seeing two TVs, but he never seemed that drunk. Even his voice sounded different, more conversational, which is the kind of thing you notice with someone who normally gives you orders. I can't recall a single incident where anything more happened. I'm sure it was also in his head that he was in front of his kids, so he wasn't going to take his pants off and climb a tree in the backyard.

I don't know how much his dues were, but I'm sure the whole thing was a ruse to get away from the family for a few hours, a practice I wholeheartedly endorse for any married guy. Once a week would be even better. As kids, we always had reasons to break off on our own and do things after school. Parents were stuck. Aside from the drives and Dad's Legion visits, they were there most of the time at night.

In a lot of ways now, I feel like Dad when I drink, simply paying dues at my own legion hall, wherever that may be. Most times, I'm meeting a friend in a bar, hanging out, getting caught up, trading music, not drinking more than a few. There are a lot of places in Manhattan that have great happy-hour specials. It only adds to that Legion effect for me, although without fail, every damn bar I go to with a friend, there's only room for one at the bar, so we have to get a booth. I'm assuming most people at the bar around that time are regulars, and I've never been a regular at any bar, never liked to drink *that* much. Even less now, much less than 10 years ago.

What are my dues? What did I do in the war? Nothing. I suspect Dad would be fine with that answer. It's a shame we never sat down and had a few beers, but it seems like the drinking ships we were on in our lives never passed in the night, as he had given up paying Legion dues completely by the time I was of drinking age.

1976: Mary Jane Peters

Just writing that name spooks me, all these years later. Mary Jane Peters was that one kid in grade and high school who caught shit from everyone. She had "cooties" whatever the hell they are. If you wanted to freak a guy out, you'd write "Mary Jane Peters + (insert guy's name here)" on any surface, and this would inspire an immediate cross-out campaign with a ballpoint pen or magic marker that would leave tears and indentations on the writing surface.

I looked in my senior yearbook, and she wasn't there. I don't know what happened to her between grade school and our last year of high school. (We were in the same grade.) She must have transferred at some point, although I can't recall when that was. I'm not even sure what town she was from in our school district. I pictured her having a hard scrabble existence, living in a crooked house on the side of a coal bank, parents with bad dental work, skinned rabbits hanging in the back yard on a clothes line.

A few years ago, one of my co-writers at *NYPress*, George Tabb, put out an excellent book about growing up Jewish in suburban Connecticut in the 1970s: *Playing Right Field: A Jew Grows in Greenwich.*

The book is written by the male Mary Jane Peters, the one kid who got his ass kicked on a regular basis, harassed constantly, raised by a maniacal father, picked on for his ethnicity and falling into the role of being "that kid." Kids have memories like elephants and will drag the tarnished image of "that kid" from grade to middle to high school. George got it in spades; the book is darkly hilarious. Frankly, I didn't like his follow-up book anywhere near as much, as George found some kind of happiness and acceptance in his life. (In my opinion, he writes much better when the odds are completely against him, and there's no hope of him ever escaping his horrible situation.)

At that time I wrote to George, confessing to him my sin of the one situation where I could have treated Mary Jane Peters humanely, but instead chose to be a typical adolescent prick. This haunts me now. I didn't do a lot of it, but the times I did do something horrible in my youth, I can recall them now clearly.

I think Mary Jane's main issue may have been that she looked odd. She was a bigger kid, not huge, but a big girl, with stringy, light-brown hair and standard-issue, cat-eye glasses that didn't do her any favors. A round face, very plain looking. Hygiene problems? I don't recall any, although I'm sure legend had it she smelled "funny" or something. She did act "weird" by asshole grade-school standards. Her manner of speech was clipped and formal which, given her working-class background like the rest of ours, stood out. I do recall her style of dress being a little run-down, a little beat-up, clearly some unironic Salvation Army duds in her spring and fall collections. This being a rural, working-class area, plenty of kids fell into that category. I was constantly wearing ragged hand-me-down pants that had clear lines in the hem where Mom had let down and brought up the length of the leg to suit whichever brother was wearing them. I don't recall her ever being abusive or strange to people. She didn't really have a chance as kids were being abusive and strange to her 24-7.

Kids would do the most incredibly insulting things to her. A big one would be for some burly guys to pick up a small guy, when the teacher wasn't around, and heave him onto her desk while she sat there. Of course, the small guy would act like he had been heaved into a sewage treatment tank, writhe in faux agony, then bolt away, screaming. Girls would pretend to see "cooties" in her hair or on her desk and scream, "Ew! Ew! Look at Mary Jane's cooties!" while everyone sitting near her would pretend to scatter away in fear.

The implication was head lice? We were checked for head lice constantly in grade school. I don't recall her ever being flagged for this. The concept was to paint her as someone who had fleas and lice, because she was weird. There was no evidence of this. All there was evidence of was kids doing what they do best: treat each other like shit. We all did this to each other in varying degrees, but no one seemed to grasp the insanity of singling out kids like Mary Jane and making her a constant recipient of irrational abuse. Most kids, it occurs to me now, were borderline psychopaths, constantly on the lookout for situations where they could humiliate another kid. Why? I guess there would be any number of reasons for that. Even in my own house where we were raised reasonably well, I can recall harrowing episodes, over nothing, really. Ditto childhood friends. I'm sure a child psychologist could separate all the bad wiring, but the basic, unavoidable truth is kids tend to be assholes. They often grow up to become even bigger assholes when they can't figure out why their personal lives are rat's nests of broken and frayed connections.

So, there's your picture of Mary Jane, this isolated person whose daily life at school was transformed into burning hell by kids who would normally blanch at the idea of lynch mobs and bullies, but for some reason suspended all logic for her. I think she did have some friends, but I'm not sure how close they were. I hope she had someone to keep her head on reasonably straight. She must have, because despite the constant harassment, she seemed fairly well-adjusted. Sure, very much on the quiet side, but again, I'm factoring in the full-court press of abuse she tolerated every day.

Let's go back to the sixth grade. One Saturday, I was riding my bike around the hospital. Along with the cemetery on the hill, Fountain Springs was famous for its hospital on the edge of town. Both the cemetery and the hospital were great places for kids to congregate, as both had open expanses of green grass at various points. In winter, we'd sleigh ride on the hill in the cemetery, and walk through the hospital grounds to get to the great hills on the country club golf course beyond a wooded area behind the hospital. (As with so many things that change with passing time, the golf course is now peppered with luxury housing units.)

We'd ride bikes around these places. The hospital had a maze of roads leading around the grounds, a very small, vaguely industrial area with a big power plant on the edge by the golf course that seemed like a haunted castle. I'd often go on bike rides around the hospital grounds to get away from it all, i.e., a small house filled with six other people, and a neighborhood crawling with too many kids on the tail end of the Baby Boom.

That day, I was riding around the hospital parking lot, when I noticed a kid slightly younger than I was, around 10, staring at me while he leaned on a car. No big deal, I thought, stare all you want, I'll do one more lap around this parking lot, and then I'll be gone. As I passed him, the kid yelled out "Asshole!" and stuck out his tongue.

What the hell, I thought, in my 12-year-old mind. Doesn't this kid know I could destroy him in a fight? What's his problem? What have I done to arouse his anger. I circled back and asked, "What's your problem?" He answered something like, you, you big dick.

As I was getting ready to get off my 21-inch Huffy with banana seat and dust the little prick, I saw two more kids approach from the hospital, a boy and a girl. For whatever reason, the lot, which had plenty of cars, was empty of other people. As they got nearer, I could see, much to my surprise, that one of them was Mary Jane Peters, apparently with a little brother, younger than the kid who was trying to pick a fight with me.

"Hi, Bill," Mary Jane called out. I was shocked that she knew my name. Sure, we were in the same sixth-grade class, but I don't recall ever speaking to her before. I wasn't one of those kids who took perverse pleasure in ragging on her. I didn't mess with anybody. I wasn't raised that way and couldn't stand when other kids would mess with me. The theme song of my youth was "Billy Don't Be a Hero" by Bo Donaldsen & the Heywoods. (If I'm being honest, it might be the theme song of my life.) While I wouldn't take part in the degradation of Mary Jane Peters, I wouldn't befriend her either.

"Hi, Mary Jane," I answered, a little befuddled.

"Don't mind my brother, he fights with everybody."

"He called me an asshole."

I can't remember the kid's name. Let's say it was Dave.

"Dave, apologize to Bill for calling him an asshole."

Dave kicked some pebbles away, eyes downcast, hands in the pockets of his shorts.

"Aw. I'm sorry for calling you an asshole. I didn't mean it."

"Thank you, Dave," Mary Jane said, "that was nice of you."

Dave asked if he could ride my bike. I think that was the real reason he called me an asshole. He coveted my bike, which was no great shakes, but I gather Mary Jane's family wasn't in great shape financially. While I let Dave ride my bike around the parking lot, Mary Jane and I had a conversation, I can't recall exactly what it was about. I gathered she was there to visit a sick relative, and her parents were still inside during visiting hours, telling the kids to go out and play.

What I recall thinking was, she's normal. She's a nice person. Good manners. Reasonably intelligent. Lucid, although the word "lucid" would not have materialized in my 12-year-old mind. I would have expected her to be a cauldron of bitterness and rage over the constant abuse. She still seemed weird, with her formal, clipped way of speaking, like we were at a tea party. Certainly no more weird than other kids, and far less hostile. Eventually, her parents came out, Dave, who now seemed happy, gave me my bike, and I rode off into the late spring evening, mind partially blown by this unexpected encounter with a legendary cootie.

How was I going to handle this new knowledge? Probably no differently than I had. The conversation wasn't so revelatory or exciting that I left thinking, "I've found a new friend!" I surely wasn't attracted to her. It was a nice moment where I got to extend an olive branch across that pre-adolescent sea of misunderstanding, to see that this person who was treated like a monster wasn't all that different. I'd say "hi" to her in the hall, talk to her on occasion. I was convinced that much would change. I wasn't the kind of person that I'd pretend something hadn't happened and present her with a stone face.

I go to school on Monday. All is well in my neck of the classroom. At a study hall before lunch, I hear a commotion over near Mary Jane's desk, which isn't unusual. Coarse laughter, finger pointing, the usual. One of the more popular girls in the class blurts out, hey everybody, read this, as she holds up a notebook, apparently Mary Jane's notebook. Mary Jane sits there staring straight ahead.

On the back of the notebook is a huge heart with an arrow through it, and written on the inside, in florid blue script is "Mary Jane + Bill."

Two days after our quiet hospital parking lot interlude. Who else could it be? I could see that she was so not used to basic kindness from kids that once I showed her some, she went completely overboard and had developed a crush on me. While I should have been thrilled that any girl felt that way about me, this felt more like being chased by a bear covered in burning shit. I was terrified that everyone would find out Mary Jane meant me. There were a lot of Bill's around. Kids knew I had no contact with her, positive or negative. No one immediately suspected. Maybe she meant a troll named Bill who lived under the bridge by the interstate?

Ms. Popularity started grilling Mary Jane in front of everyone; it was like an episode of Phil Donahue where he had a Nazi or someone of that ilk in front a grumbling, angry audience. They wanted payback, answers, recriminations.

"So, Mary Jane, who's your new boyfriend, this 'Bill' – do we know him?"

Mary Jane sat there, staring straight ahead, as she always had when kids pulled this kind of abusive crap on her. Thank God she was playing dead again. If she had pointed or looked at me, I think I might have burst into flames. Please recall I was a chubby kid. I guess I was cute enough, but chubby kids tend not to be sex symbols of any sorts to pre-pubescent girls. I wasn't hot stuff by anyone's standards. The concept that Mary Jane would suddenly fixate on chubby, smart-guy Bill on the other side of the class room didn't seem to enter anyone's mind. There wasn't any connection. If I had been some Rob Lowe-looking kid, then it could have been implied that Mary Jane had become infatuated with an unobtainable god.

I can't recall Ms. Popularity's name, but I recall we got along, because she was a "smart kid" too. (Yes, even smart kids acted like animals.) Smart, but nasty, like an egg-sucking dog. I think as a joke, she called across the room, "Hey, Bill, did you know Mary Jane is in love with you?"

I was on the spot. Ms. Popularity's voice was dripping with sarcasm, like she was sharing an inside joke with me (in front of 30 other kids with everything but a spotlight on her). She knew it couldn't be me. I had to play along because if I had shrugged and told the truth, it would have blown everyone's mind: "Yeah, she does mean me. I ran into Mary Jane in the hospital parking lot on Saturday, we talked, and while I thought we made a nice connection, we're certainly not in love, or at least I know I'm not. Mary Jane, you're a good person, even better in light of all the shit you take from these regrettable goons, but I have to make it clear that I see us being 'just friends' much as none of us like to hear that.

We get along. You're cool. Let's be friends, because I don't want that boyfriend/girlfriend thing with you, OK?"

I recognized I had to completely reject Mary Jane in front of a kangaroo court of 12-year-olds who would never understand that sort of humane, rational answer. Their response would have been to start chanting: "Mary Jane and Bill/Sitting in a tree/K-I-S-S-I-N-G ..." You can't reason with shitheads, a point driven home many times before and since. I made a sour-puss face.

"Oh, no! Not me! I don't want to get cooties! I would kiss Mr. Savage first!"

(Mr. Savage was our sixth-grade home-room teacher. I don't think he was gay. The implication, of course, was that I would rather make it with a man than Mary Jane, thus alleviating me from even the slightest suspicion that I would have anything to do with Mary Jane. Of course, the thought of me kissing Mr. Savage was an outrageous bon mot, clearly aimed at the cheap seats, some dime-store homophobia in lieu of a fart joke.)

Ms. Popularity laughed. Everyone did. Except Mary Jane. Who sat there, stone faced. She glanced at me momentarily, and in that glance, I could see something breaking. Not her heart. I don't think that was possible after all she'd been through in the past few years. It might have been her faith in common decency, that one person could treat her with such kindness, and then carelessly turn around two days later and lay a brutal smackdown on her in public that would destroy all previous goodwill.

I had gone over to the dark side and felt like an asshole, made all the worse by the approving howls of laughter around me. I was one of them now, one of the pricks who delighted in humiliating this poor girl who had never harmed anyone. The Beatles were huge on my playlist at the time, and the instrumental portion of "I Want You (She's So Heavy)" was playing in my head. Evil-sounding stuff.

It was a perfect storm of bad circumstance. Mary Jane hadn't meant other people to see her secret heart. It was on the back of the notebook, no doubt snatched from her desk by one of the cretins as a prank. I guess she wrote that so she could have some physical evidence of kindness that existed after the fact. Ms. Popularity saw her chance for another moment in the spotlight, grabbed it, then dragged me into it, not grasping that I really was this mythical "Bill" referred to in the heart. Like another infamous Bill many years later, my policy of self-preservation became obvious: deny, deny, deny. They never did find out who "Bill" was. A few days later, she had put a big "X" through my name in the heart and told everyone she and Bill had "broken up."

I've surely mistreated people since, sometimes on purpose, but that was one instance in my life when I hung someone out to dry when I should have made a stand against the ass-backwards world we live in. Didn't happen, at least not on my watch. I don't want to romanticize the plight of Mary Jane; she was a kid who got picked on too much and learned to live with it. By the same token, I don't want to play down what an awful thing that was I did to her. It still bothers me now that I shit on my principles to save myself from a moment of the humiliation she experienced on a daily basis.

Where is she now? Who knows. I couldn't answer that question in 1982, much less now. When did she break off from the rest of us? I wish I could pinpoint that. A few of us like to fantasize that at one of our reunions, kids like Mary Jane will show up looking like Cindy Crawford in a French maid outfit, toting a flamethrower and lighting couples on fire as they slow-dance to "Keep on Loving You" by REO Speedwagon. That never happened either. I hope she turned out all right. I suspect she did, as the inundation of darkness she received as a kid no doubt prepared her for adulthood. People do come out the other end of experiences like that, often with a depth and understanding that attractive, popular kids could never grasp. It still grates on me that I made life that much harder for her.

1977 Good-Bad but Not Evil

Living next to a schoolyard, I'm privy to overhearing the wondrous dialogue of teenagers. It's a public school, looks to be grades 7 and 8. These kids should be 14 and under. Some of them are obviously older, having flunked grades a few times.

A criticism kids receive is that they're unaware of mortality and repercussions to their actions. It's my take that they should be unaware of their mortality at that age, and repercussions, like anything else, are best learned through experience. My main criticism is how bone stupid so many kids are. Unforgivably stupid. As if they wake up every morning with the sole purpose of dumbing themselves down as much as humanly possible. Stupidity beyond arrogance. The kind of stupidity that's darkly nurtured, like a serial killer slowly weaving together the dark threads of his ugly future.

I wonder how many of them are playing stupid. Some are. Because I can remember a few kids growing up who were smart, but did everything they could to hide it, not only from adults, but from other kids, too.

The classic example of this was Roachey – a nickname based on his last name. We got to know each other in the fifth grade, and at that time, he was a smart kid. With fifth grade, a lot of us had to transfer over from our old grade school next to my house in Fountain Springs to the middle school in Girardville, and Roachey was one of those kids already there. Thus, even though this kid was bright as hell, the teachers had a strange way of being careful around him, like he was a bomb about to go off.

They must have been seeing signs all along. Girardville was known for being rough around the edges, and even an intelligent, well-behaved kid was raised with that hard sense of place. There was always some weird character quirk that suggested he'd be as happy whipping another kid with a jump rope as learning about geometry. This was Roachey. He was hardly a mean kid, just volatile, and most likely with odd parents. I remember him once telling a class that he got into a fight with his father while they were watching a TV special on famines in Africa. His father was pointing at the distended bellies of malnourished children and saying, "Look at how fat those kids are! They don't need any more food!" Not quite grasping the relation between starvation and distended abdomens. Roachey calmly pointed out to him that this was a sign of malnutrition. His father called him a moron. No matter what Roachey said, his father remained convinced that these kids were chubby, well-fed bullshit artists.

With that kind of parentage, you're in for a rough ride. As we got into high school, Roachey's fate kicked in. His grades started slipping. Drug intake began and flourished. He got into senseless trouble and hanging out with nothing but stoners. He was a Neil Young fanatic, and I can remember him wowing a few dozen people in the cafeteria by playing a note-perfect rendition of "Hotel California" on a 12-string guitar. I still remember sitting with him listening to Pink Floyd's *The Wall*, which I had heard on WMMR in its entirety on Thanksgiving morning of 1979. A week later, we both listened to a tape version in his brother's car, with our mouths hanging open at how good it was.

At the same time, I can recall him cocking off to our 8th grade math teacher, who was notorious for grabbing kids by the hair and using their heads like a gearshifter, a fate Roachey realized many times over. He'd get A's and B's on all the tests, then flunk the class because he rarely showed up. There was a thin line between a smart ass who knew the boundaries (like me), and a kid who either knew the boundaries and didn't respect them, or was so wired that he was bound to fail.

Roachey was brilliant in a lot of ways, but on a downward slide at the same time. He ended up getting his girlfriend pregnant and dropping out, at which point I lost track. A few years later, while I was at Penn State, I was back home one weekend at Holiday Lanes. I was shooting pool with my friend George when I had to make room for the guy with a beard at the next table making a side shot. He said, "Thanks, Bill." He looked at me. Jesus Christ, it was Roachey. He looked like Jesus Christ. We talked a bit; he was working in a factory at the time and seemed relatively sane. We left it at that, since I hadn't seen him in a few years, and we'd gone off in different directions. We had been the best of friends up through eighth grade. Again, that was the time when he started sliding over to the dark side of high-school, and I wasn't along for the ride. It seems silly now, but there was surely a dividing line then, clear-cut definitions of the social groups. You could navigate between each, but ultimately one would claim you as a member. Roachey had headed for the smoke-filled van in the parking lot, and that van drove off without me, "Hey Hey, My My" blasting from the Sparkomatic cassette player.

I've since heard he went through some bad spells: drugs, getting busted, having discussions about space aliens with various old friends, finding Jesus, who knows what else. I hope he's come out the other end. I think the nightmare for him would be to end up like his father, certain of "truths" that were really lies, and content in that certainty.

Danny was another story, along with his third cousin Mary. These were kids in my hometown. At least partially. Danny's family was related to that of Tommy One-Nut. Tommy was a kid who started out in life innocently enough, a good kid, but soon gravitated to the "bad kid" crowd led by Larry C, which led to him joining a Pennsylvania biker gang. He got his name from supposedly having only one testicle. No one knew for sure, no one cared enough to find out, it was a cool nickname. The rest of his family turned out fine, not sure what happened to make him go astray. Rumors of crystal meth dealing and addiction marked his adulthood. He died one night after losing control of his chopper. There's still an informal memorial along the road where this happened.

Danny and his family were Tommy One-Nut's relatives from Virginia who came and went. One year, Danny would be in our school, the next he'd be back in Virginia, seemingly on a whim. I don't know what his father did for a living, but it was flexible. Both Danny's and Tommy One-Nut's families were related to Mary's family. I didn't know how.

Mary was a strange girl. I recall her as being a gawky teenager with a mild southern accent and a haunted way about her. Her family lived over by the dugout: a large piece of land "dug out" from the surrounding woods. For some reason, all the people who lived over by the dugout were weird, almost like the "bad" part of town, if our small town had any.

I've recently seen an old picture of her, standing next to my sister while she tinkered on the play-by-number organ in Dad's room. The girl was beautiful in that wispy Joni Mitchell way, a fragile, dark beauty to her. None of this occurred to me at the time, as I was around eight, and she was a teenager. She was a floating member of that older gang of bad kids. (I think we were on a late-arriving curve with the 60s. A high-school yearbook from 1968 would be filled with beehive hairdos and crew cuts. A yearbook from 1974 looked like a Woodstock primer: long hair, beads, drugged-out eyes.)

The one thing Mary was noted for was her love of pop music. She toted around a portable record player everywhere she went. At any given time she had dozens of 45 singles, the top hits of the day, so we had a portable soundtrack to our lives. I don't recall her playing favorites with any genre or artists. You'd hear "Gypsies, Tramps and Thieves" by

Cher next to "Can't Get Enough of Your Love" by Bad Company. She loved those records with all her heart. One of her gangly arms was probably longer than the other from toting that portable player everywhere.

Getting back to Danny, he was like a mini-rebel. By rebel, I mean a soldier who fought for the Confederate Army under General Lee. The guy was a pure Southerner: a full-on, drawling accent, long, red hair that would flop over his forehead the same way Jerry Lee Lewis' would when banging on his piano, and a real mean streak to his character. For reasons I can't remember, every time Danny saw me, he had to fight me. Only me. We liked each other. He liked to fight more than he liked me. I was much bigger than he was. He loved to wrestle, so we'd get into these half-assed wrestling matches that would end with both of us red-faced, me having him in a headlock, telling him to say uncle, and him responding, "Nev-ah, yew yankee bastard!" I'd let him go, and we'd sit there, blushing and glaring at each other, before one of us would start laughing, and we'd become friends again. This happened nearly every time he saw me in the neighborhood. He was chewing tobacco by the time he was 10.

Despite our combative ways, we got along like gangbusters. Much as with Roachey, I could see the smart kid underneath the redneck façade. We played chess all the time in the fifth grade, and each of our games would end the same way. I'd think I had Danny cornered, and he'd make some incredible move, drawl "check mate" in that Virginian accent, coolly slide his chair out and walk away, to the men's room to take a piss. Most likely on the radiator.

Unlike Roachey, Danny didn't have any scholastic aptitude. He never took to school in any way, nearly flunking every class he took. He had a strong compassionate streak in him, much more than your average kid would show. I remember him eyeing a meter maid as we were out at recess in front of the school. She was ticketing cars for which the meter had zeroed-- cars in front of houses. Danny ran over to her and said, "Don't you feel ashamed ticketing cars for people parking in front of their houses? These are poor people living around here. They shouldn't have to pay to park in front of their houses. Why don't you have a heart and tear up those tickets?"

The meter maid reported him to the principal, who gave him a few whacks with The Hand: a large piece of black wood in the shape of a hand that bad kids would get spanked with on special occasions. My ass never got touched by The Hand. Danny's ass may have had finger imprints tattooed on each cheek.

I mention Danny and Mary together, because they were involved in a strange series of incidents. One thing I didn't note about Mary, and may be mistaken to attribute anything more to it than a passing memory that could be wrong, but she was also known for messing around with the older guys. I don't know what went on with sex and the older kids. It stood to reason that since so many of them were getting high and going off the rails, they might have been getting laid, too, or at least experimenting.

There was a field across from our house, a patch of land that the township owned between our neighbor Bubba's house, and Soytz's trailer. Really not that much land, about the size of two tennis courts. The township rarely took care of it, and as a result, this piece of land became like a small jungle, with bull grass rising six feet high, and an open sewage ditch sitting at one end of the field. There were snakes in there; we'd often find the hatched eggs.

Once every summer, the patch of land would be mowed to host the volunteer fire company's annual block party, complete with a small ferris wheel, donkey rides, balloon dart boards, a bingo tent, ping-pong/goldfish bowl tables, bleenies, fried pierogies, blind pigeons, dixie cups of warm RC Cola, the huge vat of bean soup and the inevitable beer truck with the chicken-wire fence surrounding it, most of the men spending the night there getting hammered as they didn't have to drive home. I remember playing tackle with the other kids in front of the wood bandstand while a local cover band blasted through CCR's "Proud Mary" and "Traveling Band." I even recall David, Bubba's older brother, and Soytz's son Lee walking around in his uniform a few times between tours of duty in Vietnam.

Weeks later, the patch of land would turn unruly, becoming an unofficial dark place for us kids, a black forest to be avoided, unless you wanted to hide. We'd build paths in it so that we could take a short cut through the field instead of taking roads that were 50 feet away. (Soytz, or Lee, eventually bought the lot and started mowing it. Now it's an open plot of land, sans the mystery of childhood imagination.)

Either there or in the adjacent cemetery, Mary would get frisky with some of the older guys. What they did, I have no idea: kissing, groping, maybe the occasional hand job. I don't know. I doubt Mary was the only one. I think some of those older teenage girls, some of whom had the countenance of biker mommas with their feathered roach clips and hip-hugging bell-bottoms, learned a few new tricks in that bull grass, or on the cemetery hill at night, hiding behind a tombstone any time the occasional dog walker would saunter by.

The freaky part was the time Mary took Danny into the bull-grass field. No one knows what happened. The implication was that these cousins, with southern accents, fooled around. He was about 10; she was 14 or so. It was a scandal. I'm not sure if it reached the adult level of scandal, but we kids were scandalized, shocked that something like this would happen. Danny wasn't talking, nor was Mary. Kids liked to think they were cool and could roll with anything, but cousins making out? It wasn't right.

A few weeks after that, who knows what psychological turmoil ensued, another odd, even more troubling episode occurred. I remember the day: overcast, with a low bank of fog hanging over the neighborhood. It was morning. For reasons unknown, Mary had left her portable record player on a wall in the schoolyard, with all her 45 singles. Tommy One-Nut and Danny came by. I was there with a few kids hanging out, getting ready to play some baseball in the schoolyard.

Next thing I knew, Tommy had opened the lid on Mary's record player and was flipping through her vast collection of singles. Danny picked one up and flung it into the air. The black 45 rose, like a clay pigeon used in skeet shooting, disappeared into the fog, then seconds later came crashing down on the street 30 yards away. I knew from being a kid that the crashing sound was the hook, the unavoidable attraction to doing something wrong and destructive. We all knew that crashing sound from junkyards: smashing Pepsi bottles with rocks and BB guns, breaking fluorescent lights on rocks, beating in the screen of a tv set with an aluminum bat. Fun stuff like that. There was a small junkyard like that in the woods just up from the dugout where we indulged in such pleasures. The sound of a 45 disintegrating on the road held that same negative allure.

Within seconds, Danny and Tommy were lobbing each 45 into the air, making sure to first call out the song title on each disc, sometimes singing the title if they knew the song's melody:

Tommy: *Life Is a Rock but the Radio Rolled Me*! (whizzing sound of disc in air, smash, laughter)

Danny: *One Tin Soldier* rides away! (whizzing sound of disc in air, smash, laughter)

Tommy: *That's the Night That the Lights Went Out in Georgia*! (whizzing sound of disc in air, smash, laughter)

Danny: I got a pair of brand new rollerskates, he got a *Brand New Key*! (whizzing sound of disc in air, smash, laughter)

I hauled ass. Brother M was fanatical for pop rock and had an equally large and impressive 45 collection that he'd play on his stereo in the basement. (All those singles tragically disappeared in the mid-80s, victims of Mom's need to purge junk that wasn't hers.) I knew if I'd done the same to his collection, he'd have sawed my head off with a butter knife. I knew what music meant to him. I knew what it meant to Mary. (It was starting to mean the same thing to me.) You didn't mess with people's possessions like that, much less something as crucial as their favorite music. It was a truly mean-spirited thing to do, an indication of how crooked Tommy One-Nut's path would soon become. Danny had no excuse. He got caught up in the moment and made a bad mistake.

When Mary came by the schoolyard later, saw the contents of her record collection in small pieces on the road, her record player left empty. She sat down on the stone wall of the schoolyard and started wailing, an awful, keening sound. I was watching from the house, afraid to go outside, lest I get blamed, or she asked me what happened. I wanted no part of it.

All I know is that the girl was heartbroken, destroyed in some sense, partially because she'd lost the one thing in life she loved, but also, as she soon found out, it was two of her relatives who had done this to her. I don't think she ever spoke to them again. I'm not sure what happened to her after that. I do know she slowly built up another 45 collection and was a lot more careful with it. In my memory, she disappears right there, but I'm sure we all went on being aware of each other's paths a good few years after that. Tommy One-Nut took his strange path that led over the high side of a lonely road late one night. I have no idea what happened to Danny.

1977: Music Class

I've been thinking about the music classes we had in grade school. Do schools even have music classes anymore? Music teachers? I imagine private schools do, but I'm not sure if such a thing is still a priority with public schools. They must, if they want to have marching bands in their high schools. I don't picture many kids learning the piccolo or tuba of their own free volition.

One of the rare things I'll bust my parents on is that they should have made us all learn an instrument. I was practically begging for a piano or keyboard of some sort when I was a kid. We had the play-by-number organ in Dad's room that I learned. After mastering the play-by-number book, I would take the sheet music from Sister K's flute charts (she played that in the marching band) and transpose the notes to numbers. "Everything's Coming Up Roses" is burned in my mind as a result. Unfortunately, I think the coolest song they did was "Love Is Alive" by Gary Wright, which sounded insane on a play-by-number organ. I had to work in numbers/notes transcribing sessions between Sister K's flute practice in the room, which usually amounted to her playing Chicago's "Colour My World" and "Theme from Star Wars" all night. (I have fond memories of stealing her huge, rectangular, white-fur band hat and playing air guitar to Jimi Hendrix with that white plastic strap pressing on my chin.)

That's about as far as I got. Brother M bought a dumpy used acoustic guitar somewhere. We all tried and failed at learning it, not even sure how to tune the damn thing. All we had was an instructional manual featuring the silhouette of a cowboy playing guitar to a full moon on the cover. I'm sure those familiar with rudimentary guitar remember the title of the book, which I've forgotten. Without a teacher, it was a waste of time. It seemed like most "musical" kids came from families where their parents or older siblings played instruments, too, and the kids would pick it up as they went along.

The music classes we took as part of the curriculum in school were something else entirely. I recall them lasting up through the 8th grade and being an excuse for most kids to goof off. Music teachers tended to be a weird lot. The weirdest was Mr. M in our 5th and 6th grade classes, a small guy who looked like a skinny eskimo and was prissy. I remember the time a bunch of bigger kids saw him on the sidewalk in front of the school wearing a gigantic parka. The kids surrounded him, poking fun at his choice in outerwear. All he did was stomp his foot and say, "Are you done with this infantile tom foolery? This type of cavalier behavior is unacceptable!"

The kids didn't get into trouble. Your average male teacher would have beat their asses black and blue, which wasn't a capital offense back then.

By the same token, the 7th and 8th grade music teacher, Bruce M, who had Bruce Dern's intense demeanor, yet was about 5' 2", never had any respect issues with kids. I once saw him make Rick G, the toughest kid in our grade, weep after getting him in a headlock. Rick was about four inches taller and 50 lbs. heavier than him at the time. Mr. M was a bad ass. He was a pretty good guy if he liked you, and he liked most kids. He was in a band in the 60s but never quite made it. Thus, he gigged around with his band locally, making good money in the process. He could make all the girls cry by playing "Nadia's Theme" on the piano.

Music class started out being fun, because when you're seven years old, it's a kick to sing out loud with a group of other kids. We'd have a ball singing "Senor Delgato" and "Old McDonald." Growing up in the 70s, we could have been singing "Desperado" and "Space Oddity" in their music classes. Unless you were lucky enough to have hippie music teachers, guess again. Contemporary music was looked at as barbaric and inferior. I also couldn't see us grooving to "Satisfaction" and "Stairway to Heaven" – hard group sing-a-longs and strange lyrics for kids to be singing. I once recall we had a mandatory talent contest in the second grade, which amounted to nearly every kid doing an acapella version of Three Dog Night's "Joy to the World." I'm picturing myself in my skintight, plaid, red bell-bottoms, doing my Brady Bunch dance moves and fearfully warbling "Jeremiah was a bullfrog" in front of 20 other equally scared shitless kids waiting their turn to be publicly humiliated.

The only times I can recall having real fun in music class were when we'd break out the percussion instruments, With the teacher's encouragement, we'd get a tribal rhythm thing going, sometimes to the tune of "Simon Says" by the 1910 Fruitgum Company. That was our "play time" song where we'd rock out before taking naps on wrestling mats set up in the coat room. (Why can't work be like this?) There'd be 20 kids banging away on tambourines, jawbones, bongos, cymbals, woodblocks, maracas, snare drums, and sometimes each other for the more forward youths. The teacher would have to flash the lights off and on and raise her voice to let us know we were going too apeshit.

Later, Bruce M got the school to buy him a Moog Synthesizer. This was 1978, and synthesizers were still a relatively new instrument on the music scene. He had a few classes where he tried to teach us how to use it that ended with everyone making the synthesizer blast out a farting sound, thus reducing all of us to tears of laughter. We loved playing with that thing. There were a few talented older kids in Mr. M's homeroom who knew how to play the thing and were doing Moog versions of "Nights in White Satin" and "Iron Man." He should have had a class focused solely on playing that synthesizer, but that would have been a pretty radical departure for a rural high school in the 70s.

The other music teacher we called Catfish because of his waxed mustache that finished in points on each cheek.

He was a strange guy, but I recall learning a lot in his class. He once asked us all to discuss our favorite songs and why we liked them. As usual, when he asked for volunteers, no one raised a hand. He took the liberty of leading by example. "Well, I know you children might not believe this," Catfish said, "but I like a lot of contemporary rock music. Neil Diamond is a wonderful performing artist with a full sense of melody, production and arrangement. I'm also very fond of the orchestral rock band, Electric Light Orchestra. Do any of you kids like ELO?"

I loved ELO. Along with Queen, they were my favorite non-60s bands in my teenage years. I loved how they wove strains of classical and opera into their music. ELO spoke to me with their yearning ballads of unrequited love and that sense of a mystical world out of reach. Both bands really knew how to rock, whether it was "Do Ya" or "We Will Rock You." Did I raise my hand? Are you kidding me? Colluding with Catfish? An adult with a waxed mustache? I'd have cut my arm off before I raised it!

The end game for kids who loved music class was the glee club. Teenage guys dressed in blazers and striped clip-on ties, singing shit like "Sunrise/Sunset" and "What I Did for Love" -- sometimes in period costume, dressed like peasants, Hawaiian natives, or zoot-suited street hoods in a back alley. You'd get the more industrious/smarter athletes doing this stuff, too, along with the handful of bullied guys and Broadway show-tune girls with genuine talent. Glee Club was the gayest activity officially sanctioned in high school, yet you had a few guys in it who could most likely kick your ass. I can still recall quarterback Dave M, in a monk's robe along with all the other Glee Club guys, squatting onstage and singing that "Always Thought That I'd Be an Apostle" song from *Jesus Christ Superstar*. Dave looked a little too into it, like he was having a religious conversion.

Most glee-club stuff had that strange barbershop quartet, "middle-aged people gathered 'round the parlor piano" vibe to it. They should have given the guys Rob Roy's and let them loosen their clip-ons, so that they could properly ooze into "Blue Velvet" and "Fly Me to the Moon." I grew to like that sort of 1940s-60s pop but hated it with a passion back then. I can still recall poking fun at Mom in the kitchen while she played big-band music on the local AM radio station while kneading ground beef and eggs into meat loaf. Meanwhile, I was listening to The Alan Parsons Project and thinking that made me musically superior, while Cole Porter rolled over in his grave.

The real way I came to love music, all kinds, was by simple attrition: older siblings passing on their tastes, and rapidly developing my own by the late 70s. So many great musicians of the 70s had the moment The Beatles appeared on *The Ed Sullivan Show* burned into their collective conscious. I don't think there was any one 70s event like that. We all had our moments.

Mine was patiently waiting for Mom while she did her business at the Citizens National Bank in Gordon, leaving me to switch the car keys over to A/C and listen to the AM radio in her Skylark station wagon. Sometime in the spring of 1976. That's when "Bohemian Rhapsody" gently wafted from those tinny car speakers on the dashboard.

I couldn't believe it. Brian Wilson would later say that song scared him. (I gather he might have been high as a kite at the time.) It was one of those moments where I couldn't move; I had to sit there and listen. (I'd have a similar moment years later hearing The Police's "Every Breath You Take" while driving to the local Penn State campus. That song registered from the first note and now feels like a dark, gentle, summer memory of the early 80s as strong as any real one from my life.)

Mom didn't appear to sense any religious conversion when she came out with Dad's paycheck money in her purse.

The kid who was sitting in that station wagon was not the same person after hearing that song. It was like I had been punched in the chest and fallen into a bed of stars. My teenage years would be punctuated with revelations like that, although most would involve writers like William S. Burroughs, Kurt Vonnegut and Hunter S. Thompson.

Shit we weren't being taught in school! I was learning on my own. So it went with music, from rock, to new wave, to punk, to country, to R&B, to soul, even minor forays into early hiphop, followed closely by reggae, celtic, jazz, Big Band, doubling back on disco, lounge, classical, African, Brazilian … it goes on to this day. I surely heard great rock music before that moment, one of those moments listening to the "Hey Jude" 45 in neighbor Bubba's house one day in the early 70s. (We would later dramatically plunge into backyard swimming pools by timing our jumps to Lennon's opening scream in "Revolution.") Or first hearing Elton John's "Crocodile Rock" blasting from Mom's kitchen radio and feeling electrified by that thunderbolt of goofy 70s pop.

Steve S, one of the older kids in the neighborhood, the son of one of the doctors at the hospital, landed the lead role in *Godspell* for the high-school musical in his senior year. A daring choice for a musical at the time, as schools shied away from recent, rock-based material for presentations. He might have been chosen for his red hair, the same as the star in the movie of the musical, but he tore it up and seemed like a rock star, if only for a few months. He would later become a tax attorney.

The only kid in our neighborhood who picked up the ball musically was Scupper. His real name was Lee. As with the earlier story about Soytz, Scupper's permanent nickname came from a mispronunciation, this time his own. He had a slight speech impediment, and one day when we were wrapping up a baseball game, he called out, "I'm going home for scupper," instead of "supper." It stuck.

Scupper was known for two things: being a wiry, hard-to-tackle kid on the football field, and for being the only kid who knew how to play guitar. He tried to form a band one summer's day on Bubba's back porch, hopelessly teaching a few talentless kids how to play Deep Purple's "Smoke on the Water." It was a waste of time. I recall Jerry E, an excitable, sometimes nuts, kid who lived next to Joey C, sitting in on drums, wearing a fake blonde wig with a witch's hat. I can't recall who was on bass. The only thing that made sense was Scupper's infamous opening chords to that song, followed by a directionless bass and Jerry E making a disgraceful racket on the drums while screeching the song's lyrics. (Jerry could wail. He used to serenade me in the schoolyard by shrieking the song "Little Willie" by Sweet simply because of the first-name matches. When Jerry sang those lyrics at me, often while performing a lascivious dance that was something like Iggy Pop being attacked by a swarm of bees, it felt more like a threat than a celebration.)

I wish I had a recording of that fateful afternoon. I would guess those guys sounded exactly like The Sex Pistols, about two years before that band existed. They weren't alone. Most guy in the mid-70s bashing out rock and roll like that in garages and basements sounded just as raw, loud and borderline talentless. In their case, it was all in fun and went nowhere.

Scupper went on to front various heavy-metal trios, playing locally, making money at block parties, wedding and fire halls. I'll be damned ... just googled his name and found him fronting a local Pennsylvania rock band called Red Halo. God bless him for keeping the faith.

1977: The Closet in Dad's Room

An odd thing about kids is how they can achieve far more than they're capable of, but only when there is some dubious reward. I'm thinking of my brothers and I a few weeks before Christmas. Pick any Christmas between, say, 1972 and 1977. In our early stages, we believed in Santa. We visited him at the Mother's Memorial in Ashland routinely, where he showed up on the back of a fire truck, and excitedly read off our laundry list of toys we wanted him to bring. We'd see him at the firehouse, too, which had Christmas parties for all the kids in town. (Of course, Santa sometimes reeked of Pabst Blue Ribbon.) We believed in Santa Claus … but we knew the closet in our Dad's room.

The closet in Dad's room was where our parents stored the presents they were buying us in the weeks leading up to Christmas. We'd see them coming home from shopping trips after work, vainly trying to hide the names on the bags: Boscovs, Sears, Pomeroys, Listening Booth. Up to Dad's room they'd go. Close the door. Shuffling sounds. Door creaks. Hot damn, they're putting our shit in the closet for safe keeping!

Even earlier than that, we could rationalize that Santa would break into our house and leave everything in Dad's closet because he'd be too busy to come down our chimney on Christmas Eve night. After awhile, no, we knew Santa Claus existed in theory, and accepted this, knowing all the goodies were sitting in that closet.

It wasn't enough to let them sit there for weeks leading up to Christmas. We needed visual evidence that our shit was there. We had to see it, take the stuff out of the shopping bags, hold the boxes, and know we were getting these wonderful presents.

This is where the diabolical brilliance of children comes into play. My brothers were handy with tools, in this case, the properly-sized screwdriver. That closet door was locked. Granted, an older, feeble lock that could have been picked if we were so inclined. Like seasoned bank thieves, my brothers thought it made more sense to simply remove that ancient lock apparatus that was screwed to the wooden closet door. (As it turned out, Dad's force-fed, Saturday-morning mechanic sessions weren't a complete waste of time.)

This wasn't as easy as you'd think. The key was to not chip any of the yellow paint. The screws were painted over, so we'd have to get an old cloth, not too thick, and wrap it around the screwdriver. There were at least two screws and accompanying gaskets that we'd have to assiduously remove from the casing holding the lock, pry it off without chipping any paint on the wood door, then reassemble it all afterwards, like marines re-assembling their rifles blind-folded.

That was the first part of the mission. The second was to take a mental picture of the closet layout. If our parents were smarter, they would have stacked a ton of shit – old board games, winter coats, shoe racks – against the inside of the door, made note of the order it was stacked and wrote it down. So that when they went in again, they could check if these items had been moved, as they would have if we'd swung the door open and the bags came crashing down on us.

We were that meticulous, sometimes even writing down the order of the bags stacked in the closet, but usually taking that mental snapshot of what was there so that when my parents went in again, they wouldn't recognize that we had been in there on our recon mission. I'm surprised we didn't wear gloves to hide our finger prints.

Previewing the booty was incredible. Such a rush of excitement to realize what we had asked for, we would be getting. I recall this feeling with records, and two in particular: Queen's *News of the World* and Electric Light Orchestra's *Out of the Blue*. Christmas 1977. I loved those albums, floored by both, the last really good album by both bands. I could imagine Dad buying these albums at Listening Booth, thinking, what in the hell is this kid listening to, but it got worse than that! Both albums inspire teenage memories of rushing upstairs, slapping on the Radio Shack Nova 40 headphones, cracking open the cellophane, breathing in that new album smell, opening the gatefold cover, dropping the needle on the vinyl, and getting lost in the music for a good few hours. Sitting there on the bed, facing the stereo, with headphones on, reading the lyrics and liner notes. How many hours did I spend in that pose for the next few years as I absorbed the bedrock sounds of my musical education?

So, early December 1977, my brothers and I would be in that closet, looking at stuff like this, never taking more than five or 10 minutes. We'd be wary of any sounds: a car approaching, a door slamming, footsteps on the street outside, as presumably our parents could come home any minute and catch us up there. Putting everything back was a painstaking process. Meticulous order had to be observed for replacing the bags exactly where they were, and then rescrewing the lock to the wooden door. It wasn't easy! We'd do it routinely, a few times every Christmas season, to see if anything new had been added to the collection in the ensuing weeks.

When I think about Christmas, I don't think about love, or baby Jesus, or even the presents themselves. I think about activities like those noted above that are indelibly stamped on my mind.

Midnight Mass on Christmas Eve was also one of those things, one of the few uncomplicated memories I have of my childhood Catholicism. In short, it was a beauty. A candlelight mass at midnight, with full choir, and the congregation bearing candles, all other lights dimmed or off, the priest swinging his can of burning incense. A magical mass that was always Standing Room Only. We'd get a free box of chocolates on the way out. The capper would be coming home to find all our presents laid out (our parents would bag this mass for that reason), tearing them open, and having a blast.

Why we didn't do that every year, I don't know, as it was a perfect formula. When we didn't go to that midnight mass, the same thing inevitably happened: us waking up at two or three on Christmas morning and busting downstairs to open the presents that our parents had laid out an hour or two earlier. We never could make it to a typical Christmas morning to rip open the presents. Christmas Day itself was always sleepy and anti-climactic.

In our teen years, I distinctly recall bagging the early Christmas Eve mass, which was nowhere near as magical as the midnight one. A typical mass around four in the afternoon, we were given the choice of going then or Christmas morning. We liberated ourselves from the responsibility of church-going. Not to belabor the point, but I sincerely disliked church.

The one year that sticks in my mind was all of us going to Long John Silver's and having a fish dinner, a bunch of teenagers, in our Sunday finest. It felt too weird. I didn't like Long John Silver's to begin with. I could sense the guilt floating around the table at that meal, that maybe we should have just gone to church. It's one of those gloomy memories of my teen years, like waiting in a mall parking lot for the driver (usually Mom) to show up. It was such a depressing few minutes. Every time I hear "I Never Cry" by Alice Cooper, I can remember waiting for Mom one Christmas season in the Cressona Mall parking lot, on a dark snowy night while that song played on the radio. Bagging church at any time felt like that: watching and waiting. Waiting for the bells to ring, or the driver to show up, setting us free to go back to our normal lives, where we didn't have to indulge in these charades.

1977: The Confession

Kevin and Pat Hanlon were always fighting each other. Pat was two years older than Kevin, my age, and a great friend up until our public/Catholic-school separation. We first met in 1970 when their family moved from Ashland town to our more rural setting in Fountain Springs. I recall their house slowly being built on the north side of the schoolyard. Mom must have known there were two little boys moving in who wanted to meet me as she said, "Why don't you go say hello to our new neighbors?" while cooking dinner. Their mother must have told them the same thing.

They met me halfway at the edge of our backyard by the outhouse. Pat had a toy ukulele that played "My Darling Clementine" when the hand-crank on its side was turned. He was singing that as we met, and we took turns making up lyrics beyond the title. Kevin kept saying things to me, but it sounded like another language. Pat explained that he had a speech impediment that his parents said would go away in a year or two, and he had to act as Kevin's translator in the meantime. I could tell that Kevin got upset when Pat explained this, like he was sharing a family secret. After we said goodbye, I recall watching them walk away, glad that I had new friends. I rested my hand on a stand-pipe next to the outhouse. Little did I know there was a bumblebee hiding inside it that stung me on the palm of my right hand. I cried out in pain, the angry red stigmata already forming, and ran howling back to Mom who didn't know what the hell was happening. That was a common state of being the Hanlons inspired.

The Hanlon Brother history was peppered with this sort of tension and violence. Like the time we were playing bullfighter in their house. Pat played the matador. Kevin as always was the charging bull. Instead of a cape, Pat used the front door to the house, not quite grasping in his child's mind that there was a glass storm door on the other side of the thick wooden door.

Pat cried, "Òle, òle, òle!" After shuffling his feet and snorting, Kevin charged, his index fingers raised on each side of his head to mimic bullhorns. Pat swung open the wooden door, and Kevin smashed straight through the glass, slamming onto the cement of their front walk. Their dog Schultz, a boxer, wearing a white medical cone around his head, went berserk when he saw Kevin sprawled on the sidewalk covered in blood and broken glass, and jumped on Pat. Mrs. Scanlon just about lost her mind when she came upon this wailing nightmare scenario.

Months later, Kevin nearly poked out Pat's right eye with a pair of scissors while they made paper snowflakes. Pat wore an eye patch for a few months and eventually glasses as a result of the injury. It's hard to say if the incident was retaliation or their subtle form of communication.

Kevin and Pat's fights came about during the games we kids played. Pat was a good athlete, the kind of kid who could try any sport and immediately pick it up. What Kevin lacked in skill, he made up for in size. Although most of the kids were older than Kevin, he was bigger than they were. Kevin was one of those strange kids who didn't follow the unspoken rule that older kids had to be dominant. No one dominated Kevin, except Pat, who was smaller than Kevin but more agile. Every time the kids played whatever sport was in season, Kevin and Pat had to be on different sides. Pat was usually the team captain, and one of the older boys was the other team captain, which was already an unspoken sign of resentment to Kevin. It was understood that Pat would never choose Kevin for his team. The point was moot, though. Invariably, because of his size and brute force, Kevin would be the first kid picked on the other team.

The games were harsh enough to begin with. Kids doing splits, having their noses broken, being gouged in the eyes.

The general rule was no blood, no foul, and if there was blood, a debate on whether to penalize. Anything went.

A few minutes into each game, Pat and Kevin would start going at each other. If it was baseball, Pat would throw fastballs inside on Kevin, and Kevin would return the favor by blocking the plate when Pat came around to score from third, even if the play wasn't close. Football was the worst because they could physically attack each other and get away with it. In the neighborhood games, every kid feared being hit by Kevin. The unsuspecting victim would feel a hard wind blow against his back, and then Kevin would drive his body into the ground. The last thing the kid would see was the ball rolling away on the grass. He'd lie there shaking and whimpering like a dreaming dog. All he would remember was being too hurt to cry, wondering if he'd ever walk again. He'd taste grass and dirt in my mouth but not have the will to spit it out. After a few moments, his teeth would start tingling, and then he'd feel a pain in his sides as if he had laughed too hard. Everyone would stand around staring at him. Kevin would ask him if he was all right, and he would nod. The rest of that game, maybe even the rest of that season, the kid would be a non-entity on the field, unless he was on Kevin's side.

Pat and Kevin antagonized each other with looks at first, and then words. Trash talking was unusual back then; you only did it if you were going to fight someone. Kevin would start calling Pat stuff like "hot-dogging faggot." Pat got the best of Kevin by insinuating that Kevin jerked off in the bathroom with their mother's copies of *Ladies Home Journal*. The way he said it, not even as a taunt, more as a matter of fact, insinuated that there must have been some truth in it. Kevin was also famous for sticking his hand into the butt of his pants then smelling his fingers. It was strange stuff, but most of us did the same thing, only not in public. This gave Pat plenty of ammunition when taunting Kevin.

The taunting went on until a play came along that gave them chance to go at each other, usually a potential quarterback sack on Pat. Sometimes it was so obvious that Pat would throw the ball directly at Kevin as a way of getting the first shot in. Kevin would tackle Pat, and they'd start a vicious fight the likes of which no one else in the neighborhood had ever been in. Full swinging, face biting, scratching: they were worse than women. Both would start crying as they fought, sobbing openly as they grunted and cursed each other. The other kids were so used to these outbreaks that they would gather around and mentally take notes on what to do if they ever got into a real fight. That feeling of a fight -- pure tension and fear -- was never there when Pat and Kevin went at it. It seemed natural, like it wouldn't be a complete game unless Pat and Kevin had it out.

After a minute or two, they'd be wrapped around each other throwing painless rabbit punches, both breathless and exhausted. One or the other would start laughing, and the other would join in. Soon, they'd be rolling on the grass or macadam, arm in arm, laughing at each other. They'd get up with their bruises and bloody noses, slapping each other on the back and wiping their tears.

This strange ritual went on for years, until one fateful Saturday in the winter when Pat and Kevin went to confession at our church across the cemetery. Like most of the other Catholic kids, the brothers were in the habit of going the first Saturday of every month, just enough time to compile enough sins to make it worthwhile for the priest. They never knew who was on the other side of the screen. The priests in the surrounding parishes had a way of trading off with each other so that a certain priest wouldn't hear the sins from his own parish.

Most of the parishioners knew enough to whisper their sins. The church was deathly quiet on those Saturday afternoons, with only a few people in the pews whispering their penances, and the rest waiting in line by the confessional booths.

That Saturday, Pat had probably copped to the sort of low-level, immaterial sins the rest of us did, like stealing a bunch of nickels and dimes he had found buried between the sofa pillows after his father had taken a nap. And, of course, using the Lord's name in vain, which seemed to be every kid's ace in the hole.

As Pat whispered his penance with the other parishioners, he heard Kevin reciting the act of contrition in the booth. It was winter, and the church was unusually quiet, with a blanketing snow falling outside. There was Pat, a few other kids and a dozen old ladies in the church.

"Bless me father, for I have sinned ..." Kevin started. In the portions where the priest would speak, Pat heard only indecipherable whispers and thought for sure that Kevin would be reprimanded for talking too loud. He went through his contrition and started listing his sins, which Pat heard as if Kevin were sitting next to him. Pat glanced around, and he could tell that everyone else was hearing this, too, as they hid their faces in their praying hands.

"I called my brother a lot of bad words. I punched one of my friends in school on the jaw and hurt him. And forgive me, father, but I touched myself last night."

There were a few more whispers.

"In the bathroom before I went to bed."

More whispers.

"My mother's *Ladies Home Journal* magazine and two tissues."

Those gentle whispers.

"Forgive me, father. It won't happen again."

Pat was in tears, as were the other kids praying or waiting in line. The old ladies had pretended not to hear and fixed their eyes on the floor, realizing that they would have been out of line to raise their voices over a confession no one but the priest was supposed to have heard. Kevin came out of the booth, blushing over his sins, not realizing everyone else knew them.

When they got out in the parking lot, Pat cut into him.

"Asshole, don't you know *National Geographic* has better spank material than *Ladies Home Journal*?"

"What are you talking about?" Kevin asked.

The other kids were gathering around, certain that another Hanlon brawl was about to erupt.

"Don't you know everybody heard you in the confession booth? What, did you think I was Jesus or somehow reading your mind?"

Kevin's face turned beet red. He looked around at the other kids, all of whom were too embarrassed, and afraid, to return his gaze. Pat had his chin up. It was as though he was a lawyer who knew all the answers and only asked questions that proved this.

Instead of attacking Pat, Kevin started to cry. Not a sobbing cry, but more his eyes watering too hard to stop. He kept staring at Pat, whom it dawned on that this was no longer funny. Most likely, Pat already knew Kevin's sin of masturbation. He might have been dreaming that he was surrounded by white doves, which after a peaceful moment, would flap their wings and fly away. Pat would wake up, realizing that the sound of wings flapping was Kevin jerking off in his lower bunk bed. He would never let on to Kevin that he was awake. It seemed too embarrassing.

The other kids started walking away, leaving only the brothers in the snowy parking lot. Eventually, they walked home together, not looking at or speaking to each other.

No one ever gave Kevin a hard time about his confession, lest he beat them to death. Besides, it would have been hard to hold Kevin accountable for something we were all doing like monkeys in a zoo. After that day at Confession, Kevin and Pat never fought in public again. On the other hand, they didn't seem as close, moving in different social circles, eventually different adult lives miles away from each other. Whatever compelled them to beat the shit out of each other no longer mattered.

1978: Point Pleasant

Any time I hear the song "Can We Still Be Friends" by Todd Rundgren, I have two reactions. The first is a mild sort of revulsion. Not at the song itself, which is a great pop song, but at the song's message. I'm far more in the "We Can't Be Friends" camp after a relationship tanks.

The second reaction, more a memory, is to recall summers visiting Uncle Bill in Point Pleasant: our annual trip to the Jersey shore. The reason this song sparks the memory is because the summer Todd Rundgren put out his *Hermit of Mink Hollow* album, Brother M was playing the eight track of it to death in his car. Thus, everywhere we drove that summer, that album, and that song in particular, was playing. It didn't register with me as a kid, but that was the summer he graduated high school, and he must have tied in that exhilarating sense of freedom with that album. The song sounds like a faded summer memory. I also get the same Point Pleasant vibe from "Down by the Seaside" by Led Zeppelin. Brother M was dogging *Physical Graffiti*, too, on his car's eight track, and that song naturally stuck.

Coming down from the Coal Region of Pennsylvania, the Jersey shore was like another world, one that made us feel inferior. Brother J and I had deep baseball and lawn-mowing tans. You could see the distinct tan lines on our mid-biceps where our t-shirts ended: turkey-meat white above the line and bronze below. Ditto our legs in terms of wearing shorts. We looked like dicks compared to the completely-bronzed, blonde surfer dudes who were all over the beach. It seemed like all the kids were extras out of some Beach Boys video. I envied those kids that all they seemed to do all summer long was surf, while we played ball and mowed lawns in the mountains.

I still get excited every time I lay eyes on the ocean, after not seeing it for months or years at a time. You'd be surprised how little of it you see it in New York City, unless you work on the southern tip of Manhattan. I walk over the 59th Street Bridge routinely and see the massive East River flowing into the sea, but it's not the same. There's just something about approaching a sandy beach head, walking up the wooden planks, then coming over the brim to see the ocean spread over the horizon, the waves rolling into shore, the sound of their crashing, the wind.

At Point Pleasant, we'd immediately find a spot to put down our towels then get into the water ASAP. Body surfing was all we knew how to do, not hard, and exciting when we got the knack. Many times, we got tumbled, swallowing that bitter-tasting salt water, getting bruised, losing our trunks and standing up dazed with our dicks hanging out. It was fun as hell and never got old. The surfers were usually down at the other end of the beach, and they had an attitude to boot. This was their turf, and they knew we were tourists. I don't recall ever taking any shit from these kids, but they kept to themselves and vice-versa.

Dad stayed back home in Pennsylvania. He never liked traveling anywhere past the county line, and I can only recall him coming down to Point Pleasant once. Mom would take us, although we didn't feel really cool until Brother M was old enough to drive. We tooled around playing Prog Rock on the eight track with our Cousin John, who was that rare friendly surfer. (For the record, he was heavily into KISS, Yes and Jethro Tull at the time, which seemed kind of silly then, but now seems cool as everyone and his brother was dogging Springsteen to death. I once asked John how he felt about Springsteen, and he shrugged, said, I don't know, it's not my kind of music. He seemed strangely ambivalent given that Springsteen was a local boy made good.)

I can vouch that when *Jaws* came out in 1975, people were afraid to swim in the ocean after seeing it. I was one of them when Mom drove us down a few weeks later. I recall timidly asking Aunt Ellen about the possibility of sharks in the water, and she sighed, having heard this question a few times already from other visiting relatives. I asked Cousin John and he said, yeah, we see sharks every now and then while surfing. Well, what do you do, I asked. We move down to the other end of the beach, he answered nonchalantly. It made no sense to me given the horror of that movie. I got over my fear and went in, although not too far. That fear was gone the following years, possibly because the *Jaws* sequels sucked so bad!

Mom burned easy, so she covered herself at the beach, sat under an umbrella, and was content to watch us having fun. I can see now that this is a parent's right, and she must have been in heaven watching us cut loose like that. What really grated on me, then and now, is that while Mom was watching us, there was a gaggle of middle-aged women disapprovingly casting sideways glances at Mom. They were the color of lobsters, and it occurs to me now that these were snobby New York City-area housewives who had beach houses in Point Pleasant who got bronzed every summer. Doing nothing, lying in the sun. While Mom busted her ass taking care of four kids and was grateful to have a few days off. Even then, I sensed these women were looking down on us. Mom clearly sensed it, too, and I despised them. In all fairness, it was a private beach, their beach. Uncle Bill's annual summer job when not teaching high-school Spanish was to put on a pith helmet and check passes at the small boardwalk entrance to the beach. Thus, we could spend time at a more local beach instead of crowded public beaches.

I remember how accommodating Uncle Bill was, too. Before this, up in the attic of our house I would often stumble across old high-school text books that were clearly from the 1930s. There was a complete set of Shakespeare. Paging through, I would see that someone had left notations in the margins, instructions to a younger reader, but every now and then, a stern, "This passage is immoral" underlined notation would appear. That had to be Uncle Bill, who would eventually become a teacher and was forever a staunch Catholic. He was always looking out for Dad, his younger brother, guiding him. Uncle Bill didn't care if Shakespeare had survived the centuries; the immortal bard wasn't going to get away with pulchritude in the eyes of God.

He also had a father's patience. When he learned that I was toying with a relief-pitcher role on my Little League team (I was a terrible relief pitcher), he made a point of taking a few afternoons to train me in the street in front of his house. I was all over the place with my pitches, making him routinely get up and chase the ball dozens of yards down the block. He never gave up and offered nothing but encouragement. I never forgot how attentive and sharp he was. Probably a strict disciplinarian, too, but I could sense the heart underneath and responded well to him.

For all my memories of beach insecurity, we had great times down there. Hitting the beach in the morning, coming back to Uncle Bill's house for lunch, heading out again for the afternoon, then coming back and using his cool outdoor shower to get clean for dinner, the smell of the sea in the air all the while. It seemed like our finger and toe nails grew exponentially while were down there. Whatever cuts, scars or scabs we had, they seemed to magically heal in the ocean water. We invariably got sunburned some time during the trip. There was constantly sand in our sneakers and water seeping out our ears. All of this was so cool to a bunch of redneck kids who lived over a hundred miles from the ocean.

1978: Misfits

Sometime in the mid-70s I fell in love with The Kinks, after a few years of hearing the song "Lola" on the radio. I thought it was the most intelligent, funny song I'd ever heard, and it rocked. Most songs that rocked had no meaning. They were Robert Plant yowling "baby, baby, baby" over and over. With "Lola," I could hear the story of a guy going to a nightclub in London, meeting what he thinks is the love of his life, then realizing Lola was either a drag queen or a masculine woman. It didn't seem to matter which.

The Kinks were all over AOR radio back then, along with early hits like "You Really Got Me" getting regular play on AM radio. I can't recall when I bought the monumental two-record set, *The Kinks Kronikles*, but that day changed my life, as I heard all the great album tracks they weren't playing on the radio: "Shangri-La," "Autumn Almanac," "Get Back in Line," etc. Nearly every song floored me. I had been a huge Elton John fan, but he was blowing wind by the time of his *Blue Moves* album. The other key bands for me from that time, ELO and Queen, were great at what they did, but not quite what The Kinks were all about.

In 1977 radio was playing the shit out of their current album cuts, "Jukebox Music" and "Sleepwalker," which weren't bad, but nowhere near as good as the stuff on *Kronikles*. Every time I'd go to the record store, I'd see the bargain bin full of weird Kinks "concept" albums, some on the ubiquitous Pickwick record label. (For the uninitiated, Pickwick picked up albums that had bombed and reissued them with no-frills vinyl and packaging. If a rock star had an album on Pickwick, he knew hard times). I wasn't buying, yet.

A year passed, and in the spring of 1978, I heard a song on the radio that I knew was by The Kinks but had never heard before. Back then, I wasn't so quick to assume this was new material. A few years earlier, I had heard The Beatles song "We Can Work It Out" on the radio and assumed it was a Paul McCartney & Wings song I didn't know. Understand I was 11 or so, a Wings fan, not well-versed enough to know that was clearly Lennon on the harmony vocal, and at that point only had The Beatles "Blue" greatest hits album. So much of their back catalog was new to me. Some of the greatest listening experiences of my teenage years were going back and buying all those Beatles, Stones, Who and Kinks albums (at least the ones still in print), hearing landmark songs for the first time and having enough listening experience to know it.

This song had a beautiful opening riff on acoustic guitar that repeated itself before Ray Davies came in with those first few lines about sleeping in fields and feeling lost in life.

It was one of those songs that made me stop what I was doing and listen. That happened all the time with Kinks songs, because the words mattered. I was in my bedroom, doing homework at night while listening to WMMR out of

Philly on the radio. As with all great songs, I got it on the first listen. There are good songs that grow on you, but it's been my experience that great ones hit you like a baseball bat upside the head.

Let's go back to 1978. I'm 14 at the time. I have goofy headphone hair shaped by wearing Radio Shack Nova 40 headphones, the only good product the Radio Shack ever produced. (The in-house brand name for small electronic products was Realistic. Their shit was realistic; it broke down all the time.) I went through two pairs in the 70s and 80s, using them religiously. Those were the days of dropping a needle on the start of the album, playing it all the way through Side 1, flipping it, and then Side 2, a 40-minute endeavor I repeated thousands of times.

I had acne. I never got it bad, just enough to be annoying. I wore flannel shirts all the time: my choice of clothes when not wearing goofy band, movie or comedian t-shirts. Throw in jeans and sneakers, and that was my daily wardrobe.

I was a smart kid, but not too smart. My problem in school wasn't so much lack of discipline as not caring enough about grades. I got B's and A's with ease. When it got to be crunch time in Math and Science, my least favorite subjects, I'd even get C's. With Math, I hit a wall with Calculus. I recall Mr. W's terrifying class, where he'd constantly yell at kids, sometimes throwing dusty chalk erasers when it was clear they had no idea how to handle the basic equation he had scrawled on the blackboard. I got a zero on one quiz, the same as my old friend, Hot Rod. Both of us sat there, grinning at our shared misfortune. Mr. W caught us: "What are you guys laughing about?! I could bring *my dog* in here, have him put *a paw print* on this quiz and get the same grade as both of you!" That was a mistake as we both envisioned a bedraggled mutt at the desk next to us doing exactly that and broke into hysterics. That was a *long*, unhappy class.

I was good at sports, but not inclined to join the high-school teams. I tried basketball and golf, but gave up both by my junior year. I didn't do drugs, but knew plenty of kids who did, and would go on knowing them, simply because we were kids, in that groove of knowing each other by proximity and habit.

My friends were a like-minded group of stranded kids who weren't "cool" by any standards, nor were the objects of derision. We were a pretty good bunch of guys: loyal, smart, not prone to head games, great senses of humor, which we should have exploited a lot more under the circumstances. The popular kids didn't think we were popular enough, the jocks not athletic enough, the stoners not stoned enough. "Low profile" would be an apt description. You could be part of our gang, if you could find it, and didn't mind our befuddlement with all things important to your average teenager.

There was Tony from Ringtown and Rich from Wilberton #1. (There was a Wilberton #2, and I defy anyone from either town to tell me the difference.) We called Rich "Balloon Ass" as a play on his surname. Both were great at Math, smarter than the obvious suspects in the top-class rankings, but nowhere near as well-rounded. Tony was forever trying to challenge Balloon Ass' insane mathematical genius, made all the crazier by the fact that his English skills were so rudimentary that he routinely used the phrase "dat dere tingy" to say "that thing."

There was Schwamy (nickname based on surname) who transferred from Delaware when his parents moved to Ashland, with his berserk imagination that came out in hand-written cartoons recasting The Brady Bunch as The Manson Family. (His photo mash-up of me in my 20s holding a Black Velvet Christ painting, with my current face photo-shopped in Christ's place, serves as my "About the Author" photo.) Most nights found Tony and Schwamy looking for adventure in Tony's VW Rabbit, forever blasting Van Halen at ear-bleed volume. They usually ended up at the arcade at the Schuylkill Mall, blowing through Tony's painstakingly saved collection of bicentennial quarters on video games like Donkey Kong and Pac Man.

There was old friend George whom I had known since we were four, on the same doomed Little League team, later driving around all night in his souped-up 76 Nova with tailpipes and cassette deck. His older brother Johnny taught Social Studies and took a perverse delight in ranking on Schwamy, once telling him there was a place for kids like him … on Mars. On another occasion, Johnny had asked us to write down three things we wanted to be when we grew up. Most kids wanted to be doctors, teachers, carpenters, engineers, nurses, etc. Schwamy's answer: "I want to be a gynecologist in Hollywood, or a hot-dog vendor on the beach in Hawaii, or Cindy Crawford's bicycle seat." Johnny paused for a moment, his mind blown, before muttering, "Why am I not surprised?"

There was Lee, who had a whole other set of friends based on his wrestling and track skills, but often found his way to our invisible lunch table to share laughs and insults. We were constantly sparring in English Lit classes; each grasped how smart the other was, but refused to yield. More on Lee later. Ditto, Hot Rod, our complicated relationship going back to grade school.

Paul Y floated in and out of our group, way out once he started dating a girl a few grades behind us, and things got serious in that "John and Yoko" way teenage guys succumb to. Schwamy couldn't stand him, based on his eternal, droning question: "Schwam … how'd the Phillies do?" Schwamy understood that Paul didn't give a damn about the Phillies and was subtly making fun of his baseball obsession. I knew Paul from grade school. He lived out the road in Fountain Springs, and we rode his mini-bike on the trail in the woods behind Route 61 all the way back to our cemetery. I still have a three-line scar branded on my right knee from the time I crashed the bike against my leg while wearing shorts with the engine running hot.

It's odd to me now that when I heard "Misfits" for the first time, it struck me with a thunderbolt of recognition that I was a misfit. I had always felt out of place in some sense and still do now. At the time, I didn't know it was a condition many people feel in the same way, too. I can look back now and see that I really wasn't the huge misfit I made myself out to be: I was a normal kid, all things considered. Very bizarre and developed sense of humor for my age, smarter and more well-read than your average kid, but aside from that, about as normal as a teenage kid could be. "Misfits" is a romantic ballad, and I gather there were kids and even older listeners who took it upon themselves to romanticize their plight like I was doing.

I could point out kids who were misfits. The handful of teenage guys in my class who were obviously gay and catching shit from all sorts of demented goons on a daily basis. The kid who smelled like shit and wore heavy metal t-shirts. Those wayward kids who seemed like they'd be happier jumping boxcars headed west than sitting in "the rubber room" (where the bad kids went for punishment). The large kids who "overheard" fat jokes and comments all day, every day. The homely girls no one would pay attention to, much less ask out. They weren't waving their freak flags high. These were kids who seemed on the verge of being invisible, or willing themselves to be so. There was nothing romantic about it.

What got to me about "Misfits," as with so many other Ray Davies song, was it made the unusual universal. Ray let me know he understood that we're all strange in some sense, and it's all right. The song's bridge noted that misfits were everywhere; they were all of us.

The song has a sense of building, like any good ballad. "Misfits" has a few of the moments when the song fades to silence, then fades back in on an organ note, or the signature riff repeated on acoustic guitar. This song wasn't a hit; I'm not even sure if it was released a single. The big song from the *Misfits* album was "A Rock 'N' Roll Fantasy," a similar song in sound and theme. Ray sang about his uncertainty with the band's future, and his decision to keep on going because there were people out there who loved his music more than he did. The song seemed a bit cheesy and dishonest to me. Of course, he wasn't going to stop making music, what else was he going to do? "Misfits" seemed real to me, like Ray was walking with me through those nutty high-school halls, where everything seemed to be some desperate competition I wanted no part of. Kids either chased that brass ring or turned too easily towards bitterness and rejection.

A cool thing about The Kinks that I discovered in my senior year. I was in Mr. Welker's Nuclear Science class, which I'll describe more fully later. Being a smart kid, I was in these smart-kid classes with that mix of eggheads and go-getters. Some kids were smart. Some were smart and popular (i.e., into sports and school-related activities). Some were popular and faking the smartness to the best of their abilities. That class was no different. We all got along on that weird sort of "smart kid" wavelength.

One day, we went on a field trip to the Berwick power plant, not a nuclear reactor, but it's a power plant. Mr. Welker knew people there so we could get a detailed tour of how the place worked.

The tour went as planned. We all wore hardhats and had a ball, being out of school, middle of May, 17 years old, about to graduate: a great time. On the way back, we had the van to ourselves. Since Mr. Welker knew we were "good kids," he trusted that we wouldn't go apeshit and tear the thing up. We didn't. As we were pulling out of Berwick, Mike and Dave, best friends on the football team, pulled out a portable tape recorder and popped in a tape. I figured,

"Jocks. Nice guys, but probably assholes when it comes to music. Here comes Journey, or Styx, or Def Leppard."

They popped in *The Kinks Kronikles* and were blasting "Waterloo Sunset"! I freaked out, as I was one of about five kids, the others soulful, musically-inclined stoners, who seemed to know or care who The Kinks were. I asked them how they got into The Kinks, and just like me, hearing songs on the radio, a stray King Biscuit Flower Hour here and there, etc. They said they played the album all the time after practice. I tried to imagine a busful of jocks grooving to "David Watts" and couldn't. That was Dave and Mike, two cool kids who surprised me that day, but I should have seen it coming.

That was the point of "Misfits." I took a good look around, and there were two kids on that bus like me in some deeper sense that I'd never considered.

1978: Sampson and Leo

Getting a haircut in Astoria now is an international experience for me. I take a long walk down Steinway Street towards 30th Avenue, through Little Egypt, with its periodic clumps of Middle-Eastern guys bantering in front of the hookah cafes, some international soccer channel playing inside, a night game in Tunisia, that strong, sweet hookah smell hovering over the block.

I get my haircut before hitting the gym and ordering take-out Lamb Biryani from the Nepalese restaurant on Steinway. The barbershop is run by two Russian guys, both good barbers. One is quiet and studious, the other chatty. He keeps a parrot in a cage next to his chair to charm younger customers. I've noticed he's also trying to sell suits, cologne and gadgets on the side.

This used to be old John's shop, but he retired recently and passed the business off to them. John was a big, old Russian, bald on top, pictures of him in the army with more hair and less weight next to his mirror, among the phalanx of family photos. He worked with his son who had a big, wavy, hair-metal mullet, a real head of hair, the kind I expect to see on a non-balding Russian barber in Queens. He was forever fending off barbershop suppliers and street hustlers selling porn DVD's who would wander in from the street.

A few years ago, I was getting my hair cut by old John when I heard the son mutter, "Oh, shit, here comes the cry baby." I couldn't look out the window, but I could see in the mirror, a man and woman dragging a small boy down the sidewalk. They looked to be of Eastern-European descent, from somewhere in that hazy crossroad between Middle-Eastern and Western cultures.

They burst through the door, and the kid was pitching a fit. The scene in *The Omen* where they try to take Damien to church? This was the same freak out. The kid was howling like he was about to be circumcised with a butter knife. His hair wasn't that long, straight and black, halfway over his ear and down his neck. Tears, screaming, desperate pleas in their native tongue. Hippies getting forced buzz cuts in a rural, American jail circa 1968 after a routine traffic stop were probably less emphatic.

It took me back to my childhood haircuts that were equally traumatizing. God bless Leo the barber – he was a kind man. But when Mom would drag me into his barbershop in Ashland, it was always a bad trip. She was in the habit of letting my hair get long as a small boy – not hippie long, but shaggy. "Wide" would be a better description. We joked that if Dad or any of us let our hair grow out, we'd have dreadlocks.

Leo specialized in one thing and one thing only: crew cuts. You could sit there and give him five minutes of detailed instructions. Didn't matter. You'd always end up with the same box-headed crew cut. He cut hair like The Ramones made music: two minutes, electricity buzzing, and you were gone. The only difference was Leo didn't count off,

"One - Two - Three - Four" before dive-bombing in with his clippers.

His son who worked with him, Leo Jr., understood that the 70s weren't the 50s, but it was always a gamble whose chair would come open first. Their reading material was *The Policeman's Gazette*, *Grit*, The American Legion magazine, *Highlights* (please refer to "The Drill" chapter from 1974 to understand why this terrified me) and comic books, the only time I read these things. Both of them were classic barbers who gave crying, little boys lollipops.

When I see small kids crying nowadays over what I recognize as reasonable, longish haircuts, I have to laugh. Because Leo would give a kid reason to cry – it was like joining the army. It was that radical a departure from what he had previously seen in the mirror, a total sheep-shearing experience that would leave most kids either wet-eyed or wailing. The apologetic, post-haircut sucker was meager solace. You could have given me a complete set of Phillies baseball cards, and I still would have felt violated afterwards. I cried because of two things: the sense of impending change, and the act of something, even if it was only hair, being cut off my body. It scared me in a very real sense.

My mid-teen hair length pushed the boundaries of good taste and parental disapproval. I laugh now looking at the pictures but still recall Dad grumbling that I was long overdue for a haircut. Bushy, unkempt, pointing at weird angles. Just bad 70s hair. The longer it grew, the more you could tell I was wearing headphones all the time. It was a bad look, but I was far from alone. Most guys had these shaggy, combed-straight-down haircuts, much longer than mine, accented by hideous-looking, peach-fuzz mustaches and sideburns.

Leo would get his clippers humming, and that was all she wrote. The dramatic transformation Leo wrought was jarring. Strangers probably thought I was talking to Jesus in the form of a burning bush or family dog, and had symbolically chopped all my hair off to spiritually cleanse myself. This was how DeNiro had his hair in *Taxi Driver* before he got the mohawk.

I would take a lot of crap from the guys at school. Not as much as I'd give to Tony, whose barber meted out the same, rigid punishment, a Prince Valiant/Moe Howard-style bowl cut every few months. I would drive him into a seething, ass-kicking rage by running Three Stooges riffs on him all day: making that Curly Howard "woob-woob-woob" sound, or doing that freaky finger-snapping/hand waving routine Curly would do to Moe before getting finger-poked in the eyes.

The most notorious session in my teens occurred when Old Leo actually shaved spots into each side of my head, inadvertently giving me a cool punk cut. I couldn't believe it. While all my friends were laughing and calling me Johnny Rotten, I was mortified that he had gone beyond the normal military cut. He must have accidentally pressed the electric clipper all the way through to the skin. Kids would playfully taunt someone about "getting their ears moved" or "getting run over by a lawn mower." One of Leo's cuts would have kids asking me when I was shipping out to Paris Island, after a month of helping Charlie and Tex tune up the dune buggies at Spahn Ranch.

1979: Brown Paper Bag in the Trunk

Everyone has a drunk story. You'll read mine later. I feel an urge now to tell one of Brother M's amazing drunk stories, as it underlines so much of what went on between him and our father, that weird dance a parent does when the oldest sibling of a group of kids goes off the rails. I can see now as an adult that this must have scared the shit out of our parents. The oldest son, formerly a straight-A student, falls in with the drug crowd (an alarming number of driving-age kids in our town) and immediately starts free-falling on levels that are shocking and new to them. They could handle kids being prickly and combative. A kid driving his car into the side of a hill, appearing like a stoned ogre in the living room at three in the morning, covered in dirt and weeds, the cop who escorted him to the door, telling them, "He gets a free pass this time, but not next"?

That's not even the story I'm thinking about. There are a few. Brother M broke in our parents for the rest of us, but the rest of us never got anywhere near that out there, which must have been a huge relief. I shied away from drugs as a teenager and college student simply because I saw the older kids in my neighborhood have problems with them a few years earlier. Of course, I experimented in college, but I can count those experiences on two hands ... or one hand that looks like two? I must admit, those were some wonderful nights, particularly when magic mushrooms were involved. I never picked up any habit or social structure that encouraged prolonged drug use.

The story I'm thinking of ended unceremoniously. On a summer day, my father was working on some minor issue with Brother M's car. He needed to get the jack out of the trunk. He went back to the trunk, opened it, stood there for a few minutes looking into it, started shaking his head and muttering to himself, left the trunk open, but decided it would be a better idea to skip working on the car and mow the lawn instead.

The end. But the end was a beginning. I watched all this happening from the back porch, can't recall exactly what I was doing, but I do recall Dad muttering to himself, small curse words like "god damn" and "son of a bitch." Since he left the trunk open, I couldn't help but walk by a few minutes later to see whatever had set him off.

I was met by the smell of stale beer. The whole trunk reeked of it. There were no beer cans or bottles. The trunk itself looked like any trunk: spare tire, jack, crow bar, small tool box.

And a brown paper bag that had split open enough to reveal a pair of deeply soiled underwear. Clearly a pair that had been shat in, full load. The smell of stale beer was so strong that I didn't pick up on any shit smell. Not since diaper days had I dealt with any episodes to rival something like this. Shitting your pants at any point in your life between the ages of 2 and 82, it's one for the ages.

I knew Brother M was sleeping off his stew. Later that day, he needed to hit the record store at the mall, possibly to pick up a new Todd Rundgren eight track, and I asked if I could tag along. I told him about Dad's situation with the trunk, and his reaction, which had Brother M laughing his ass off. It was then that I got the back story on the paper bag, the beer and the soiled underwear.

As usual at that point in the late 70s, he had worked a shift at the Acme supermarket in Shenandoah. (Coincidentally, he had another story of shitting his pants there one day when one of his coworkers played the prank of locking all the men's room stalls from the inside. This forced him to attempt crawling over the top, which is where he lost the battle and dropped a load. He went back to work with a meat-butcher's smock to cover the fact that he was bare-assed underneath.)

He wasn't working that night. Those nights, he hooked up with some friends, with beer and whatever drugs were handy at the time, to cruise, which simply meant listening to rock-and-roll eight tracks while driving around all night. Doesn't sound like much, but we all did it eventually (sober in my case), as teenagers back then loved to go out in groups, be in cars at night, amongst their kind, listening to rock and roll, doing nothing but driving around for hours. I can't recall how many times I did this as a teenager. I can look back now and see that we were reveling in a sense of spare time we took for granted. Even when I get spare time like that now, it doesn't occur to me to hook up with guys my age and listen to music while we drive at night. I wish it would, because I miss those casual, goofy, fun times we often had. Everything I do as an adult feels so weighted with intent and direction; being directionless in small increments has its merits.

As the night wore on, he found himself driving alone while killing a six pack, surely too drunk and high for his own good, much less for driving. Drunk driving was not the crime of the century back then. Guys would often get into cars with beers, not necessarily drunk, but the simple act of getting into a car with a beer is a bit shocking now. We all drove drunk at least a few times in our youth back then. A cop was as likely to tell you to go home and don't do it again back in the 70s and 80s, unless you had been in an accident or staggering drunk.

Well, strange things happen sometimes when you get that loose. In Brother M's case, he shat his pants, again. Just happened. Probably sharted, and things devolved from there. He pulled over in a Burger King parking lot and thought, "How am I ever going to go home like this?" He was wearing his white pants, a snazzy dresser at the time, and the pants were luckily not stained. The underwear looked like a road map of hell, where the rivers ran brown.

So, under those harsh parking-lot lights, keeping a keen eye out for cops or other sane humans, he opened up the door, took off his pants, stood up, shook out a few lumps and got his underwear off. The smart thing would have been to abandon them right there. Our parents were raised in the Depression and had drilled into us that nothing must be wasted. In a way, it was heroic that Brother M had tried to save his irreversibly soiled underwear. He was paying tribute to our parents, even if they could never see it that way. He seemed to be thinking, "I can salvage this horribly shit-stained pair of cheap white underpants."

Well, he couldn't, but not for lack of trying. He poured a beer on the underwear and scrubbed, hard. Another beer. He must have sensed some kind of progress as he kept at them. What to do with this underwear. He had the paper bag for the six pack. Why not put the underwear in the paper bag, put it in the trunk, and the next day, go get it and see if there was any way to salvage it or at the least throw it away. That's the only explanation I could have for why he didn't leave that shitty underwear in the parking lot. He was so high that a sentimental sense of honoring our parents by not littering or abandoning a piece of clothing they had paid for kicked in. He couldn't do either.

You do strange things when you're high. One of those strange things is adhering to a gentle code of morality that would escape you while sober. Because you're high, you feel a yearning to be good in some higher sense. So, you convince yourself that if you do something honorable while you're high, you're striving to be a good person despite being hideously wrecked. I've been there; we all have.

Brother M could be a prickly kid and was surely hell on wheels as a teenager. I gather a moment like that, alone in that parking lot, trying to figure a way out of an impossible situation, the better angels of his soul came shining through. In ways he thought were enlightening and honorable. I'm willing to bet he was listening to "Ten Years Gone" by Led

Zeppelin on the eight track and feeling spiritual. Not quite realizing his version of being an enlightened human being meant our father, a few hours later in the harsh morning light, opening the trunk of his car and having a deep WTF moment decades before WTF moments were noted as such.

Dad never mentioned the situation to anyone. Had I not been on the back porch, the whole thing would have quietly passed as opposed to entering the hallowed halls of teenage legend. I felt like that tree in a forest that hears another tree fall. It happened, and I was there to prove it. I suspect there were many other odd little instances like this in Brother M's teenage years where there was no one else around to verify that the falling tree had made a sound.

1979: Fore!

Technically, golf was a high-school sport, but come on. Golfers tend to be athletes on the same physical level as bowlers or badminton players. A few words about the sport of golf: I hate it. I didn't back then. Golf made sense to me, although I found it to be a frustrating sport, one that would allow me to reach a certain mediocre plateau and never move beyond. It's a game that requires precise coordination, years of practice and inexplicable natural ability, like that of a distance runner or major-league pitcher. I recall many afternoons throwing a club farther than I had hit a ball, or yelling louder and more viciously than Johnny Rotten could ever hope to. It was a game of existential crisis.

Brother J got into golf first, as did next-door neighbor, Bubba. I started following them out for nine holes at the skimpy local course. Soon, we were all saving lawn-mowing money to buy our own clubs and bags. (I would have saved for golf shoes, but they were the kind of footwear I associated with barbershop quartets: glaring, two-tone leather shoes that were ready-to-wear with black socks and bermuda shorts.)

When the time came, we joined the golf team in high school. We were good in sports but shied away from the high-school versions with their lame social protocols. Golf had none of the brutal popularity vibes that all major high-school sports put out.

Socioeconomically speaking, golf was a sport I should have been nowhere near. Other kids playing were often the children of doctors, lawyers, business owners, dentists, school principals, etc. Dad was a factory worker; I should have been like Tom Cruise in *All the Right Moves*. But I was more like Anthony Michael Hall in *The Breakfast Club*. Making all the wrong moves.

As a result, I simply played the game and tried to avoid the smug, country-club silliness that was rampant even at the cheap public courses. I made it a point to take off my t-shirt and get a tan, tying the t-shirt around my bag's strap in lieu of the fancy lamb's wool holder wealthier players had. It was punk-rock golfing: pair of shorts, white socks and black Converse Chuck E. Taylor high-tops. I would have been cool, only that golf is beyond even the boomerang effect of anti-cool.

To join the golf team, all you had to do was approach the coach, whom we called Duke, the high school's geometry teacher, and ask. Immediate acceptance: no one was ever turned away, as so few kids came out that we were often short a few players (five varsity and five junior-varsity). Every August, practice started around the same time as the football team, meaning that we could play at the local course for free as many times as we wanted. Even better, when the season started in earnest (running concurrent with football), we got out of school for matches (twice a week), and if it was an "away" match, that meant getting out after lunch period.

The only catch was being on the golf team meant the word "dildo" flashed over our heads in neon letters all day at school. We had to wear our uniforms the day of a match: white, short-sleeved knit shirts. In a working-class high school where flannel shirts and long-sleeved Ozzy Osbourne concert t-shirts ruled, it was like walking around dressed as a giant penis. Kids would bark out "fag" and "blow me" in the hallway. Or "fore" or "Here comes Arnold Palmer!" We had to leave our clubs in Duke's classroom at the start of the day. Most afternoons in the fall, Duke taught a remedial math class for the more "challenged" students. When it was time to leave for a match, we'd go to his classroom and find trailer-park nimrods using our clubs to play air guitar or beat each other on the head.

The worst was being stuck on the mini-bus while the football team passed, which would happen in late summer when we had our first few matches. They'd file by in their pads and cleats, sweaty and filthy from practice, archetypes of virility, glaring at us like we were all dressed in drag as Judy Garland and blowing them kisses. I still recall one particularly vicious kid laying in with the usual homophobic bluster that, I imagine, is still a hallmark of low-brow, high-school harassment. A decade later, I distinctly remember him coming out of the closet and getting paralyzed from the neck down in an automobile accident in the span of a few months. The Lord works in mysterious ways. Perhaps He plays golf?

I didn't quite understand the homophobic comments. There was nothing gay about golf. Boring and uncool, yes, but not gay. Football is a sport where men hug and fondle each other constantly. No same-sex partners touch each other in golf. Football has positions like "wide receiver" and "tight end." Linebacker sounds suspiciously similar to "fudge packer." Just saying.

Our golf team was awful. Even with the few rich kids on the team -- one of them had a putting green in his backyard – we were simply out-gunned by the wealthier teams "south of the mountain." Schuylkill County is cut into north and south by the Broad Mountain, the north side tending to be the grittier working-class towns, and the south the more affluent. The kids from south of the mountain were incredible golfers, raised playing the game, practicing routinely on much better courses, one of them being the county's premier country-club course, filled with challenging, dog-leg par fives and sloping, bi-level greens. They mostly looked and acted like James Spader in *Pretty in Pink*. We had crappy, flat farm pastures that felt like pitch-and-putt courses in comparison. Playing their courses was like a teenage rock band going from a garage to Madison Square Garden.

As a result, our motto was, "Later for the agony of defeat." Duke couldn't care less. He would often take the edge off another ragged school day at the clubhouse bar while we were getting kicked around the course. My first JV match, our lead golfer, Paul, got up in front of at least two dozen people and took the opening swing. He drove a huge, mossy divot 30 yards. His ball went 50 feet straight up in the air and came back down again at his feet. Duke put his face in his hands and made a beeline for the clubhouse. We nearly pissed ourselves laughing, although none of us would fare much better. The other team stared on in disbelief.

We were so bad that we'd strike deals with the other team. Yes, we knew we were going to lose, but we bartered with them to knock points off our embarrassingly high scores. We'd offer to buy them Cokes in the clubhouse. Or make bets, like the time I knocked five strokes off my score by sinking a 15-foot putt using my putter like a pool cue. One kid had a baseball bat in his bag and when his opponent wasn't looking, would get off an amazing shot, hitting a ball 300 yards onto the green, although he could normally hit only 150 yards.

Those were fun times, to be out of school on beautiful fall afternoons, wandering green, open fields, playing into the dusk, even if we sucked and usually lost. Let me note here that it was almost exclusively male, although a few teams would have one or two females. Panther Valley had a buxom young woman on its team, and we all had mental images of ourselves wildly banging her on one of those well-coiffed greens in the middle of the course. As nerdy teenagers, we had about as much chance of that as beating Jack Nicklaus.

One guy looked like Freddie Mercury with wire-frame glasses. Another had a permanently red face; he looked like he was blushing or having a heart attack. We wore silly golf hats that are now cool but made us look like jackasses in the early 80s. On drives back from matches, the kids who couldn't fit into the mini-bus, packed with our clubs, would ride along in a teammate's car, jamming on golf-team music: Devo, Kraftwerk and The Cars. We were certain Ric Ocasek was on the golf team in high school.

The irony of all this? The football players who harassed us now golf. You can see them on the courses early Saturday morning, dragging their big, tired asses into electric carts and reminiscing over the good old days when they could openly harass anyone and get away with it. Revenge of sorts? Hell, I'm not doing appreciably better. I did stop playing almost immediately after high school, as if I were living my life in reverse. I imagine that in my 60s, I'll drive around with other senior citizens and knock down mailboxes with baseball bats.

What does it mean now? I don't know. Being on the golf team, I wasn't popular. It didn't get me laid. Abusive pricks occasionally gave me a hard time for being on the team.

It was great training for adulthood. The quiet resolve I learned as a high-school golfer has served me well. I often think back to the denouement of my golf career: the opportunity in my senior year to purchase a letterman's jacket for my participation in a high-school sport. They were beauties: red wool bodies with white leather sleeves and red-and-blue cuffs. The kind of things Knute Rockne wore, and The Beach Boys wrote "Be True to Your School" about, with our high-school's letters proudly emblazoned on the left breast. My parents were willing to put out the reasonable sum for me to get one, but I held off. Not out of any disrespect or defiance of the high-school athletics hierarchy; I simply thought a navy-blue windbreaker with my name stenciled rodeo-style on the left breast would have been cooler.

1980: Duke

I still haven't cracked the nut on women. Any man who thinks he has must be delusional. You can be married for decades, and you're still going to be in the dark on any number of issues. I'm single and don't lose any sleep over this. The secret to happiness is not to lose sleep over issues like this, which is how couples stay married for decades. Life gets situational after awhile, and you roll with whatever comes your way.

I wouldn't know it at the time, but in high school, I was setting up patterns with women that play out to this day. Which is to say getting myself into impossible situations that are not impossible to begin with, but reveal themselves to be in short order. The first time was trying to win away a very smart, pretty girl from her longstanding boyfriend, who happened to be a badass on our champion wrestling team. I nearly got my ass beat a few times, and certainly should have, but somehow escaped with only a broken heart. (I would meet them again at my 10th high-school reunion as they got married right out of high school and stayed together. They were both so cool and kind with me, for which I'll be eternally grateful. What could have been a very long night turned out to be night of revelations and an unexpected reappraisal of those years, which were nowhere as bad as I imagined them being through my 20s.)

After that first debacle of going for a girl who was taken, I was understandably gun shy about these matters. Way too gun shy. To say I didn't get laid in high school is a radical under-statement! I would find myself getting into these odd situations where I'd gaze at some girl for weeks or months on end, with her gazing back. Which didn't necessarily mean the door was open.

Such a case happened with Helen in my sophomore year, with her a grade ahead. A very pretty girl, smallish, smart. Dating an ape. One of the guys on the football team who was an average kid, not that big or tough, but hung out with other vaguely "bad" guys who never did anything all that wrong. High school was all about image as opposed to action, and it worked most of the time. If I had been really smart, if a guy any age wants to be smart, he should ask himself why a woman he's attracted to is with a boring jackass, and perhaps draw the conclusion that maybe she's not all that. The even worse conclusion: why is he routinely attracted to this type of woman?

I spent months making eyes at this woman, as she did with me. All the while, dating this other guy with no end in sight. One day, an older friend in her class saw me looking at her, asked why I didn't ask her out. I told him the obvious answer. He shrugged, went over to her, told her I liked her and was wondering if she would go out with me. I was incensed at the time, but the guy made a great point to me. What was there to lose? Chances are the answer would be no, already taken, thanks anyway, but I'd be no better or worse off than before. That's how this one played out. I do recall later that day, making eye contact with her as my bus pulled away from the school. She had the saddest look in her eye, acknowledging that there was some quiet bridge between us she wasn't willing to cross.

The whole time this quiet flirtation played out, I was listening to the Genesis album *Duke* which had come out that spring. Even now, seeing that album cover makes me think of Helen and that quiet teenage despair. Nothing happened, but something happened. The album's vague concept is a character, Duke, guiding a woman to stardom. She leaves him behind when she becomes a star, leaving him older, wiser and heartbroken. Of course, I wasn't Duke – this girl was a year older and not a star – but I related to that same sense of heartbroken wisdom. A good "romantic failure" song to pine over is "Please Don't Ask" from this album. I remember playing that song over and over, thinking, "What an intelligent song about losing hope. No bitterness or melodrama. Just the truth."

Genesis got a bad rap after Peter Gabriel left, the consensus being they were a lesser band because Gabriel was the creative focal point of the band, and responsible for most of those interesting, stream-of-conscious lyrics. The band didn't skip a beat, even if they weren't as hip as solo Gabriel. They shared writing credits on every song. When Phil Collins took over the lead vocals, his voice sounded almost exactly like Gabriel's. The lyrics might have changed a little, but they were still good. The bad rap was they were still doing what was Prog Rock at a time when it was slowly fading out, while Gabriel was doing more commercial material with great success.

I bought all those post Gabriel albums, once on vinyl and re-upped on CD: *A Trick of the Tail, Wind & Wuthering, And Then There Were Three, Duke, Abacab*. That's where I stopped, as *Abacab* was the band skulking towards the 80s pop-rock monster they would become through Collins' far more slick solo albums. Along with *Duke* that ill-fated spring of 1980, I was dogging two other big Genesis ballads that best represented my teenage state of perpetual blue balls and broken heart: "Ripples" and "Afterglow." Both songs about leaving and heartbreak, both sung by Phil Collins in that post-Gabriel period. Emotionally accurate songs to play when you're a screwed-up teenager with the world crashing down because the love of your life is unobtainable. A drive to the convenience store to pick up milk for your Mom feels like a windswept journey on a ghost ship in the Azores.

There's a larger story to tell in the fantasy life of 70s teenage rock fans in which their rote American surroundings are in direct contrast with the romantic imagery placed in their imaginations by bands like Genesis, Queen, Led Zeppelin, etc. All I know is there were plenty of guys driving around in Ford Pintos who thought they were on camels in the Sahara when listening to "Kashmir." Of course, drugs may have had something to do with that also. The same mild self-deception came into play with matters of the heart, too, thus we all felt like Fabio on the cover of a romance novel every now and then.

1980: Baloney in a Nutshell

On a trip back to Pennsylvania a few years ago, I opened the county newspaper and was shocked to find that Mr. Welker, my old high-school chemistry teacher, had passed on in his 80s.

Mr. Welker was one of those love/hate teachers. A lot of kids hated him at the time, but later admitted they learned a lot under this tutelage. When I forwarded the obituary to Brother M, the best he could come up with was, "Not one of my favorite instructors, although I think his intentions were good." The rest was remembering how he'd dropped out of Mr. Welker's class and had received a stern lecture about his (surely lost) future. Brother M did have logistical issues with adult authority figures in his late teen years. Mr. Welker had his short-term future pegged: gone to hell in a hand basket.

I got along swimmingly with the guy, or about as swimmingly as a goofball teenager could with a strict disciplinarian. He was by no means a nasty teacher. Just hard: my way or the highway, learn this, or get the hell out of my class. He was physically imposing, too, a large, burly man, with a pronounced forehead, and most noticeable of all, an orange tint to his skin. Like Homer Simpson. He felt like a space alien to many of us, a more intelligent being we couldn't quite understand, sent here to educate us.

The only really bad thing I remember about him was his habit of injecting his personal politics into his class, which was Chemistry, i.e., had nothing to do with politics. I found plenty of left-leaning instructors doing the same (particularly in college), but Mr. Welker leaned right and was convinced every generation that came of age after the Korean War was doomed.

This was funny when he routinely attacked "Hanoi Jane" Fonda, whom he despised equally for her Vietnam-era antics and her starring role in the then hugely popular movie,

The China Syndrome. One of Mr. Welker's auxiliary jobs when he wasn't teaching was to help out at the Three Mile Island nuclear power plant in Harrisburg, as he also had a strong background in Nuclear Science. Not sure exactly what he did, but he was well-regarded there. As you may recall, there was a core meltdown at Three Mile Island in the spring of 1979, the exact same predicament detailed in *The China Syndrome*, which came out days before the real-life accident.

When he'd go off on his Hanoi Jane rambles, he'd be on fire. Telling us what a nuclear meltdown was really like, how the movie totally botched it and blew it out of proportion. The problem was, I never knew if I could trust him as a valid source. Sure, he knew infinitely more than I did about the topic; he worked there. How much of his bile (usually apropos of nothing) was because he: a. worked there and had a professional stake in nuclear power being presented as positively as possible; and b. really hated Jane Fonda.

"All I can say is, by the year 2000, go talk to Jane Fonda when your electric bill is hundreds of dollars of month, and most of that is quietly being provided by nuclear power," he'd say. He wasn't too far off the mark. I'll never forget once, though, raising my hand and somberly stating, "I don't know, Mr. Welker, what you're saying sounds like baloney in a nutshell."

I had employed a double-zinger on him: using his two favorite catch phrases, "baloney" and "in a nutshell." He knew it, breaking into that weird, hard laugh of his, like a dog choking up grass, and said, "Mr. Repsher, if you don't start paying closer attention, your grade for this class is going to be baloney in a nutshell."

I also recall a more hippy-ish female student blurting out, "Mr. Welker, are you telling us that Jackson Browne is wrong about this?" He was one of the many pop-music "No Nukes" spokespeople railing against the nuclear industry at the time. Mr. Welker's reply: "So it goes from Glenn Miller disappearing in a plane while serving his country in World War II to self-serving hippies spouting off about topics they know nothing about." He threw his hands up and walked away, knowing in his heart we were all doomed, listening to frilly, careless rock stars instead of a guy who knew what he was talking about.

On that same note, I'll never forget his reaction the morning after John Lennon was murdered. That was a shocking incident for all of society, whether you were a Beatles fan or not. Most of the kids at school weren't big Beatles fans, but surely knew of them as they were omnipresent in our pop-music culture, much more so than today (and they're very present today). If you were a teenage kid into music, at some point, you went through your Beatles phase and really "got" the band, despite being a toddler when they broke up. Besides which, they were still putting out music. I was a huge McCartney fan, and Lennon had put out *Double Fantasy*. (Brother J and I went halfway on that album and were luke warm on it. Loved a few of the Lennon songs, some were too hokey, the Yoko material was not our bag. Still, when one of Sister K's friends offered to buy the album for $20 a week after his death, we refused.)

That morning, we piled into Chemistry class, some kids like me, stone-faced and out of it, still in shock, but honestly, most kids were not feeling any remorse. Mr. Welker barked out, "OK, everybody, let's get over this 'John Lennon hoopla' and move on, I don't recall people getting this upset over Glenn Miller's plane gone missing. It's only music, and this is Chemistry."

Most kids sat there open-mouthed. I'm sure I was one of them. It made no sense to take a swipe at Lennon hours after his passing. In retrospect, I gathered he was getting a bellyful of John Lennon all morning on the news and from everyone around him, and he'd had enough. I hated him for a few days after that, but it wore off. Frankly, what he had said wasn't much different from what our parents were saying. I suspect Mr. Welker's discomfort wasn't provided by or aimed at students. Most of the teachers at our high school at the time were in their 20s and early 30s, children of the 60s and surely devastated Beatles fans. I suspect he was sitting in those smoke-filled teacher lounges and listening to other teachers carry on about John Lennon.

His class normally wasn't that controversial. It was Chemistry. He drilled it into us, having us memorize the periodic table, key formulas and calculations, the whole shebang. You either learned that bedrock knowledge by rote, or you got the hell out. To get an A in his class was a monumental achievement and generally indicative of someone who was headed towards a science-based career. I was a solid B student in his class and didn't even like Science. It was that sink-or-swim. It was a gut check to see how much of this material you could inundate yourself with and process in a test situation. I passed, nearly got an A, too, but didn't push myself that hard.

A typical Welkerian touch: he loved this particular Texas Instruments calculator that did logarithms, a big deal at the time, as he recalled doing this on an abacus back in the 40s. (I even recall him having an abacus in the class room and teaching us how to use it!) The Texas Instruments calculator with logarithm function? For him, it was like the invention of the iPod. He demanded that we all go out and buy that same calculator, nothing else would do. He would teach us how to do the calculations manually so we grasped the principle, then we'd use the calculator to save time.

Calculators at the turn of the 1980s were coming into vogue. You could get a basic one for under $10, but battery-operated, as solar panels on small devices like this had yet to go mass market. The Texas Instruments one was special, and as I recall, cost upwards of $20, but not much more. Mine is still back in "my" drawer in the living-room desk back home. It sits there in its denim-blue carrying case, out-moded by smaller, faster, solar-panel calculators that came in its wake. I also recall the buttons clicked when you pressed them.

The thing with this calculator, though, was that blue, soft-leather case came with a loop so you could attach it to your belt. "Now, I'm not going to tell you people how to dress," Mr. Welker said that first day in class, "but if I were you, I would attach the Texas Instruments calculator to your belt, much like I do, and keep it there, because you'll be using this calculator constantly."

You could tell how much of Mr. Welker's Kool-Aid a kid drank by whether he wore his calculator on his belt, like a gunslinger. Forget about pocket protectors: a teenage male would get his ass kicked on principle for wearing one. I don't recall one single female student doing this. I do recall a handful of guys, who were not the smartest kids in class, but we really taken in by Mr. Welker's sales pitch. As with so many nerdy things in high school, you may as well have worn a white t-shirt with the word "DICK" emblazoned on the chest in gigantic ALL CAPS scarlet letters. A kid who did that would take endless shit. The usual gag was to temporarily strap your own Texas Instruments calculator to your belt and pretend to have a showdown with the kid, both of you unzipping the case, drawing out your calculator, flicking it on and seeing who could find the square root of 586 first.

I had two legendary incidents in Mr. Welker's class, along with all the hard work and studying. As noted, we got along pretty well. I had two brothers and a sister pass before me through his classes, so he got the impression he could trust me as a student. Brother M came off as an under-achieving charlatan, while Brother J and Sister K diligently B'd it through his class. I was a "good kid," which wasn't necessarily a blessing as a teenager. I may have chafed at Mr. Welker's politics and discipline, but I saw through the bullshit and absorbed whatever he had to offer as an instructor.

The first incident was Dress-Up Day, which the school would have once every semester, a chance for kids to dress like adults, for guys to put on ties and suit coats, and girls to wear nice dresses and such to school. As opposed to our normal uniforms of concert t-shirts, flannel shirts, cruddy jeans and sneakers. It was a big deal to put on the dog in high school, save for that small cache of students who normally dressed well.

Dress-Up Day, Chemistry class rolls around, and Mr. Welker has scheduled an experiment in the lab next to our desks in his classroom. We loved doing this because it could be dangerous and risky at times if you didn't do things right. Shit was always happening, phosphorous burning too much, sulfur smells emanating from mixed liquids, etc. He drilled us on how to use bunsen burners, as you could imagine the danger of 20 teenagers lighting these up simultaneously without any training. We all had our hand-held flint devices, and our burners that we'd hook up to our individual gas pipes. Turn on the pipes, hear that telltale hiss, then flick the burner on with the flint.

I must have been groggy that day because I did something unforgiveable: accidentally hooked up my bunsen burner to the water pipe adjacent to the gas. I was dressed up that day. Everyone around me was, too. I turned on the pipe, didn't hear the gas, picked up my bunsen burner to see what was wrong, which pulled off the small hose leading to the pipe, spraying water over everyone within five feet of the pipe.

Of course, the class went nuts. Understand that kids had lit their burners, and scattered when they got splashed, nearly burning themselves in the process. It was mayhem for a few seconds, but blew over quickly, although I surely pissed off those kids around me. To Mr. Welker's credit, I don't recall him punishing me, but giving me a stern warning. I'm surprised this didn't happen more with the gas and water pipes right next to each other.

The second incident was a test we had in the last semester of our senior year in Mr. Welker's Nuclear Science class. That class was a mistake on my part as I hadn't anticipated how lackadaisical I'd feel towards academics in that last few weeks of high school. I was cruising towards the finish line, already accepted at Penn State, felt I had nothing to lose. Inject into this mindset Mr. Welker, teaching a relatively new and very difficult class that he had a burning passion for, and it was an educational disaster.

Even the kids who were good at Math and Science were tanking the class. It was hard! Unlike his earlier Hanoi Jane rants, this was actual Nuclear Science, and most of us weren't cut out for it. I recall one girl really taking to it, and sure enough, she did pursue Nuclear Science in college. Most of us were totally lost in this class, from the first week on. Since it was our last semester and all of us were already college bound, no one was sweating it, save those kids who kept desperate tabs on their Grade Point Average.

The last week of school, we had our final exam, which was an all-essay extravaganza as opposed to the usual sections of Multiple Choice, True/False and such. Normally, I'd be over-joyed with this development as I could write them in my sleep. But I had two problems here: I was totally flummoxed by Nuclear Science, and my study habits were completely shot with freedom from high school so close we could smell it like blossom on the wind.

That was the last test I took in high school, and in uncharacteristic fashion got a C Minus on it, which was cause for great joy. Because I knew jackshit about the topics at hand and truly deserved an F. I can't recall the exact questions, but each one I turned into a free-form exploration of the universe, gearing the first and last paragraphs towards the question at hand, but in between rambling a cut-up style of writing much like William S. Burroughs used in his novels. I had read *Naked Lunch* earlier in the year and was entering my Beat Writer phase with Kerouac, Ginsberg, etc.

It didn't take me long to realize writing like that wasn't my forte, but you need to do these things first to realize you're no good at them.

The one question that stood out was the last: explain in detail the theory of Black Holes. We all know what black holes in space are, but I recalled we had a special class and film about the topic which went into detail about their discovery, the differing theories about what they are, what it would be like to enter one, etc. Interesting stuff, but I was zoned out at the time and not paying attention at all. Not studying a lick either. Those few weeks, every night found me shooting pool at near-by Holiday Lanes with old pal George, who was much better than I was because he had a pool table in his parents' basement, so I had to practice hard to beat him. I spent much more time shooting pool that last month of school than studying, a malady many of classmates suffered from their entire high-school career.

I explored a racial component to the Black Hole Theory, tying in the Civil Rights movement and the band Earth Wind & Fire into what happens when a burned-out star enters a black hole. I pictured the Black Hole as nightclub in Harlem, and the burned-out star being singer Tom Jones. And so it went. I think I had Tom and the members of Earth Wind and Fire beating up a gang of KKK rednecks from the 1930s who had slipped into a time-space continuum and ended up in their black hole. The essay ended with me clicking together the heels of my black Chuck E. Taylor Converse hightops and chanting "there's no place like home," tying into my theory that Dorothy from *The Wizard of Oz* had been in a black hole, and that movie was what really went on in there as opposed to gaseous explosions and super novas.

It was a tour de force of "no longer give a shit" babble from a kid woefully unprepared to handle that or any other essay question in a test. By all rights, I should have flunked. Mr. Welker gave me a C Minus, on the test and in the class. Not just that – I had friends in that class who studied their asses off for that test and got C Minuses, too. I guess they simply had the wrong answers, as opposed to imaginatively wrong answers like mine that at least demonstrated creative thinking.

Whatever the case, I'll never forget how nice he was to cut me that slack on the way out. I tend to remember the good things more than the bad with Mr. Welker. He once told us the story of how he and a few of his friends, back during the Depression, had swiped a shipment of potassium from the lab for the sole purpose of throwing it into a nearby creek to watch it explode. This had to be done carefully, constructing a slingshot, as throwing it by hand into the water could result in an explosion they couldn't escape. He detailed the whole process, how they set up the slingshot between two trees, moved two large rocks they could hide behind, constructed informal mirror/cardboard periscopes (another thing we made in his class) so they could watch, and communicated the joy they had in blowing the shit out of that creek. None of them had anticipated the number of dead fish their depth charge would unveil. There was his signature dog-choking laughter and twinkle in his eye as he told the story.

1980: Ringtown

We used to tease kids from Ringtown by taking the melody for Glenn Campbell's hit song "Rhinestone Cowboy" and instead singing, "Like a Ringtown farmer ..." There are a lot of farming communities in Pennsylvania. Within our school district, there were other farm towns, like Gordon and Lavelle. The drive between those towns provided overwhelming whiffs of cow manure in summer time.

While it would be lost on outsiders, all these small towns have their own vibe, which will often manifest itself in the kids. With farm towns like the rural patches around Gordon and Lavelle, the kids were physical, due to their proximity to farm animals and the need to interact with them. I know that sounds weird – I don't mean to imply bestiality – but when you work on a farm, you're herding and feeding goats, pigs, cows, etc. You get into it with them sometimes, holding them down for shots or brands, treating sick animals, etc.

Our high-school championship wrestling teams of the 70s and 80s were stocked with Ringtown kids: big, physical kids who liked to grapple. Even now, farming high schools like Tri-Valley, despite being very small population-wise, will often field state-finalist caliber wrestling teams. It's a weird thing with farm kids.

I don't think Robin and old friend Tony came from farming families, but both did enough work on farms as kids, and lived around plenty of other farmers, that they had the same rollicking, physical vibe. They administered "titty twisters" on guys in their peer group: grabbing a guy's chest as hard as possible, pinching down and twisting. I'd imagine this would be much more painful for a full-breasted woman, but it hurt like hell, too, when done on a guy. Robin was strong as an ox; if he caught you in a titty twister, the pain could be excruciating. Followed by him braying out his horse-like laugh.

Another odd thing we did in that Beavis-and-Butthead phase of life. Any time we disagreed with what one of us was saying, provided no teachers were around, rather than say something witty like "you're full of shit," we'd ball up one of our hands into a fist, place it directly underneath the chin of the kid making the questionable statement, and then make a "pwt-pwt-pwt" sound to imitate a squirting oil can. What we were really doing was pretending our outstretched arm and fist was a penis, and we were ejaculating on the offending party's face as a sign of disrespect. That oil-can sound ... I've never heard my penis make a sound in any state of being. I guess when you're 14 years old and learning how to use the thing in new and exciting ways, the first time you see it in action, you imagine it making that sound.

Those Ringtown kids were always grabbing each other: headlocks, full nelsons, hammerlocks. When I say they seemed gay, I don't mean "effeminate" gay. I mean "prison shower sex" gay, guys grabbing each other in deeply physical ways that were rude. Granted, most boys rough-housed in varying degrees, but with Ringtown kids, it was a relentless art form. It was nothing to pass by a study hall or gym class in repose and see two Ringtown guys, red-faced and gasping, locked up with each other in some physical challenge. Arm wrestling was big, too. Girls would be sitting at the surrounding desks doing homework, while two Ringtown guys would be popping neck veins and sweating bullets in an arm-wrestling death match. (I kept waiting for one of them to lean over and gently kiss the other on the cheek.)

You'd think I wouldn't get along with guys like this, but one other thing about Ringtown kids: most of them were good-natured and friendly. As time went along, I got tired of the endless arm-wrestling matches and silly physical crap that seemed like a subliminal mating ritual. But the kids I knew from Ringtown tended to be open and friendly, regardless of social status.

I should mention social status, because that was the strange (but good) thing about Robin. This is a guy who spent the first two decades of his life doing everything possible to go off the rails (drugs, dropping out, rampant teen sex, going AWOL in the Navy and eventually getting discharged, etc.), yet is now a plant manager for a pet foods manufacturer, making great money and living in a quiet rural/suburban town with a few kids. I recall him dropping out of high school in 1980, having flunked a year and suffering the indignation of being dislocated from his same-age friends. By all rights, I had figured this guy to be a corpse long before 30.

How did he get there? A reversal of fortune? I gather that he's as perplexed that he's made it this far and is, in fact, excelling in life. I once asked him if something must have happened to make him shift gears, he said, no, I knew I was a good worker, I hated school and had more of a wild side when I was a kid.

Which was an understatement! He had Tony and me in tears with some of his stories. The time he and Tony watched a notoriously gamey kid in our school take a dump in the locker-room shower after gym class. Or when he screwed his then-girlfriend in the vestibule of the auditorium during a presentation. (I vaguely remember this as I was in the auditorium that day and the rumor had spread like wild fire. I thought it was a joke at the time, but he verified that they did have sex.) Or routinely driving his motorcycle at over 100 mph down a long pot-holed hill leading into Ringtown. Or having one of his naval officers hit on him in a hotel room while on R&R in Connecticut (hopping naked into bed with Robin, throwing his bare leg over his waist and whispering "roll over" into Robin's ear, which he did, punching the officer square in the face, then taking off with nothing but his pants on and catching a taxi back to base).

The guy's a repository of these sort of wild stories, his favorites being all the times he's been caught having sex with various girlfriends and then wives in public or while visiting relatives. He seems to take a perverse delight in calculated risks like yanking up his wife's dress with her parents on the porch and banging out a quick one on the living-room sofa. He detailed getting caught once, bare-assed and romping full-gun in a guest room. His mother-in-law opened the door without knocking, letting out a shriek. I can only imagine her horror to witness this red-haired beast romping porn-star style with her little princess. The following dinner must have been memorable for everyone.

Robin wore leather pants to school, sometimes with a matching vest, the gayest thing I recall anyone in our high-school wearing. He was a Judas Priest fan. Like millions of other Priest fans, Robin had no idea Rob Halford was gay and into hard-core S&M, thus the leather outfit he wore into metal's rough-hewed legend, with all these aggressively heterosexual kids none the wiser. There was no mistaking Robin for being gay. The guy was like a modern-day centaur galloping through the countryside in a permanent rutting season, leaving hoof marks and stains on many family-car seat covers.

Before he joined the Navy, after dropping out of high school, he worked with Brother J at Hess' gas station in Frackville on night shift. This only gave him more time to rut, as he outlined a few instances of partying customers taking up his offer to come back at his break time and get the van rocking. Pumping gas on night shift is a rough job: shady characters, gypsy travelers, drunken kids and adults, a lot of down time as the night wears on. The gas freezes on your hands when it gets colder. J recalled the weird conversations he and Robin would have early in the morning, reminiscent of a perverted *Waiting for Godot*:

Robin: What would happen if you crazy-glued your dick to someone's forehead?

J: I imagine you'd have your dick crazy-glued to someone's forehead.

Robin: I know, I know. But, what would you do?

J: I'd stand there thinking, "I have my dick crazy-glued to this person's forehead." And that person would think, "This guy's dick is crazy-glued to my forehead."

Robin: I know, I know. But how would you get out of it?

J: I think a better question might be how would you get into it.

With Robin, the possibility of crazy-gluing his dick to someone's forehead was very real. Just to see what would happen. I couldn't help but think when I heard him recount these many bizarre stories what an odd life he had leading into his adulthood. The last time I saw him in our youth, I didn't know it, but he was AWOL from the Navy for the first time. He was riding around on his motorcycle, with what would become his first wife (not sure if she was pregnant at the time or shortly thereafter). When I heard he'd gone AWOL and then been caught and thrown in the brig for 90 days, I thought, here we go. Apparently, he did the same thing again a year later, only this time, the Navy threw him out after this stint in the brig. All this transpired before he was 21 years old.

What I'm not seeing with him is all those years in between, much like no one knows what happened to Jesus' missing years. I know the basic story line: drummed out of the service, feeling low, gets a job driving trucks, which grows into these various managerial spots resulting in plant manager years later, all the while married and having kids, so he has these things to anchor him. As opposed to the footloose and fancy-free kid I knew who nearly blew out his candle before legally becoming an adult. I remember the time he and Schwamy, while out driving drunk, sheared off a telephone pole in Pottsville and somehow got out of the situation, with Robin's mother blaming Schwamy for the incident (although he was not driving and nearly got his head caved in when the pole crashed down on the car).

He once asked me if I knew the whereabouts of many of the infamous, fellow drug-addled kids from our class, the ones who got high in the wooded area on the north side of the school before lumbering back to doze in meaningless classes. I told him they were all living on Mars with Jesus Christ. Because I have no idea what happened to a lot of the kids, save I suspect they've had a rough time unless they, like him, snapped out of that teenage drug lethargy. The few times I've seen Robin since then, that wild energy he had as a kid erupts, and vivid memories of embarrassing and odd situations come flooding out, like some bizarre form of group therapy. It's rare that I laugh so hard as an adult.

1980: Winter Ball

On a Christmas bus trip back to Pennsylvania a few years ago, I was struck by the sight of so many unattended basketball rims in schoolyards and driveways, and how much I used to play basketball as a kid.

Basketball came in on the tail end of football in our neighborhood sports world, which meant early December. We'd all put down the football and spend more time getting into basketball games in the schoolyard. Football, after a certain point, would only occur if it snowed, and we could indulge in those much-loved "snow games." (I really didn't enjoy playing football after awhile. We were all getting too big to be doing this without supervision or protection, and I didn't see the point of getting my head kicked in to prove what a bad-ass I was in the neighborhood.)

I loved basketball simply because I was good at it. Football and baseball, I'd usually get picked middle of the pack. We were all reasonably good players. If a kid wasn't, he simply stopped playing. There wasn't much of that "last guy picked" vibe so many disgruntled adults complain about regarding their youth. Basketball, I was the one. I either picked the team or was the first picked. For one reason only: my set shot was 80% accurate, some days closer to 90%. Sounds outrageous? It was. I could score from anywhere on the court, the farther away, the better. Put two guys on me, and I'd still score. It was a rare game where I'd screw the pooch and make my team lose by errant hot-dogging. We'd normally play to 50 or 100, by ones, depending on how much time we had. These games would get nutty, like a board game that drags on for hours and finds the fortune of the players changing dramatically over time. A team would be down 75-40 and end up winning 100-97.

Did this prowess on the court transfer to high-school ball? No, despite the coaches I had in junior high and freshman year seeing I could put the ball in from all over the court. We'd have free-throw drills at the end of each practice, the object being keep going until you miss a shot. I'd normally go through 30 shots before missing. When I got into games, again, I could hit from anywhere.

The problem? Defensively, I was an average player, surely nothing special. I didn't understand plays, as we never used them in neighborhood ball. The plays seemed designed to get the ball as close to the rim as possible; I wasn't nearly as good inside as I was out. My specialty was swishing the ball from the side court just outside the three-point line. Another thing I had to realize was there were other guys in the school who were just better than I was. This guy Nick in particular, who's now a state cop, was a great all-around player, an even better long shooter than I was. I would back him up after the coach toyed with starting me, but put me down when he saw I wasn't fitting into the other roles. Too short to be a center, not quick enough for guard, and the other forward was a great defender, if nothing special offensively.

After freshman year, I stopped playing for the high-school team. What do I remember most about that season? Winter. Steamed-up windows on school buses driving through the snow, to cramped rural gyms, wearing our uniforms under our clothes, so we could strip off like Superman and be ready for the court. And Billy Joel's album *The Stranger.* One of the kids had it on eight-track and played it incessantly. (It came out in the fall of 1977, but rest assured, it was still being played to death years later.) The album is burned into my mind for that reason. Every time I hear the title track, I feel like it's winter, and I'm on my way to a game in Pottsville or Shamokin. We even nicknamed the cute cheerleader/starting-guard couple "Brenda and Eddie" after the characters from the song, "Scenes from an Italian Restaurant."

I'll also never forget the one gym we played, might have been in Tamaqua or Mahanoy City. The walls of the gym were covered with blue mats displaying stick figures engaging in various sports: football, baseball, basketball, etc. Behind each rim, strategically placed, were mats depicting wrestlers: one stick figure behind another one, grabbing him by the shoulders as the front one was slouched over. It looked exactly like two guys having sex and would have made a very cool symbol for a gay bar in an Olympic village. Without fail, it cracked us up every time we came down the court and couldn't help but glimpse it behind the backboard. We lost when we played there simply because we were laughing so hard the whole time.

Another thing that occurred to me later: I was simply more geared towards the rim, type and height, of the backboard in the schoolyard, a rusting old hunk of metal on an uphill incline. It was two inches shorter than a regulation rim, and bent down in front. I spent hundreds of hours practicing on this rim. My touch was geared towards that specific type of shooting, which does make a difference when playing on a regulation-length basket on a flat wood surface. I was still a pretty good shot, but not the dead-eye I was on that shitty schoolyard court.

When I say I played day and night, I'm not joking. Many times, I'd be up there alone, sometimes in the dark, shooting by the light of the moon, and making it. I learned to judge my shots by the feel of the ball leaving my fingertips, not what I was seeing, and I'd be just as accurate at night. That wasn't such an abnormal thing in winter. We wouldn't play after dark, meaning after 5:00 in December and January. There was nothing unusual with shooting baskets after dark, and it wasn't like I was out there until midnight. Most nights, I'd wrap it up by 7:00. Pat Hanlon would come down and join me in a game of Horse some nights. (Horse was simply matching a guy's shot, or acquiring letters to spell the word "horse" if you missed.)

If it snowed, I was the first one out there to shovel out the court after helping to clear out our cars and walkways.

This is what I was thinking about most on that bus drive home. None of the kids along the way loved the game enough to shovel out the court, which meant a lack of resolve to me. I'd shovel just enough to have a foot or two outside the normal lines of play. We found that the concept of showing up dressed for the tundra was ludicrous. We had rubber balls for days like this, as opposed to leather, so they'd bounce in sub-freezing weather. We'd start playing, and surely be sweating our asses off after about 20 points on either side. The play along the lines could be intense and often ended with guys splayed out in the snow along the sides, a kick if one wasn't too embarrassed over how he got there.

The best nights, though, were me alone out there, shooting under a full moon, court freshly shoveled. I could see my breath in the dark, feel the cold air in my lungs, pumping in shot after shot from way outside. I'm not sure what I was thinking. Before high-school, I thought I was going to be a star, as we all do with various sports when we were kids. I'd feel the same playing tennis a few years later, and would become a good player, but nothing like a professional, or even great amateur. After I gave up on high-school basketball, it occurred to me that I simply liked playing the game, this way, with no designed plays and no player set to be the star. Whoever had the hot hand, feed him the ball and let him do his thing. That was usually me in the schoolyard. When I was by myself, it was a good way to get out of the house, get some fresh air and do something constructive, even if it had no net effect that I could use in the "real world." A waste of time? Sure, but I wasn't hurting anybody, and my "alone" time as a kid was severely curtailed by seven people in a house meant for four. And a neighborhood full of howling, tail-end baby boomers always up to semi-evil shit. It was a pleasure to be able to do something I was good at, by myself, on a winter's night. I can see the ghost of my teenage self back there, in his ragged hand-me-down clothes, hooded sweatshirt and kelly-green Philadelphia Eagles knit cap, bouncing the ball, throwing it in the air, satisfying swoosh and snap of ball hitting nothing but net, ball bounces, repeat about 150 times, maybe humming a Supertramp song every now and then, coming in for some hot chocolate and a night of bad TV. Anything seemed possible on those nights in the middle of nowhere, even if nothing ever happened.

1981: Hot Snakes

Grandma passed on in 1981, a few days before my birthday in June. In her early 80s. Six years earlier, she had suffered a massive stroke that did a number on her memory and cognitive abilities. At the time, and being a kid, I rolled with it, not knowing any better.

I wouldn't say it was like growing up with death in the house, but it was growing up with the recognition of someone very old who had been dealt a grievous blow. My teenage years, that time of blooming and discovery, were shaded with the knowledge of old age and impending death. I don't consider that a bad thing. A worse thing would have been to have her shuttled off to an old-folk's home, which was not an option.

Before the stroke, Grandma had been the matriarch: mother to four sons and a daughter she had raised through the Depression and sent off to fight in World War II. Her husband, my grandfather, died before I was born, in his mid-50s. He worked in the mines, not sure if he was a coal miner or not, but I know he worked at the mines. When there was work. Dad would tell us that during the Depression, guys at the mines got to work one day a week so they'd have enough money to afford basic food and housing needs but not much else. We were forever getting the "baked-bean sandwich" lecture from Dad. He and his brothers got one each for breakfast and one for dinner. That was their food intake for the day for years running. To raise five kids in that time must have been something, but they were far from alone.

For years, Grandma kept a little flag in a drawer that was given to mothers of soldiers in World War II to designate how many sons they had in the war. Hers had four stars (red on a field of white with red stripes on the edges) for her boys. Aunt Ruth was in the WACS, but I guess that didn't merit as a star. Uncle Jack was in a bomber (a near death sentence), Uncle Bill in the jungles of New Guinea, not sure what Uncle Vince did, and Dad, in his previously noted boot-camp accident and post-war Germany adventures.

These people had been through a world of shit by the time they were 25; there's a reason that generation wanted to settle down, fast. My uncles and aunt went off in their own directions, but Dad stayed home after wandering the world as an army mechanic for roughly 10 years. He gave college a try, didn't like it. He spent a short time working with Uncle Bob, in his carpenter shop in Pottsville, but found his way into factory work at Allied Chemical in Marlin. How he came to take care of Grandma and live at home was a slow process of discovery that this was how life was going to be. I grew up with an unrealistic view of home ownership as a result; I thought everyone paid their mother $1.00 for a house, and it was theirs.

It was mostly a blessing to have her there. One of my earliest childhood memories is Grandma leading me to the upstairs bathroom, after I had shit my diapers, a full load, and had me sit on the toilet, while she picked out each turd by hand and dropped it into the water between my legs. While I sat there, slack-jawed and shit-assed. This blew my mind as much now as it did then. I'd post a "kids, don't try this at home" warning here, but I think most people get the picture.

She'd do hardcore things like that. Things that said, "I love you, little boy," but also, "I'm harder than you." I can imagine a woman who raised kids through the above-noted storm of circumstances must have been hard as nails.

The most memorable incident for me was Hot Snakes. That part of Pennsylvania qualifies as deep country, even now. In various pictures from the 1940s through the 1950s, there's a wilderness beyond our backyard, where houses were starting to be built in the 60s and 70s. Thankfully, not many were built, and the woods crept right up to the cemetery on the hill, still do.

In the spring, sometimes we'd find snakes in the backyard: copperheads. Never got bit, but they scared the hell out of me. They came out of the woods at night to seek warmth, which they'd find on cement that absorbed and held heat longer than woods and grass. On those breezy April mornings, you'd sometimes look out the kitchen window at the backyard, and there'd be a snake or two sunning themselves on the sidewalk. Sooner or later, they'd leave, but the idea of them being that close to kids and pets wasn't cool with anyone in the neighborhood.

Grandma did her thing, at least on one occasion, not sure if this was a regular occurrence. She went out with a baseball bat and beat two copperhead snakes to death on the pavement. The picture is long gone – I wish I still had it – but there was a polaroid taken of her standing with the two "hot snakes," one in each hand, smiling as the spring sun rose behind her.

She was tough. I noted earlier: "mostly a blessing." The downside was hardline Catholicism. I mean full-on, "if I had my way, you'd all be priests" Irish Catholicism. When Dad married Mom, the filthy Protestant, he may as well have married a topless native from the Amazon jungle; the level of acceptance would have been comparable. It was almost a "mixed" marriage, something staunch Catholics did not advocate. Marrying Mom was the best thing Dad ever did, because her sweet and open view of the world perfectly offset his more hardened, stoic take on things. It wasn't as bad as the actual Catholic/Protestant "troubles" in Ireland, but it was surely frowned upon.

Especially by Grandma. Mom won her over: remember her always extended hand. At least I never remember them arguing about religion, mostly because Mom was a non-practicing Protestant, and Dad bagged church religiously. As long as the kids were raised Catholic! Grandma was the Catholic enforcer, and she put us through the paces. Routine confession, all the classes involved with catechism, confirmation, etc.

Luckily, we dodged being sent to Catholic school because it cost extra as opposed to a free public-school education. We also dodged being altar boys. How, I don't know, as I know Grandma was hot on having this happen. Thank Christ she never got her way, given the risqué adventures of "Father Bendover."

Catholicism was a constant under-current in the house, and the quiet message was that Mom was an outsider. I grew leery of religion as a result. When you're raised in a house by a woman you know is true, who would give her life for you, and you're being fed the subtle message that she's somehow lesser because of her religion, you either reject the person or the concept of religion. Seeing as how Grandma was forcing religion down our throats like castor oil, and Mom lived like a saint, or the nearest approximation a working-class girl from Pottsville could offer, you can guess which side I leaned towards. I never fully rejected Catholicism, but I'd be hard-pressed to call myself one. When you're raised Catholic, that sort of things sticks with you the rest of your days, and not in a bad way. Like guys who have been in the military. I'm far from a practicing Catholic and don't particularly worry about it, nor hold it against those who find value in their faith.

All along, the matriarch quality of Grandma's life was constantly driven home for me, mainly by our relatives routinely visiting the old homestead and paying tribute to her. I hardly ever see any of my cousins anymore, as we're pretty spread out. Even if we weren't, we all have our own lives now as adults. We're not like one of those extended clans where cousins are constantly flitting around each other's lives. Every summer, it was visiting time, and every few weeks, there'd be another massive family invading our already-crowded house. Kids in sleeping bags. Huge vats of baked beans. Cook outs where we could have eaten an entire cow. Amusement park visits, drive-in movies, Pioneer Tunnel tours in Ashland, constant activity of some sort. It was chaos. Upwards of 12 people in a house that would have comfortably suited four and normally held seven. It was amazing we didn't have too many memorable blowouts, but we were also on our best behavior. Looking back, I genuinely liked a lot of my relatives and recognized them as good people.

It was made clear, these visits were happening because in my uncles' and aunt's minds, this house I was being raised in was their home, too, and my grandmother was their mother, whom they still loved immensely. Again, a good thing to be exposed to that and recognize the value of someone. Do I miss those huge family convergences? Not really, but by the same token, I've realized they weren't the horrific weekends I made them out to be at the time.

Then, of course, one day around 1976 (I can't recall the exact timing), I came home from school and was told by

Mom that Grandma wouldn't be home for awhile. She'd had a stroke and needed to be in the hospital. When she came back home, it was like day and night. Before that, she had been vibrant, hands-on, wouldn't think twice about putting you over her knee and giving you a good swat for being fresh. The effects of the stroke were immediate and obvious. Slurred speech. Scrambled thoughts. Memories jarred askance. Physically, she lost a lot, moved slower, was prone to falling and hurting herself in ways that would leave her bed-ridden for days. Until one's experienced a family member going through something like this, it's hard to explain.

That was the cataclysmic change in all our lives, especially Mom's. On top of taking care of four kids – luckily we were teenagers or just getting there – she now had an elderly woman to watch over who was having a rough time dealing with every-day life. Mom, to her credit, handled it like a pro. Never once complained. Did everything and then some to make sure Grandma's life was as comfortable as possible. This would often involve bathing her, helping her up and down stairs, watching over her all day to make sure she didn't wander off, being a round-the-clock nurse that would have cost a fortune to hire. Understand that up to this point, I felt like I had two mothers, which is a great thing for any family to have.

This is also where the Catholicism got strange. Because of her stroke, Grandma could no longer attend church. With her mind wandering through her entire life, she'd often be banging on our bedroom doors at four in the morning on Sundays, telling us to "get the horses ready, we have to go over the mountain." She was referring to her childhood when she and her family would prepare a horse and buggy to take them to church in Girardville, on the other side of the large ridge past the cemetery. Since she couldn't be at church, she became obsessed with making sure we got ready for it on

Sunday morning, with the campaign usually kicking into high gear by Friday.

It was nuts. This was when my brothers and I stopped going. Sure, going through the motions, getting dressed, and leaving at the appropriate time. We'd pull up short, stop in the cemetery next to the church, and sit around the mausoleums, waiting for the bells to ring that signaled the end of mass, so we could scurry back home and make it seem like we had gone. Sister K lasted a few more years but eventually started tailing off herself in the 80s.

This became our outlaw teenage ritual. We weren't all that nuts about church to begin with, but to be harangued over it incessantly all week ... forget it. When we were in the cemetery, one of our neighbors would sometimes drive by in his utility vehicle and stare us down. Expecting what to happen, I'm not sure. (As this guy was later nailed repeatedly for tax evasion, he should have been more worried about his own problems.) We sat there and stared back. We weren't "bad" kids. Christ, we were wearing plaid pants and clip-on ties! Short hair! Just sitting there. A sane adult, like me now, would have said, "ah, kids bagging church, they're not going to cause trouble for anybody as they don't want to get caught." But he had our number! We'd also field disapproving glances from some of the "church" people when we saw them during the week. To which I thought, disapprovingly glance away! When church is made to feel like a prison sentence, no kid in his right mind will want anything to do with it.

I previously noted my grandmother's sisters all lived in the same house in Port Carbon, still a gritty town back home. Back then, I recall there were occasionally riots, the kids in that town in the 70s were particularly nuts, over what, I have no idea, probably a very bad grouping of kids (and drugs, most likely). I don't know how all the sisters ended up there. In my mind, it was raining over their house alone, like in *The Addams Family*.

After the stroke, Mom got in the habit of taking Grandma down to the house in Port Carbon much more often. She understood that whatever had happened to Grandma, the end could be near, so she wanted to ensure Grandma spent as much time as possible with her sisters. Mom's reward for this? Being called a filthy Protestant and a bum on a much more regular basis, as it was clear the sisters were inundating Grandma with anti-Protestant dialectic. Without fail, every time she came back from a visit there, the Protestant bashing rose a notch. Understand that Mom never cared about being Protestant: non-practicing, and frankly wasn't worried about what anyone else believed in. (I'm still not sure how she avoided converting to Catholicism when she married Dad as I've seen friends in the same situation soldier through "training" classes for their impending nuptials.)

This memory shades my overall memory of those women as a result. I don't hate them now. In fact, I recall how loving and warm they were to us kids, how glad they were to see us, every time. I was forever wiping my face after getting a big wet kiss from one of them, generally after hearing, "Oh, look at little Billy, all the children in Dublin look like darling Billy!" But the bullshit they put Mom through over something as pointless as religious differences. Mom never blew her top. She owed those women nothing. They weren't her blood relatives. She could have said, "Screw it, I'm never speaking to those biddies again. Someone else can take care of her, since I'm not good enough!" That never happened, because Mom knew she had to rise above. They eventually came around when it became clear a few years on that Grandma's health was truly deteriorating, and Mom was going all out to make sure all went as well as could be.

When that started happening visibly, I've blocked out a lot of it, but it surely went on for a few months. All I recall is that she started having more accidents, falling down and injuring herself more, becoming more delusional. I don't know how long this went on. Most of her post-stroke life was tolerable, but the last few months, things came apart more quickly. There were a few falls requiring hospital stays, and it was becoming clear, at least to us, that the end was near. For a kid, this was an odd experience; I'd never watched anyone go into decline over a period of time. I didn't know she was dying. People want to believe the best when it comes to situations like this, like a bad spell is happening, and things will get better. But there are points in life where things don't get better and only get worse.

I recall the last fall, that June in 1981, a perfect summer evening. Sister K went into the bathroom and found Grandma on the floor, unconscious. Immediately, she called 911. I still remember what a nice summer day that was, twilight, fireflies coming out, crickets starting to chirp. When the attendants wheeled Grandma by the screen door in the kitchen, where Brother J and I were, her eyes caught ours, and I'd never seen such a look of sorrow and longing, which I now recognize as "goodbye." At the time I wasn't sure how to interpret it. J blurted out, "This is it. I think she's gone this time." I didn't know what to think.

Sure enough, that was it, we never saw her alive again. She passed away in her sleep early the next morning at the hospital.

The next few days were absolute chaos. I don't know how many people converged on the house: dozens. All her children came with their families. All her friends showed up, some traveling miles to be there, a few dozen older people who must have known her decades ago, showed up for the wake and funeral. A few were legendary bums who only went to funerals to get a free meal. It was like a sad circus, with a lot of crying and eating. Food everywhere. As a kid who lived there, I felt territorial towards the house, but that feeling was forfeited for a few days, absolute madness. I was too blown out first by her death, and then by this whirlwind of activity, with relatives and strangers, that I didn't know what was going on. I remember us kids sitting in the living room on the morning of her funeral in our pajamas, too freaked out to move. It seemed as though a few dozen people converged on the house in less than an hour. We had to get dressed and use the bathrooms. We couldn't, as there was a constant stream of visitors in and out. When we finally got ourselves together, we were late for our own grandmother's funeral.

All I remember about the funeral is that during the burial, my brothers and I sat at the top of the hill in the cemetery, away from the action, and took our shoes and socks off because it was so damn hot. We were wearing collared shirts and ties, which was something we rarely did and never in summer. Everything about the day was disorienting and off. The Temptations song "I Wish It Would Rain" made sense on a hot, sunny day like that, a day that would have found us normally mowing lawns or playing tennis out at the high school. Dad waved us down, so we put our socks and shoes back on for the ceremony. Afterwards, going back to our house, there were far more people I didn't know in and around the house, along with the relatives I recognized as being part of Grandma's life over the past decade. Whether people were annoyed by our "antics," I have no idea. They weren't antics. We were shocked by her death and had virtually no space to gather our wits and relax from the next morning after she passed on.

Brother J and I found our way upstairs, got into our shorts and t-shirts, went to the Schuylkill Mall and caught *Raiders of the Lost Ark*. I'll always have a soft spot for that movie for the simple reason that it gave me a chance to disengage for an hour or two from a bad situation. Afterwards, we drove around as much as possible, got home around sundown, and the crowd had dwindled to our uncles and their families, still a horde of people, but at least we knew them. Everyone left the next morning. I can recognize now, for Dad and his siblings, that was it: their father had passed on many years earlier, and now their mother was gone.

A crazy few days, and I turned 17 while all this was going on! That milestone birthday came and went without a trace, over-shadowed by a far deeper event. I wish there's more I could remember. I'm sure pictures and chats with family members would dredge up a ton of details, most of them good. These days, Grandma is more a fiber of my being than an actual memory. If there's any toughness in me, and there is, I know where it came from. I think this is what happens when people pass on, and then decades pass. All that's left is whatever they put into you in the first place. Sometimes it's hard to remember how this happened.

1982: Freeze Frame!

Let me take you back to the winter of 1981, leading into 1982. Last year of high school. While everyone else is listening to Van Halen, Journey and Styx, I'm mainly into 60s Brit Pop and New Wave, which isn't winning me any popularity contests. New Wave was "fag" music back then. I still remember trying to sell one of the guys in gym class on Elvis Costello. He laughed at me: "Just look at the guy! You know he's a fag by the glasses! They'd be steaming up while he was blowing me!"

Never mind that this guy had a full-length poster of a heavily made-up Freddie Mercury in a silver lame unitard posted in his locker. (As an aside, I had a picture of the Swami Prabhupada that Brother J had pulled from a brochure he received from Hare Krishnas at Penn State. I admired the Swami's gold Rolex visible beneath his beads and flowers.) We were all willfully naïve about such matters back then, but everyone intrinsically sensed New Wave was for fags and nerds. (Although a few years ago, I did an informal survey for the Class of 82's favorite song based on choices from our yearbook. It turned out to be "I Love Rock and Roll" by Joan Jett and The Blackhearts, a mainstay of the feathered roach-clip set, but rocking hard enough to draw in enough guys to win.)

Into this atmosphere stepped The J. Geils Band. I knew about them from their last big hit, "Love Stinks" – a great song, surely their best. Until that point, for me, they had been a seedy blues rock band with a weird lead singer. I wasn't on hand for the glory days of their first few albums in the early 70s. I knew "Give It to Me" from hearing it on radio (WZZO from Allentown, WMMR and WYSP from Philly), but that was about it. I picked up a greatest hits album around that time, of which their live cover of the Motown classic "Where

Did Our Love Go" registered, but most of it seemed like warmed-over blues rock.

While I didn't go particularly nuts for the *Freeze Frame* album, old friend George did, buying it on cassette and wearing it out. The band had huge hits with the title track and "Angel Is the Centerfold." The album was geared towards a more teen audience as the band aged and recognized they had to change to survive. George was particularly enamored of the last song, "Piss on the Wall," in which lead singer Peter Wolf disregards world events to focus on, well, the title says it all. A dumb, juvenile song that I have a hard time listening to today, but it made perfect sense to a bunch of disaffected 17-year-old kids.

Freeze Frame became the cruise tape of our senior year. Of course, George was a strange guy to begin with. Any time we pulled into one of those sleepy Coal Region towns in his souped-up 76 Nova, it was customary to roll down the windows and blast the ultimate freakout song on his cassette deck: "Baby Elephant Walk" by The Lawrence Welk Orchestra. All kidding aside, that is a great piece of music, written by Henry Mancini, but not something a kid who was dogging the hell out of the first two Ozzy Osbourne albums would normally listen to. He also had a cassette of The Ink Spots greatest hits borrowed from his Dad, so we'd use something like "I'm Not Trying to Set the World on Fire" as the freakout song.

George also had a yen for Frank Zappa, thus *Joe's Garage* is another album that brings back 1982 to me, the title track and "Catholic Girls" in particular. George leaned more metal than my pop-rock tastes, but at least he was listening to cool shit in general, along with the inevitable Sammy Hagar albums. My greatest influence was getting him to buy *The Slider* by T. Rex. He cursed me for it over the first two weeks, glam-rock gobbledygook about cosmic seas and bumble bees, then couldn't stop playing it the rest of the summer.

At that time, neighbor Bubba was in his first year at an electronics school in the Lehigh Valley, outside of Allentown. He was living in a nondescript apartment complex outside the city limits with another guy from our home area who also was a low-level drug dealer. Their place was a shamble, which is what you'd expect from two 19-year-old kids on their own for the first time. Both would later transfer to a school in Ohio that would fizzle into a false lead. The roommate, whom I'll call Ray, was a nice enough guy, big, friendly. He often told the story of one of his customers being so desperate for pot that she'd regularly fellate him while he was on the toilet. Pretty ragged stuff, but in light of his legendary bowel movements, this was even more gruesome. I have no reason to doubt this wasn't true. Who would boast about such a thing?

The only thing I can recall about their apartment is a *Conan the Barbarian* movie poster on the wall. I'm sure there was furniture, but whatever it was, it came from the family rec room or the local Salvation Army.

How I came to see this place was George scored tickets to see The J. Geils Band at Stabler Arena in Bethlehem. It was perfect timing. February 6, 1982. The week of the show, the *Freeze Frame* album went to the top of the Billboard charts, the band's first and only #1 album. We knew they'd be psyched to play that show, a hard-touring bar band from Boston who finally hit it big. My parents decided it was OK for me to go; I'd never been to a rock concert. Brother M had flamed out to a rock and roll soundtrack, so my parents were acutely aware of the present dangers, but figured I wasn't going to stumble down that path.

George had four tickets. (Each ticket coast around $10.00, which is how my mind, even now, relates to what one should pay to see a band. I felt like an asshole spending $65.00 to see Springsteen a few years ago.) We were clearly going. None of the other guys in our circle of friends seemed to give a shit. Most were surprised that I wanted to go, but I could guess The J. Geils Band was a damn good live band, on top of which I had started to like the album. A few phone calls were made. It was decided that Ray and Bubba would take the two remaining tickets and would let us use their place as a launch/crash pad for the show. My parents made it clear: this was no overnight visit, see the show, and come straight back. This would entail getting back at around 1:00 or 2:00 the next morning, as Allentown was over an hour drive south. Holiday Lanes would have to get by without us for one night.

There was snow on the ground, and I was mildly surprised that Bubba was living in such a hovel. In retrospect, his place was surely no worse than many other student apartments I'd see in the next few years at Penn State. Kids willfully lived like bums, couldn't afford good furniture and were clearly set-up for a transient existence with maybe a few youthful touchstones – posters, bongs, stereos, albums – thrown in to make it more "homey."

Ray and Bubba took us out to dinner (fast food). The whole time, Ray was smoking hash. I didn't have any. I didn't need to have any. The simple act of breathing the same air in a closed car in the middle of winter gave me a contact high. It was a giddy hash high, a lot of laughing, spacing out. We got stupid. At one point we got out of the car on a back road to take pictures with a camera one of us must have had. I had discovered a bunch of brown, plastic flower pots in the backseat that, when worn on our heads, looked exactly like the futuristic hats that the band Devo wore as part of their stage show.

Lord, I wish I still had this picture. Somewhere, there's that picture of me at seventeen, rake thin in my huge navy peacoat, leaning against a used car in the country, snow all around, sun is out, wearing my Grandmother's cat-eye shades and this asinine plastic flower pot on my head, a stoned smile on my face, arms crossed. If I could get that picture back, I'd frame it and call it "Youth." Even thinking about that picture makes me recall the best aspects of being a kid: directionless, weightless, having fun in the moment, maybe $30.00 to my name, a Bad Company cassette blasting from the Sparkomatic, three other guys in the same head making snow angels in a farmer's field outside of Allentown.

That giddy high extended to the show. I can't recall what substances were being imbibed. I know Bubba and George were drinking beer, although I can't recall what brand. I might have had a beer or two but wasn't drunk.

This was how concerts went back then: everybody got stoned. Beer was the least of it. Most people were high as kites, hours before the show, and barely able to stand at the show. I recall being incredibly excited as we got there. There was literally a pot cloud hovering over the crowd. It was impossible not to be high unless you wore a gas mask. For better or worse, that's how I remember arena concerts from the 80s. I'm sure they were even more druggy in the 70s. Everyone self-medicated in the hours leading up to the event. (This would grate on me when I saw The Kinks there twice later in the 80s and realized most of their newer fans were frat boys.)

Jon Butcher Axis was the opening band. They came and went. I recall liking them, but not rushing out to buy their album. (A year later in the same arena, I'd see a defiant INXS get booed off the stage opening for The Kinks, shortly before they took off like a rocket.)

Lights went out minutes after the Butcher loadout, and the crowd started howling in anticipation. The stage exploded in flashpots, with Peter Wolf hopping around like a frog, to the tune of "Come Back" a disco-sounding song from their *Love Stinks* album. It was exciting as hell. The band had it down. Wolf was a consummate front man, had a variety of dance moves he used throughout the show. His favorite was rapidly circling his hands in front of his stomach and finishing the flourish with a jump or 60s dance move. Their harmonica player, Magic Dick, had a visual presence with his big white-boy afro and, I didn't know it at the time with nothing to compare it against, played well. During the song "Musta Got Lost" – a minor hit from the mid-70s I hadn't known – Wolf jumped into the crowd and got passed around like a returning hero. The band was over-joyed to finally have a #1 album. On top of having a #1 single that fall with "Angel Is the Centerfold," this was as good as it got for them. (Wolf and the rest of the band had an acrimonious breakup a year or two later, with Wolf having middling success as a solo artist and the rest of the band putting out the regrettable *You're Gettin' Even While I'm Gettin' Odd*, featuring the non-hit "Californicatin" that I foolishly bought.)

I should note here that we never stopped wearing the flower pots on our heads. Normally, this would cause consternation, but seeing as how we were surrounded by stoned masses and arena employees who had "seen it all," weird teenage rednecks with flower pots on their heads wasn't that big a deal. I recall Bubba and I going down to our section entrance a few times and square dancing.

The concert was a blast, one of the better shows I've seen. I also think that was the only time I've ever seen a band with a #1 album on the charts. My tastes were such that this was never much of an issue, although Bowie had a Top 10 album with *Let's Dance* when I saw the Serious Moonlight tour a few years later at Hershey Park Arena.

The concert ended with the band forming a human pyramid onstage, with keyboardist Seth Justman, the smallest guy in the band, climbing on top to extend his right hand, palm up at the audience. The band did the exact same thing in their "Freeze Frame" video. A palm/hand print had been the band's insignia since featuring it on the cover of their *Sanctuary* album a few years earlier.

For how exciting all that was, heading back to Bubba's apartment was a bit of a letdown. Everyone was wasted physically after getting blasted in one form or another for a good part of the day. I don't know why I did this, but I pissed in their bathtub. This must have been around 11:00 or midnight. I hadn't forgotten that I promised my parents I'd come home after the show. It didn't appear that this would happen. George was blotto. Bubba was pretty gone, too. Ray was stoned. If I had any sense, I'd have called my parents and woven a yarn about everyone being too tired to drive back, and it would make better sense to come back tomorrow morning, could I stay overnight please? All things considered, it would have been the safest option.

Instead, I busted Bubba's balls. George hadn't driven his souped-up Nova to the show. Bubba had been home that Saturday and drove all of us down in his car and was expected to drive us back. I think part of the problem also was Ray was a bit of a nut. The guy was large. I knew he was a drug dealer. While he was friendly, he also put out a strange vibe while stoned that made you feel like you might wake up with a steak knife in your back and him laughing maniacally in the corner.

While I didn't pitch a fit, I laid on a thick guilt trip ("Dude, you made a promise to get us home tonight, now keep it!") and wouldn't let up. I recall walking with George along the shoulder of the nearby interstate that ran a few dozen yards from their apartment. He was pissed, too. We wandered like that for a few minutes before we finally saw Bubba emerge from the skanky apartment and yell, "All right, I'll take you home. You bunch of pussies."

We had a muted ride home after a strange, stoned day and a great concert. Once Bubba got behind the wheel, we were fine. The driving helped re-focus him, and I suspect had we crashed out there, I would have awoken the next morning to the sound of Ray's gurgling bong, and another half day of lazing around in a druggy haze before getting the hell out of there. By the time we got back, I was glad I had busted his balls. I gathered he didn't mind taking a long ride with his childhood friends as a brief respite from the wacky lifestyle he had going on at the time.

That was it, the first concert. If only Mom hadn't thrown out that $15 concert shirt I bought that night, featuring The J. Geils Band in that pyramid on the front, and the big hand print on the back. Along with the Bowie Serious Moonlight muscle shirt I later bought, I could have E-Bayed those things for at least $50 a piece to some retro-seeking hipster. Then again, I'm spared the depression of trying them on and having them fit me like a tube top.

1982: Harry Chapin Vs. The Clash

Ms. Murphy was one of my favorite English teachers. She was somewhere in her 20s, pretty, had made a brief excursion to New York earlier to see if she could make it as a model but ended up coming back to Pennsylvania to attend college. She became a teacher in that wave of 60s kids that swept into our school system in the 70s and was known for her big, horsey laugh, which seemed out of place on such an attractive woman.

It wasn't unusual for teachers to bring rock records into class for a theme or lesson, usually English class, anything to kickstart kids into writing a tolerable 500-word essay. I still remember how hard it was for so many kids to write anything. They couldn't formulate their thoughts into even the most basic themes. Your average kid in high school, despite reading plenty of books along the way, newspapers every day, magazines routinely, couldn't put together a single, readable paragraph. There would be kids in high school writing short essays that read like a second grader describing the sky. All because they froze up and viewed this as something they never tried before, and would be judged harshly because they didn't know what they were doing. That rigid sense of impending doom is something that would freeze up any writer.

Thus, some music to open up the kids creatively. For one writing class, she brought in a Harry Chapin album, probably because he was an old folkie she could relate to with good, clear lyrics. Chapin had passed away the previous summer in an automobile accident on the Long Island Expressway. We all knew "Cats in the Cradle," a massive 70s hit absorbed into our musical DNA. But not much else. So she started playing his hit album *Verities and Balderdash* on the portable turntable. (I remember this album because Brother M freaked out over it upon its release in the mid-70s; he zoned in on "30,000 Pounds of Bananas" as the song was about a banana truck having an accident outside Scranton, PA.)

Some kids started to snicker. Folk music. This is the guy who did "Cats in the Cradle"? Oh, man, what next, John Denver? That's how kids are: they laugh at new things they don't understand, and most kids surely weren't on the aging folk-singer bandwagon. Hell, most of them thought Styx was better than The Beatles. I couldn't blame everything on drugs; it was lack of taste.

I don't think she dragged the needle across the record to make that horrible scratching sound, but everything stopped cold. Ms. Murphy freaked out. Tears in her eyes. Raised voice, nearly screaming, words along the lines of, "Harry Chapin was one of the best folk singers who ever lived, and I will not have you laugh at him like this when he died a few months ago. I try to broaden your horizons, and this is what I get in return?"

Most kids were shamed enough to stop snickering and avoid eye contact. We sat there in silence while she quietly wept at her desk, clearly having one of those "where did my life go wrong" moments.

Honestly? I thought Harry Chapin sucked! I've since become more of a fan, have about a dozen of his tracks on the iPod, and get the pop-folk, story/song vibe he had going. His image had that "hairy-chested, pop-folk singer wearing boots and taking himself way too seriously" vibe about him. Started in the 60s by Barry McGuire with his made-to-order topical song, "Eve of Destruction." We'd all seen too many variety shows on TV that would feature this soulful, macho troubadour, like Neil Diamond or Gordon Lightfoot, gazing off in the middle distance, gold medallion gleaming on hairy chest, because his leisure suit with ruffled sleeves was open to his navel, while an orchestra swelled behind him. The whole endeavor felt like a 10-ton bag of shit falling from the sky. While the kids weren't sensitive enough to grasp that laughing at him publicly was insulting to Ms. Murphy, this is what someone like Harry Chapin represented to them.

Ms. Murphy, while not considered hip by most kids, was hip. We had another project where we had to go through old yearbooks and note changing trends among teenagers over the course of years. We found her graduation yearbook around the turn of the 70s, with her stunning picture, and the notation that she loved Jimi Hendrix! This would have been a much hipper personal tidbit to spring on the kids, but she kept it to herself. Kids regarded her as a strict disciplinarian, but I got along with her because I could see this side of her. And understand how someone born and raised when she was would be a huge Harry Chapin fan and hold that music dear to her heart.

But kids are pricks!

Later in the school year in the same class, Ms. Murphy again turned to music. This time, it was our turn. We had to bring a copy of the one song we loved the most, write an essay about why we loved it so much, and read it while the song played in the background. I'm sure I picked a Beatles or Kinks song at the time. "Lola" was my favorite song in the high-school yearbook, a choice that still works for me. Most kids picked the usual dreck floating around at the time: Journey, Styx, Boston, a long-in-the-tooth disco track, Barry Manilow. High-school girls, especially Catholic girls, loved Barry Manilow. The metal kids would bring in Sabbath or AC-DC. It was all predictable. A metal kid wouldn't bring in "At Seventeen" by Janis Ian, even though the song nailed that teenage sense of dislocation he knew intimately as a stoner. Most kids simply weren't generous or smart enough to recognize different people going through the same shit.

There was one girl in that class who freaked out everyone. She was a pretty girl, not a knockout, but I remember her being attractive, a grade behind me. I liked her, but never acted on it, which was my mistake, because I recall us making eyes at each other a few times. I would learn why in this class. The day it was her turn to read her essay, she came in "dressed like a punk."

That wasn't true. She was more new wave, like one of The Go-Go's, but close enough to punk for everyone to think she was punk. She had a neon blue headband, a sexy short leather skirt with black stockings, and a black/gold -striped top that showed off her cleavage. She looked great; all the guys were looking at her differently that day. It later occurred to me that she looked like Pat Benatar without the buck teeth.

Her composition was on The Clash, the song "Lost in the Supermarket" from the *London Calling* album. As noted earlier, at the turn of the 80s, rural America and punk music did not mix; most of those kids thought "punk" sucked. Punk meant anything from The Sex Pistols, to The Ramones, to Elvis Costello, to The Clash, to The Talking Heads ... even to Tom Petty and the Heartbreakers. Punk was really rock and roll and new wave, but had been marketed as such to be the next step in rock. Most kids were entirely comfortable with their standard-issue taste in Classic and Hard Rock, or frilly Top 40 pop.

I was one of five kids in the high school who owned any "punk" albums. At that point, we're talking the most cursory, plain collection: Elvis Costello, The Talking Heads, etc. I'd hear a song like "Mirror Star" by The Fabulous Poodles on WZZO, recognize it as a good pop song, rush out and buy it, which wasn't a mistake. Most kids would have viewed a relatively harmless, tasteful band like this as "punk" because they were British and being marketed that way.

So, this pretty girl brings in *London Calling*, which I bought the day it came out and grew to love. This alone should have cemented even a casual friendship among kindred spirits. She starts expounding on how much she connected to "Lost in the Supermarket" (I did, too, the song on the album that initially grabbed me), a disco song by artistically-expanding punks. Even worse!

Kids sat there stone-faced. If this was on a stage, a huge hook would have emerged from the side curtain to pull her off. Most kids absolutely hated punk/new-wave music. Older fans, people in college and their early 20s, were buying this music in droves. Kids would, too, shortly. The Clash would have a huge hit when *Combat Rock* came out in May 1982, but it took that long, a few years into the 80s, to slowly turn things around. At which point, MTV and synth pop took over, and things grew very strange and hollow.

I'll never forget that pretty girl in her headband, standing there about as alone as she could be, like a true punk, and listening to "Lost in the Supermarket" with her. When the song ended and it was commentary time, most kids were too embarrassed to say anything. I started a dialogue with her about the album, saying how much I liked "Train in Vain," too, and had recently bought the first two albums at Record Town in the Schuylkill Mall. The look on her face: she opened up like a flower, thank Christ, one person out there gets me! We should have left that class, arm in arm, and started a relationship right there, heavy petting while listening to "Police and Thieves" on the stereo console in her parents' living room. I had my head up my ass not to recognize this perfect opportunity: the running theme of my high-school years.

1982: My First Drunk

We must have been seventeen. George was a month older than I was and had been driving at least a year. Like every teenager in our town, we had become habitual cruisers. There was nothing else to do at night but drive around in his souped-up 76 Nova and listen to his tapes, on our way to nowhere, or more likely Holiday Lanes. By seventeen, this was old hat for us. I knew George was already going out to bush parties. (Bush party definition: drunken, rural teenagers congregated in the woods for the purposes of swilling beer, abusing various illegal substances, and perchance to dream, maybe even *getting laid*, to the tune of Ted Nugent and Aerosmith.) Next-door neighbor Bubba, two years older than George and me, had taken to partying a lot with George. It was a matter of time before I got dragged along on one of these clandestine excursions into oblivion.

Sure enough, that summer was it. Summer vacation: the only teenage luxury. I've forgotten what it's like to have three comfortable months off. There have been rare occasions as an adult when I've had three months off, but they were angst-ridden periods of unemployment and eroding bank accounts. As a teenager, I felt a rare privileged to be unemployed. It was a good feeling while it lasted: stay out all night, get up late, live like a low-budget rock star.

All I needed to complete my portrayal was a senseless episode of alcohol-induced self-immobilization, and George was about to provide for that. I can't recall the exact circumstance, but George and Bubba took it upon themselves to head out one night in June and get me wasted.

I didn't know what to expect. Back then in rural Pennsylvania, getting served in most bars was not too difficult for teenagers. Yes, sometimes a kid would get carded, which simply meant he would leave. Most likely, another bar would serve him with nary a wayward glance.

This night would be a double whammy: getting drunk and in a bar. I've since realized that drinking in a bar before 21 is an incredible adventure that becomes mundane once you can get in legally. I think that initial thrill is what keeps many people coming back to the bar: the promise of a wild night, getting out of one's head, experiencing a higher plane not possible sober, even though a simple motor function like standing at a urinal becomes a major feat of physical prowess. As time goes on, the fantasy mellows into the hard reality of avoiding reality.

We picked a non-descript bar a few miles away in Hecksherville so no one would know who we were. It was no problem getting served. We must have looked exactly how we were: three scared, nervous kids pretending to be older. The first thing I noticed after throwing down my first mouthful of Yuengling, the local beer on tap, was how awful it tasted. I'd tasted beer before, but it was dawning on me that I'd have to drink a lot more than a mouthful tonight and not make that squirrel face every time. Like a woman with Tom Petty's face and a great pair of breasts, beer had made its cruel pleasures known to me, and it wasn't love at first sight.

The game plan was to keep moving, one bar to another, town to town, our own magical mystery tour. We must have quietly sipped two beers a piece in that first bar; nothing untoward happened. This being my first time, I didn't know what would transpire and simply felt at ease with the world, which I should have taken as a sign that I was getting drunk, as the situation had my nerves jangled before sitting down at the bar.

We piled back into George's Nova and started blasting Zappa's *Sheik Yerbouti*. We were carrying on like maniacs, howling and laughing our asses off. The simple act of getting served in a bar at our age was a triumph, like breaking into the bank of adulthood and stealing what really mattered. Bubba broke out a bottle of Jack Daniels he had hidden under the seat. We all took turns at it. I thought beer was bad. To this day, J.D., that Tennessee redneck, will beat my ass with a gravel-filled wiffleball bat. Back then, it tasted like gasoline and made my eyes water. After a game sip or two, I handed it back.

Round two: same scene. Walk right in, sit right down, avoid eye contact, and order a Yuengling. It worked again! At this point, we started slipping into moods that, unknown to us then, were drinking roles we'd play as adults. George: existing in permanent state of irritation, scathingly funny, but a little woozy, as if he might doze off before insulting you. Bubba: an instigator, messing with people for no good reason, one moment enjoyable, a pain in the ass the next. Me: pensive, much more open than usual, slowing down everything around me to match my inebriated state of being.

It was around then I noticed my vision getting blurry. The edges were frayed. It was as if the world were turning into a crappy high-school film projector, the sound of flickering celluloid and that gently flashing white light. I've since seen this quality perfectly captured in the Vietnam-Vet party scene in Scorcese's *Mean Streets*, especially when Harvey Keitel tumbles to the floor, and it seems like the camera is dragging him across the floor.

Bored yet? We were too excited by the newness of it all to be bored that night. It started hitting me that this was all it amounted to: sitting down and drinking. Maybe talking to the person next to you. I could do this! There was no great mystery, no "adult" requirement to it that we didn't already possess. Frankly, most of the adults around us were acting like slobbering idiots. We fit right in.

Round three: a little weak in the knees, but still standing. Again, recollections are hazy, but I was still functioning. Back into George's Nova. Some Sammy Hagar on the tape deck this time: *Three Lock Box*. Rock and roll! Or a reasonable facsimile thereof! Bubba passed back the J.D., and this time it went down easy, no sting at all.

Another town, another bar, another barstool, another Yuengling. I wish I could pepper this story with interesting situations and wild Hunter S. Thompson style encounters with freaks and losers, but it wasn't all that dramatic. All the freaks and losers we were running into seemed normal. Maybe that was the secret of alcohol? I was finding this adventure pleasantly smooth, like the cool, clean taste of Yuengling.

Round four: it's safe to say by this point that I was completely trashed. The last thing I remember telling George was, "My gums are going numb." Which sounded like, "Mah goo ah go-uh nummmm." After that, I don't recall saying much of anything for the rest of the night. I might have been communicating with color flash cards in my mind. Yellow, dude, look, it's yellow, can't you see the color in my mind is yellow and respond accordingly? It was also at this point where I first experienced what I can only call stop-time drinking. I've felt this since, but only on a handful of occasions where the alcohol consumption was irrationally large for me.

Stop-time drinking is when you're so drunk that your mind starts working faster than your motor functions, and you wait for your body to catch up to your already-sluggish synapses. This means that you sit there and watch yourself raise your hand to the glass, lift your glass in the air, move your arm back, aim the glass at your mouth, deposit the beer into your mouth, move your arm forward, place the glass on the table, pull your hand from the glass and sit there with a look on your face as if you've invented fire. It's like an out-of-body experience where your soul forgets to leave your body, so you watch yourself from the bar-room floor. Or a mechanical fortune teller in a sideshow booth, snapping into jerking motions with a quarter deposited, the paper message clicking out of the slot reading, "No future."

I was there. My vision was all blurry and colorful; Van Gogh was my optometrist. Sounds fluttered and disintegrated. I could hear and was aware of them but did not respond. Bubba would call out my name, and I would turn my head two minutes later as an after-thought. I didn't focus on taste that first time out, but I would have eaten anything handed to me at that point: a juicy steak, a shoe, dog shit in a hot dog bun. It wouldn't have made any difference.

Round five: this is where the chickens came home to roost. God only knows what George had on the tape deck this time around. Bubba passed back the J.D., and I did my thing. When I passed it back, he and George started laughing hysterically. I had guzzled half a bottle of Jack Daniels as if it were Kool Aid.

I look back on this last bar the same way Napoleon must have looked back on Waterloo. Flaily's in Frackville. It was my ignoble undoing. I had the drill down at this point, but I still can't imagine how any bartender in his or her right mind would have served us. We were three hideously drunk teenagers, barely able to stand, blurry-eyed and slurring. We didn't just get served: the bartender hooked us up with a free pitcher of kamikazes.

For those unfamiliar with this sweet, acidic and highly-alcoholic beverage, a pitcher of kamikazes shared among three grown, sober men is enough to get all three inebriated. The state we were in, it was like Bob Dylan picking up an electric guitar at the Newport Folk Festival in 1965. Whatever world existed before this seemed tame and respectable compared to the depraved one we were entering. We would have booed ourselves but were so drunk we couldn't even say "boo."

I remember needing assistance to walk to the men's room; one of those electric jazzies I see old folks using would have been grand in this situation. Bars should keep an emergency jazzy in the corner for times like this, when one of their patrons has simply gone too far, which has happened nearly every time I've been in a bar. The world was a kaleidoscope at this point. Colors, sounds, smells, everything flashing around me like machine gunshots in a slow-motion war. Getting this drunk is like crawling so far inside yourself that you feel as though you're not looking at the world outside – you're looking at yourself from outside. You do not like or dislike what you see. You do not feel happy or sad. You bob along like a corked bottle on the ocean, the note inside blank.

It was then I found I couldn't walk. I have only been this drunk one other time, my college graduation, a three-day bacchanalia of degradation and good times. George and Bubba had to prop me up, like a wounded war hero, and drag me out to the Nova. The situation was so bad they put me in the shotgun seat that Bubba had been claiming all night. The tape deck in George's Nova had a small digital clock on its face. I remember putting one hand over an eye because I was seeing three or four clocks. George later told me that after a few minutes, I put both hands over my eyes, like the "see no evil" monkey and moaned, "I know what time it is, too late, too late," over and over.

I don't know how, but we made it back home. Bubba asked if I was all right. I grunted. He went into his house as George pulled away in the Nova. I was standing in front of my house, about two in the morning. Even this far gone, I knew I couldn't go home, even though it was five steps away. I had to get myself sober first, whatever it took.

I walked, up to the north side of the schoolyard, bordering the cemetery and woods beyond that. I sat down on some steps and tried to remember what I had for dinner. I couldn't, but that didn't matter. My mother's spaghetti and beef sauce came flying out at this point, all over the steps. A tear-jerking, rasping, gasping moan of a puke. Spaghetti was never meant to come out my nose – this I remember thinking as I watched it happen.

At this point, a car pulled up and stopped. Someone inside said something to me. I don't know how I responded, but I did. The person said something again. I responded again. The car pulled away. It might have been Jesus, the toughest guy in high school or one of Charlie's Angels offering me head. I didn't know. It didn't matter.

As with all such violent regurgitations, the immediate feeling afterwards was sheer, orgasmic bliss. A great feeling. I was still obscenely drunk, but I felt like I could at least walk now. So, I walked, with the attitude that if I roamed around the cemetery, I could get myself straight again. The walk up the cemetery hill was tough. I found myself breathing hard and sweating at the top.

The way down was worse. I had little control over my legs and found myself breaking into a slow jog that turned into a reckless shamble by the hill's bottom. I yelped as I ran, sure that I would tumble over a tombstone and crack my head open on a piece of cold, smooth marble. The night went this way, slow strain followed by frenzied release. I found myself memorizing the names on the tombstones, and feeling bad about the small stones with lambs and angels to signify the death of a child.

After a bit, I sat down near my grandparents' tombstone. Grandma had only been gone a year. I wiped the sweat from my brow with the American flag planted on my grandfather's grave, to honor his time spent in World War I. I held my head against their cold stone. Grandma wouldn't have approved. All I did was hold my head and think the clouded thoughts of a boy drunk and alone. The slight clicking sound I was hearing in the dead of night was my grandparents' skeletons turning over in their graves.

My head started spinning, and I threw up again, although not the Italian delight I had left on the schoolyard steps. It seemed that I was covering all the points of my childhood with vomit, like a dog marking his territory to find his way home. With my hands, I shoveled some dirt over the mess and stood up strong for the first time in hours. I headed back to the house, the sky still thankfully dark, and tip-toed to my room.

Lying down was a major problem. The first attempt made me violently ill, and I ran to the bathroom and vomited again. I found myself pressing my face against cold objects, in this case, the comforting porcelain of the toilet, which felt so good against my hot skin. The bathroom carpet under my legs felt as good a bed as any, and the short, blue shag tempted me greatly. I knew falling asleep on the bathroom floor wasn't right. I got up and went back to my room, this time taking my clothes off because of the sudden cold sweats that soaked my shirt.

I tried lying flat again, and this time threw up on myself. By then, I was genuinely exhausted and decided to wipe myself down with my bed sheet and throw it on the floor. I laid flat, finally, even with my bed seeming to move like Linda Blair's in *The Exorcist*. After a few minutes, the spins passed and I fell asleep.

Looking back at each step of this night, I find myself wishing the story would have ended at each one, beginning with the first beer, and ending with the next morning. In my drunken stupor, I had forgotten that Mom peeked into my room every morning to get the dirty laundry sitting by the door.

The morning after was no different. At eight sharp, she poked her head inside the door. Even drunk, I was a light sleeper, and the sound of the door knob turning woke me, although I kept my eyes shut. I heard my mother let out a slight gasp, then a moment of silence, then the door quietly shut again.

The sun was out, and I raised myself on my elbows to see what she had seen. I was naked, but had managed to put my black, Chuck E. Taylor high-tops back on. My chest was covered with dried brown vomit, which I started scratching off, like a young snake shedding his skin. My sheets were puke-streaked and balled up at the bottom of the bed.

Worst of all, and something I had no control over: I had a raging hard-on, the likes of which I awoke to every morning as a teenager.

This was a fate I would not wish on my worst enemy. My mother had seen me naked with a full erection. I decided that the world as I knew it had ended, and a new world fraught with all possibilities, good and bad, awaited. My head was pounding, and I was still tipsy. My mouth was dry, but I had no urge to drink. Grandma's lecture about the man in hell dying of thirst in a pool of cool water up to his neck came back to me clear as day.

The total failure I felt made me fearless. "What more could go wrong?" I asked myself as I slipped into my pajamas. As I walked into the kitchen, Dad took one look at me and snickered, as did Mom, who was making scrambled eggs, the sight and smell of which made me gag. My hair was plastered straight up, and Dad said I was white as a sheet. He was laughing at, not with, me, because I didn't think I could ever laugh again.

"Had a rough night?" Dad asked as he wiped his face.

I groaned at him. He started laughing again. Mom, whom I found hard to face, shoveled the eggs onto her plate.

"Want some eggs?" she asked. I shook my head and sat down at the far end of the table. My father got up and drew me a glass of water from the tap.

"I'm still drunk, Dad," I said.

He kept on laughing.

"I will never drink again," I lied. Dad couldn't stop laughing. Mom was smiling all the while, too.

"You will, Bill, you will," my father said, "but if you're smart, you won't forget this time."

He finished off his glass of water, then went out and mowed the lawn, far too early. The lawn was his car stereo, and the sound of the mower was his rock and roll. The whining of the motor ate into my skull.

Mom never referred to that morning; I am a far more relaxed and grateful man for it. The thoughts that must have went through her head as she saw me naked, puke-streaked and aroused would surely make a story far longer than this one. I have neither the inclination nor right to tell it.

1983: Hot Rod

In grade school, I had a very strange friend: Hot Rod. We were in the same grade, all the same classes. He wasn't a tough guy by any means, but he took great joy in beating me with branches during recess. Our house was right next door to the grade school. I'd go home for lunch some days. I recall eating french fries drenched in ketchup on a paper plate, watching cartoons, while Hot Rod would stand at the chain-link fence outside the living-room window, pleading with me to come out to play. This invariably meant running away from him as his mind switched into some berserk overdrive, tree branch in hand, a murderous look in his eye.

The odd part being, we were good friends. The branch-beating fetish didn't last long, a few weeks in the second grade, but it's stuck with me all these years later. I wasn't a mean kid by any stretch of the imagination; anyone raised with me can tell you that. I'm not a mean man, got my moods like everybody else, but I'm mostly kind-hearted. Strangers see this in my face all the time in New York City. Not a plus.

I'm still wondering why I didn't try to kick Hot Rod's ass back then: it would have been justified. Kids would get into scuffles, usually over nothing. I can safely say Hot Rod was a nerd. He had a tendency towards large-collared shirts and wire-frame glasses. He'd later be the first of our gang to take an errant stab at a peach-fuzz mustache. Telling him he looked like a dick would only increase his resolve.

I can also recall us laughing our asses off on many occasions. His family was from Belgium, but he was American born. His parents had thick European accents and were sweet people, but this set him apart from the rest of us. He'd often bring postcards and such to class to explain where his parents were from, most of which featured urinating statues and naked guys in helmets. This stuff was comedy gold for grade-school kids; we would piss ourselves laughing over these postcards.

Above all else, Hot Rod was known for one thing: singing. The guy was a natural performer, had a great voice, was taught how to use it from an early age. Music class would find most of us terror-stricken at the prospect of singing solo in front of everyone. It didn't help that we had to sing insane shit like "My Hat It Has Three Corners" and "Fifteen Miles on the Erie Canal." These songs were goofy and unfamiliar to us, but we learned them by heart as we sang them over and over, usually at our desks, so you could lip-synch most of the time. When it came my turn to sing solo, I'd be up there with my head down, blushing redder than a rose, murmuring in a toneless soprano, the idiotic lyrics of "Billy Boy" … while the music teacher hammered away on an out-of-tune upright piano and wondered what in the hell had gone wrong in his life.

Hot Rod would get up there, and he may as well have had a beer stein and lederhosen. He knew the lyrics, and he'd be emoting, waving his arms, walking up and down the aisles. The kids would respond to him as a performer, smiling and laughing, in disbelief that this weird kid with glasses would turn into something else when he opened his mouth to sing. A more serious song, like "Stille Genacht" ("Silent Night" in German, we learned songs in German, not sure why), he'd be leaning over the music teacher's out-of-tune piano, Dixie cup of ginger ale in hand, gazing into the eyes of the prettiest girls in class as he effortlessly reproduced the hushed tone of the night Christ was born in a manger.

As you could imagine, after the class at recess, the tougher kids in the school would sometimes have him in the corner of the schoolyard, in a headlock, muttering, "Sing for me now, songbird." At which point they'd make him sing something like "I like big dicks" in the clenched voice of a kid trying to breath with an arm around his neck. Tough guys were jealous of kids who could sing or dance. It wasn't considered manly. Maybe this is why Rod went through his tree-branch phase with me. He knew I was good enough a friend that I wouldn't reject him for letting off steam, with the knowledge that most of us felt behind the eight ball as kids.

Flash-forward a few years, and Hot Rod is the star of the glee club, with his clip-on tie, ill-fitting blazer and peach-fuzz mustache. We went on being great friends straight through high school, into our early adulthood. I can still recall him doing those nerdy glee-club presentations. It wasn't like glee clubs now, doing hip pop-rock songs from the 70s and 80s. They were doing show tunes mostly, which was ghastly uncool to 99.9% of teenagers at the time. That 0.1% percent are now out of the closet and living happily in major urban areas.

There was one weird thing he did that solidified his geek status. The concept of human beatboxes rolled around with rap in the 80s: guys imitating the sounds of funky drumming and percussion with their mouths. Acapella groups have always done that, but it became a fad in the 80s with early rap music. Hot Rod was doing this long before the trend arrived, in the late 70s. We'd be sitting there, goofing around in home room, when suddenly, Hot Rod would start beatboxing "Love Is Alive" by Gary Wright. To get that wah-wah guitar sound, he'd go "Diddle, diddle" in a high-pitched voice. Along with all the hiccups and hard blowing to illustrate the shifting between beats and chords in the music. It was seriously weird, especially when he'd air drum along with his beatboxing. You may as well have put a sign next to our group of giggling guys, wearing polyester leisure shirts with unicorns on the front, that read: "Ladies, don't bang us." If one of us had shit out pants, it would have been no more or less enticing than this.

No girls in that group, of course! It was rare that guys and girls would be friends, or in any group of friends in high school. The stoners and jocks could pull that off, but kids in the middle didn't. You'd walk around the cafeteria before the first bell (when all the buses pulled in and deposited the kids to wait in there), and nearly every group would be segregated by sex. If kids were dating, then you'd have boy-girl groups. Again, the jocks and stoners would fall into that category, which made them seem cool because they had bridged that gap of casually appearing to have friends of the opposite sex.

Hot Rod didn't get laid in high school; most of us didn't. The few who did, the situations could be awkward and forced, like throwing dicks at a dartboard to see where they'd land. Very few bull's eyes. Usually immature kids with raging hormones making questionable choices that would set the pattern for greater adulthood miscues and transgressions. Most of us fell into that category. The hesitancy and overly cautious consideration I noted earlier has been my M.O. as an adult, too. I don't mean to be negative here. Just ask yourself how many high-school sweethearts you knew who got married, much less stayed that way. I wouldn't call this learning by our mistakes so much as learning to live with them.

I note all this, because Hot Rod was a desperately horny guy. He really wanted to get laid, as we all did, but it was a burning passion for him. I can't recall if he met Cindy in high school or college. It had to be high school, because she was in ours, a few grades lower. I recall thinking she was an average-looking girl. Hot Rod knew her through various church-related singing functions. I don't think he was a burning Born Again Christian, but he was part of church groups that surely leaned in that direction. The kind of groups that had hip, young kids singing Christian-themed pop music as part of their introductory offer.

I'm sure it came to pass that Hot Rod was doing his songbird thing when Cindy laid eyes on him and saw her own little Elvis. He was a funny, charming, guy, too, so that didn't hurt, nerd or not. He was older, which a lot of nerdy, unattractive guys played to the hilt in high school with younger girls. It wasn't until our first year at a Penn State branch campus that they started becoming an item, and then he'd fill me in on the wacky stuff.

Cindy was a Born Again, but one of those typical Born Agains who swung that way because she was a naughty, naughty girl. I recall Hot Rod telling me of a routine date: "Her parents were at a Christian retreat last weekend, so I went over to her house. Knocked on the door and it didn't seem like anyone was home. I let myself in, walked over to the stairs, and looked up. Cindy was standing at the top, naked from the waist down. The way she was looking at me, I knew to go up there. I ate her out on the staircase, and she returned the favor on the living-room sofa."

Hot Rod hit jackpot every time he pulled the lever. I wouldn't call either a nymphomaniac, just two horny kids made even crazier by that thin patina of teenage pseudo-Christianity. He'd give me the weekly lowdown on their escapades, and I couldn't help but be jealous. Cindy didn't seem particularly bright or college-bound. I'm not sure where she went after high school, but it wasn't the same direction as Hot Rod. He didn't look a gift horse in the mouth, that much was certain. That first year out of high school, he was the only guy I knew who was blissfully happy in a no-bullshit relationship. Most guys with girlfriends already had that sense of a heavy anchor around their necks, with what I'd wager were choppy sex lives based on that "wait until we're married" premise. That really meant "this is as good as it's ever going to get as I find penises and sex as desirable as football and the band Rush." Cindy loved sex, Born Again or not.

I recall her being argumentative, too, so that would explain the short-term, super-nova effect she had on Hot Rod's life. I don't doubt that wherever he is now, sitting in an armchair, big-bellied, pondering his choices in life, he thinks back on that one with a smile. That had to be the one relationship where everything spiraled out of control, but he held on, knowing that this was like a star flaming through the night sky that wouldn't do so again for another 50 years, by which time he'd be dead or too old to care.

Hot Rod held on, but the flame went out. I recall some raw years right after that. He didn't go up to the main campus with me, where I had a blast and blossomed. He got a job as janitor at our old high school: sanitation engineer to be exact, when he had been studying engineering at college a year earlier. He'd tell me of scraping dried, bloody tamp-ons from the ladies' room walls with a paint chipper. His stories about feminine hygiene, and the much worse practices of women in their respective restrooms, were legendary. Strange part was he really liked working there!

Things got better after that, but that's also when we started losing touch. When I moved to New York in the late 80s, the only times I'd see him would be when I came home and went to the firehouse, where he was a volunteer fireman in his early 20s, along with a group of a dozen guys who forged a tight drinking group down there for a few years. It was a great place to hang out and get bombed on a Friday night. The place would be empty, so we'd sit in the main hall, where meetings and Bingo normally took place, and drink at the bar, putting a dollar or two in the till for every bottle of Yuengling or Miller we'd pull from the fridge. There was a pool table in the next room, and I can recall more than a few fun nights hanging out with the guys, in a place that felt like the clubhouse we never had as teenagers.

Of course, it was a guy thing, so there was that ongoing sense of all-male camaraderie we had worked to perfection in high school. Not a bad deal in high school, but being at the firehouse routinely also meant no one was moving on to relationships, so I can see that time as a holding pattern/refusal to grow up in a well-meaning sense. A few years later, guys get married, have kids, get real jobs, move away, etc. The loose ends get all tied up, one way or another.

Hot Rod went back to the branch campus, got his Associates in some type of Engineering, and then got a job as an engineer at the plastics factory Dad had worked at for decades before retiring in the early 90s. Being an engineer in that place was a pretty good deal – slightly better working conditions and great pay if a guy stuck with it, which I'm assuming Hot Rod did. I'd also heard he started singing in a country band with his older brothers, which sounds like the exact thing I'd hope he do in his life. Obviously, not appearing on CMT any time soon, but professional enough to play covers at bars, county fairs and weddings for good money in his spare time.

I can see Hot Rod up on stage, a burly guy now, some permutation of facial hair, be it a handle-bar mustache or goatee, plaid shirt, jeans, cowboy boots and hat, with two guys who look like him, blasting through "Friends in Low Places" while the crowd two-steps away and cheers loudly afterwards.

1983: The Blue Shirt

I couldn't stop staring at Lee's peach-fuzz mustache. Laid out in his coffin, he was wearing a dress shirt, hands folded over chest. It was my second wake, as Grandma had died two years earlier, so I knew how to act. Stand over the coffin for a few minutes, contemplate the corpse, then move on for the next in line. I felt insincere and self-conscious, but hadn't yet realized these were standard feelings in the presence of a corpse.

Lee threw me with that mustache. It was so cheesy looking, not like him at all. We had fallen out of touch in the latter half of our senior year of high school when he started dating a girl in that obsessive way teenage boys have. I hadn't seen him in the eight months since we graduated high school. The mustache looked fake. I wanted to reach down and tear it off, miraculously yanking him back to life and out of this charade. But I knew it wouldn't budge. Maybe it's one of those things, I thought, that hair and nails keep growing even after a person dies. Wouldn't Lee also have a five o'clock shadow? The rest of his face was as clean and ashen as a tombstone. Even his acne had disappeared.

Of course, the real reason I focused on his mustache was to deny the horror of one of my friends dying at eighteen. According to the article in the local paper, his grandfather had found him in his mother's garage working on his car with the motor running. This was in February, just after Valentine's Day. The article stated there was "no foul play" in his death. It didn't state that if he were working on the car, he would be doing so because it wasn't capable of running. If it was, he'd be tinkering with the engine, not spending the hours it would take for carbon monoxide poisoning. Lee was an intelligent kid, in no way stupid, which he would have had to been to work on a car in a closed garage. I had heard he had been drinking a lot around that time, so it's possible he could have gotten drunk, went out to the garage, started the car and passed out. I knew that dead was dead, and it made no difference, at least to me. He turned the key and faded himself out of this world.

In our Class of 82 yearbook, the first big picture is of the entire class gathered in a field behind our ugly, pillbox high school. We're all decked out in red and blue, the school colors, kids grouped together in various social castes, cheerleader girlfriends perched on jock boyfriends' shoulders, stoners slouched over and completely ignoring the camera, the great middle class of kids in between saying cheese.

The legend of this picture is Schwamy standing next to me. His shirt is an other-worldly, phosphorescent blue with what looks like a fingerprint on his left shoulder. His shirt was white that day. The photographer took six different pictures. In each one, Schwamy's whipping a bone at the camera, the middle finger of his right hand plainly visible on his left shoulder. I was doing the same, smirking the whole time, only I had my arms folded, with my hands wresting on my biceps, which ended up hidden behind the bodies in front of me. Schwamy had the shit luck of having his middle finger exposed every time. He had the fear of God put into him by the powers that be and was forced to pay for the amateurish alteration to the final picture. In that picture, Tony is on my other side, smiling like a loon, and Lee's on the other side of Tony, grinning placidly.

It is now virtually impossible to see that picture without dwelling on Schwamy's bold statement, as all the other memories around that day simply involve getting out of class and standing in a field for half an hour. Some of what we did back then has become legend, retold in tall tales over the years, in bars and living rooms, relating to a time in our lives that our minds try to tell us was free and easy, but I can usually recall as being wrought with teenage insecurities. With Lee, it bothers me that I can hardly remember a thing about him, and we were good friends for six years. All I can think about is Lee dying the way he did, although random memories of him, like his trademark cackle, surface now and then like passing shadows.

Lee's family had been plagued by bad luck. His parents split when he was a kid, with his father moving his medical practice out of town. He had two older brothers and an older sister. All of them were smart, well-adjusted kids. One of the brothers died by falling off a fire truck during a run when Lee was 12; my mother recalled him crying hysterically at the funeral. A few years later, his sister's boyfriend shot himself in the head in the driveway of his mother's house. All this transpired before Lee fell in love for the first time in our senior year. As with most kids at that time, he had no idea what he was in for. The girl was pretty, a junior with a reputation for being clean-cut and intelligent.

Whatever Lee was with his girl, I had no idea, as they both floated into that stormy, elusive world of teenage romance. Couples like this dotted the hallways between classes, necking openly and leaning as far into open lockers as they could to avoid teachers, the guy holding his arm around the girl's neck in a way that suggested a minor mood swing could find him strangling her. Most of them were doomed and blissfully unaware of it. When the inevitable break-ups occurred, stories circulated of vicious fights and occasional physical threats. That, or the wounded boy would do something melodramatic, like call the girl at 11:00 on a school night and play "Telephone Line" by the Electric Light Orchestra into the mouth piece.

It was routine behavior for a guy in love to become estranged from his friends, and Lee was no different. This coincided with our graduation, so I completely lost touch with him. I went off to the local branch of Penn State, and Lee, like a lot of kids who didn't enter college or the armed forces, had no idea what to do. I only knew he was living at home, with a minor reputation for drinking, and that he had broken up with his girlfriend, hardly an uncommon scenario at the time. Whatever transpired between them, I had no idea, save that it was over. The next time I saw him was in a funeral casket.

A strange thing happened about six years after that. I had moved to New York and was in that annoying mid-20s phase that can only be described as counterfeit middle-age. I still hear it now with twentysomethings complaining about how they feel so old, a concept laughable to anyone old enough to know better. What they mean to say is that they're clinging to a teenage sense of time. They are old by this pitiful standard but haven't adapted to the reality of time, that it keeps moving no matter how one perceives it. They're longing for a world that no longer exists. Couple this with the first few tastes of a real job with no end in sight, and it's easy to feel ancient at twenty-six.

I did what most people do in this condition: drink too much, thinking it romanticized my plight. I wasn't alone; the city was crawling with dimestore Bukowskis. We all had treasured stories of waking up on the sidewalk next to a puddle of vomit, or realizing the redhead at the bar we had thought was a dead ringer for Nicole Kidman more strongly resembled Carrot Top in the morning light.

It was in this state that I took the bus home one holiday season and went out drinking Christmas night with a few friends. Most of the bars were closed, but we found one open, a real dive in Shenandoah we usually never went to, but had no choice.

The bar had a back room with a pool table. We went back there, and sitting in the shadows was Lee's old girlfriend. She had on a spandex, leopard-skin top and a tight pair of jeans. Smoking. Still pretty, but harder around the eyes. She had road miles on her face in ways that I didn't. There was another woman with her with that same slightly used-car look.

At first, we kept our distance. After a few rounds, we found our way into a booth and started talking about legendary teachers and their quirky habits. She had the accent: that thick, Coal Region brogue of northeast Pennsylvania, a hybrid of guttural Eastern European and elongated Irish. That accent, to me, was someone's way of saying they were always going to live there: an unconscious, working-class dedication to home, even if it meant scuffling for blue-collar jobs in a place devastated by the coal boom ending decades before we were born.

We were all flirting. The thought of scoring with Lee's old girlfriend intrigued me, although I knew there was nothing romantic about a drunken romp, no matter what the personal history. As we kept drinking, it became obvious that no one would be getting laid that night. When that bridge was silently crossed, Lee's old girlfriend looked straight at me and said, "You were one of Lee's friends, weren't you?"

I could tell by the way she said it that she'd been sitting on that one all night, waiting for the right time to bring it out. We had gotten paired off at one end of the booth, and no one else could hear us. It wasn't an accusation, just an honest question. I said yes. The hardness drained from her face, and she told me as much as she was willing to tell. They were in love, things had gone wrong, and they simply had lost control of the situation. Lee was a fairly intense kid, and I suspect that played into it. Nobody's fault, just the way things played out. She didn't say when they had broken up, or what the final blow was. Her accent fell away when she spoke about this, and I could see the studious girl she had been in school lurking beneath the surface.

The worst thing she told me, and she wouldn't be specific, was that some people close to Lee had blamed her for his death. This had wounded her deeply, that her first love would have this ugly coda. She confessed in the span of a Def Leppard song on the jukebox. At the end of it, she got up, walked to the ladies room, and I sat there staring at my bottle of Yuengling. She came back a few minutes later, and I could tell that she had been crying. No one mentioned Lee again, and the night played out in that hazy, late-night drunk manner of teenage nostalgia, big plans and small talk.

The last thing I remember was stumbling to the car with my friends, looking over my shoulder and seeing her at the door of the bar at closing time. She waved at me and smiled. It was one of those frigid clear winter nights with no snow on the ground. I had long given up on church, much less the midnight mass my family would go to for Christmas. There was something in her smile and the wave of her hand that made me think of those nights. The tradition at those masses was for the priest to hand out small boxes of chocolates to the children on the steps of the church as we exited. Now that I was so much older, I was getting a hangover and mixed emotions.

At our 10th year class reunion, Lee, and a few other people from our class who had died young, were the objects of a fairly bizarre tribute. I went to the reunion over Thanksgiving weekend at a catering hall back home. Twenty-eight years old, far from middle-aged, but closing in on the brick wall of thirty. This had the potential for a terrible time, but I ended up having a ball. It was great to meet old friends again, and a pleasant surprise to find that life had beaten us down enough that even former nemeses could sit down and commiserate over a few drinks.

Off in the corner was a table with four lit candles on it to commemorate those classmates who couldn't be with us that night. Never mind that 60 classmates showed up from a class of over 200. There were plenty of living classmates who couldn't be with us that night because they hated high school and thought the reunion would be complete bullshit.

Lee was the second candle. The first was a kid named Kyle, one of Lee's friends, who had shot himself in the head at a bush party two months before graduation, inexplicably blurting out the word "cheeseballs" before pulling the trigger. (Connecting the dots years after the reunion, we learned this was a nickname for his then girlfriend, also in our class, and now also departed.) The third was a girl named Carol who had a congenital heart problem all through high school and watched her days fall in numbers even then. The fourth was Danny, who was drunk-driving home on the Broad Mountain from a block party when he veered into the wrong lane and hit another car head on.

DJs had been hired for the night, leisure-suited, morning-zoo types, and it was easy to ignore them so long as they kept a steady flow of Billy Squier, Styx and Journey. Near the end of the party, they started pulling out all the stops nostalgia-wise. I could see they were going to close out the same way every high-school dance ended back then: Skynyrd and Zeppelin, baby, "Freebird" and "Stairway to Heaven." "Freebird" came first, and it got the dance floor crowded with nearly everyone, even when the song sped up and made the guys do more than slow dance.

The song was met with a huge round of applause. From the stage, one of the DJs directed our attention to the table with the four candles, stating that this last song was for those of us who couldn't be here tonight, yes, the special ones who had left us early. I was sitting at a back table having a beer with an old friend when the gentle opening strains of "Stairway to Heaven" echoed through the hall. There was a mass exodus from the dance floor. I could hear people muttering "fuck this" and "this is sick" as they passed on the way to the bar. The DJs had hit a raw nerve with the crowd, who didn't want to see these kids we knew exploited. Death was still a new proposition to us all, especially concerning people who had been the same age as us. The dance floor was empty before Robert Plant crooned his opening line.

I hadn't seen that one coming, nor had the DJs, who snuck behind curtains and speakers when the song ended. There were scattered boos. Most people were milling around the back of the hall, men and women alike toting beer bottles in both hands before the bar closed, muttering about the DJs' tastelessness. Ten minutes later, it was old news.

I hadn't been aware of it, but Lee is buried in the small Protestant side of the cemetery on the hill, 20 feet from where I skipped so merrily that Easter Sunday in 1972. He lived in Ringtown, with its own cemetery, so this was a bit of a shock to me. Our cemetery used to have a wooden rail fence dividing the Protestant and Catholic sides. We loved dangling upside down from it by the backs of our knees, even if it meant getting splinters. The fence is gone, but I gather that sense of separation is still there, embedded in family plots that will take years to fill out.

When we were kids, that cemetery represented life more than death to us. It was a great place to sleigh ride in the winter, careening our Flexible Flyers around the tombstones on daredevil runs to the bottom of the hill. Summer nights found us telling ghost stories by those spooky graves with lit candles on them. I already noted the unfortunate details of my first drunk on the Catholic side late one night.

People came there on Sundays and major holidays to pay their respects. This looked like hell to me. Distracted parents and their ungrateful kids badgering the shit out of each other. Older people weeping by their loved ones' tombstones, planting flowers and kneeling on the grass with dazed looks on their faces. Yapping dogs on leashes marking their territories on tombstone corners.

All they were trying to do was remember. I can see that to do so with honesty and clarity is the best tribute to someone who is gone. A subtle form of hell may be the inability to remember at all, as it leaves a sort of emptiness easily mistaken for freedom. I think of Schwamy's shirt and recognize that my memory is sometimes like that bad touch-up job, substituting an unreal shade of blue for pure white, all to avoid that brazen middle finger of our youth.

1983: The Factory

    Earlier, I mentioned running into Joey Flanagan while working one summer at Dad's factory. For most of my childhood, the factory was a gray mist to me and everyone else in my family. Most guys with families in our town had working-class jobs. Mom would make a sandwich the night before. In the morning, Dad would pack the sandwich and a thermos of ice tea into a lunch pail, maybe some chips, and off he'd go in his dumpy used Dodge. A scenario played out a few hundred times all over the neighborhood. He'd leave for an 8:00 shift and come back around 4:45, usually not in a good or bad mood, sort of "another day at work" attitude I now know all too well. If I was in the yard tossing a football or baseball, he'd put down his lunch pail and join me. It was crucial for Mom to have dinner on the table right around that time. After dinner, Dad would read the paper on his sofa (he owned the damn thing, literally and figuratively), often with quarters and dimes slipping from his pants' pockets that we'd later confess to stealing, and take a nap before a night of TV.

Hardly a bad life (even if all that reads like lyrics from a Kinks song). I'll never quite get the stereotype of working-class guys sitting around a kitchen table, drunk, smoking, wearing a wife beater, and conveniently beating the wife and backhanding the kids. That wasn't us, nor many of the families I knew back then. If there were guys like that, bad news, they'd have been miserable pricks no matter what they did with their lives. It stands to reason that if you're not making a lot of money, then you shouldn't base your personal happiness on money. Not too many people seem to gather that's about the best, most sane way you can get through life, especially in our deranged culture.

Dad would go off to work at this mystical place, and that's all I ever knew about his work life. He never brought it home with him, save for the occasional conversation with Mom complaining about some jerk at the job. The only physical manifestation was a cracked fingernail on his right hand that Mom would file for him every few weeks while we watched TV. As with so many guys in the factory, he got lazy around one of the machines and nearly lost his whole finger. The greatest danger in the factory seemed to be boredom, resulting in the machines reprimanding workers for their lack of interest.

We'd go to his company-sponsored summer picnics, but those were a blast, kids everywhere, a huge cookout, games, prizes. I knew this was a respite to work as opposed to Dad's work. After my first year at the Penn State Schuylkill Campus, I lucked out and gained entry into the summer work program at Dad's factory. My two older brothers had blown off the opportunity because the financial aid they were getting for college at the time (late 70s) was phenomenal, paying for everything associated with school. Not for me. Ronald Reagan took an axe to student aid. I had to make some money if I wanted to have any spending money during the school year, and build a small nest egg for the eventual move to the main campus and an apartment.

The pay was appreciably high for the time for kids in school. Dad was pleased that I took him up on the offer. I was glad to have gainful employment, in a place where I'd have Dad to guide me around and look out for me. There were a dozen other kids in the same program, all in the same boat, working-class kids, sons and daughters of the factory. All of us were attending local colleges, looking to make some good money in the few months before the next school year began in September.

I was assigned to the maintenance division; Dad was in production. This meant we wouldn't have much contact during the day, which was for the best, as I'd see him at breaks and lunch time. Each division had a different color jumpsuit. Production was white, maintenance blue. First day was simply getting assigned two uniforms, work goggles and a hardhat, with a voucher to hit a shoe store in Minersville for a pair of steel-toed boots. It felt cool to be wearing a uniform, something I hadn't done since my Little League and basketball days in early high school.

Maintenance didn't mean sweeping up. It meant maintaining the numerous machines and heavy equipment in the factory: mechanics. I had zero mechanical aptitude thanks to Dad's Saturday-morning sessions. It didn't matter. The expectation was for kids like me to come in and simply assist on jobs, hold a wrench in place, do the grunt work of the department, sweeping floors, handling any small projects that came along that didn't require too much know-how. Another college kid, Ed, was assigned with me, a football player on scholarship to one of those small, northeast Pennsylvania colleges. The guy was built like a little bull and had the vibe of a surfer dude. We got along pretty well. The maintenance building, separate from the main factory, was a ramshackle bunker filled with greasy parts and work machines (drill presses, lathes, saws, etc.), pornography posted wherever possible. I was forever turning a corner in that place to find a poster of a naked woman bent over to show me her perfect ass.

Of course, my main memory of the factory is the guys who worked there, a motley collection of Korean War Vets (Dad was an old timer for sneaking in on the tail end of World War II), Vietnam War vets, younger guys who had no war, some druggy/wastrel types who clearly weren't going to last long and the occasional very tough broad who held her own. Ditto, the occasional black worker. The handful of black guys who worked there fit right in, were in the same boat as everyone else, got along amazingly well with a bunch of white guys who were and still are often depicted as a bunch of bigots. I found that if you worked with someone, you'd learn a lot more about them beyond race. You'd learn the truth of their nature, something more revealing than any surface value or carefully-chosen words.

In maintenance, most of the guys were gritty older Korean War vets who put out the "mechanic" vibe. I often got placed with Pete, a crusty, old guy who looked like Van Gogh with a pair of Wayfarer shades. There seemed to be some bad blood between Pete and Dad, at least that was the factory lore. Pete and I got along great, and he confided in me that he had a lot of respect for Dad, and Dad did vice-versa when I told him I was working with Pete.

The oddest pair was Al and John, two old timers near retirement who were diametrically opposed in personality, but were best friends. I wrote a one-act play about them a year later at school, "Tweety Bird and Blowfish," that the teacher went nuts about, called it the best student play he'd ever read. I simply imagined John's last day at work, and the blow it would lay on Al, who never showed his emotions, save anger and resentment, and seemed to have no one else in his life who could make him smile.

Al was a big, burly guy who clearly drank a lot and would often come in late or phone in sick. When he did come in, he'd sulk at his station by the lathe and generally not be approached by any of the managers until later in the morning. The "leave me alone" vibe he emanated would have intimidated even Lou Reed. I'd occasionally see Al get into it with a manager in a way that suggested asking him to do any kind of work when he was in his dark place was an invitation to an argument.

John was a sparkplug. My first day there, standing there like an idiot in my hyper-clean jumpsuit (most blue maintenance suits were filthy with grease and oil stains), John walked up, hugged me, and cried out, "Billy, you look just like your Dad, I'm John, let me walk you around, you and me are going to be friends." In that play title referred to above, he was Tweety Bird, a vibrant, comical guy, bald on top with pair of coke-bottle glasses that made his eyes look enormous. Small, too, about 5' 2" or so, compared to the grumbly bear of a man Al was. When I got paired off to help John, I knew I was in for a day of philosophical conversations, him talking about his wife and kids (two of whom were my age), a little work, a lot of bantering. Make no mistake, the guy worked hard, but I took note regarding the attitude he had about work, that you should enjoy doing it, see purpose in it whatever it was, and just do it.

How he and Al became best friends, I have no idea. Obviously, they worked in the same department, from what I remember, starting around the same time, too. I should mention that the factory opened for business in the early 60s, and my father was among the first few dozen employees along with John and Al. For that reason alone, I got along with Al as, like so many other guys, he saw my father in me. (I never understood that as I didn't grasp the physical resemblance, but there it was.) It was good to see that whatever Dad's reputation was at work, there were people in this place who treated me with respect as a sign of respect for him. Whatever he was doing there, he was doing it right. The guys who worked with Dad would often joke about the hiding places he had and how he knew how to kill time when necessary. I also got the vibe they were learning their jobs by watching him and were impressed with him. (Dad turned down a few opportunities to move up the corporate ladder as they would have involved pulling up roots and leaving the area. It was a chore to get Dad past the county line. All the traveling he did for a decade in the armed forces wore him out in terms of moving around.)

The main reason Ed and I were hired, beyond helping in Maintenance, was to paint the metal portion of the factory roof. There were a lot of ducts, air vents and piping that were on the roof, and they had to be weather-proofed to avoid rusting. The same with the wooden walk ways that led all along the roof, a sea of gravel with these various metallic configurations sprouting up like towns every few yards. It was a big job and would take most of the summer.

I've never been tanner than those two summers at the factory. Ed and I would go up there around 9:30, take the morning and afternoon breaks, and lunch, but most of the day was spent painting in the summer sun, in an environment that was like a desert. It only made sense to unzip the jump suit down to the waist, use the arms as a belt, and get tanned while we worked. We'd occasionally get busted for this, as one of the maintenance managers would routinely check up on us during the day. Most days were a strange, lonely hum with a paint brush. Everything hummed up there; we could hear the factory working through the sounds these ducts and pipes put out. I can't recall which, but one of the managers was a prick, an older guy, about the only guy who didn't like Dad. I took solace because a lot of guys thought this guy was an asshole. Still, I recall him dressing me down a few times for not wearing my full uniform … in 90-degree heat and direct sunlight on a roof covered with metal and gravel. We didn't take him that seriously, and he didn't take us that seriously because he knew we'd be gone soon enough. (The best managers were usually guys who had worked the factory floor for years and had been promoted to manager. For every guy like that, there were three or four who had always been nothing but managerial types with little or no feel for the men who worked for them.)

The only other major job we had, near each summer's end, was to build "coffins" for burnt-out and old dyes: long, extremely heavy metal rolls that were used to produced sheets of plastic. We were building literally coffin-style casings out of wood to hold these things. I got good at carpentry for a very short while, as we'd have to build first a proportionately-sized box, and then wooden frames inside to hold the bars on each end, finished off with a lid for the casket. We'd also drive these things to a near-by warehouse in a delivery truck (Ed drove as he knew how to drive a stick) and put them away. It was a fun job as it kept us busy for a few weeks, and we had a clear-cut goal each day.

It became a treat to take breaks as it meant human contact in the lunchroom, a gritty, no-frills place: a soda machine, some non-descript tables and metal folding chairs. But it meant "no work" and eating, so it was a good place. Guys would treat me like a novelty there because I was a college kid. I still remember reading *A Tale of Two Cities* on break there, freaking out many a coworker as the *Penthouse* "Letters" Forum was more in line, and trying to choke back tears at the book's end. There was a lot of joking, a lot of complaining. I recall one little guy with a beard who worked on the floor, complaining about the "college kids getting a tan on the roof while I work my ass off." I look back and recognize that even then, I could have kicked the shit out of him. I kept my mouth shut. This guy was an unhappy little prick. My being there was simply a lightning rod for his misery. Had he goaded me into a fight, I would have been booted off the summer program and lost a good chunk of change.

Some of the younger guys tended to be screw-ups. I don't know why as that factory was far above the working conditions of most factories in the area. There was one guy who was borderline crazy, came in one day missing his front teeth, said he had tried to bite a fire hydrant. Whether that was true or not, who knows. He probably got into a fight at a local bar and got his teeth knocked out. You never knew with him. There were some real outdoorsmen there, too. One guy told a story about running over a sea turtle while on vacation in South Carolina. Got out of his car, realized the turtle wasn't dead, so he got out a tire iron and beat it to death to make sure. Threw the turtle in the back of his pick-up and had turtle soup the rest of his vacation.

I'd check in with Dad in the lunch room, but there was no rule that we had to sit together. He was often sitting with his crew, talking shit about the day's work. I'd often be with the maintenance guys, doing the same. I recall one guy, Harry, the biggest character in the factory, who worked in the dye shop. It was Harry's job to clean the huge, smooth iron dyes that would need to go back to the factory floor ASAP so the guys in production could keep pace. In terms of the plastic, think saran wrap, or any rolls of plastic. There were hundreds of kinds of plastic products that would come out of the plant based on orders from manufacturers. One of our Christmas presents at home every year was plastic sleds made in the factory, simply rolls of thick plastic with a handle on one end. If you sprayed Pam on the bottom of those things, they were like rocket sleds.

Harry was always flirting with the women in the place, a big, burr-headed guy who was a lot like Curly in The Three Stooges. (I should also mention that there were a handful of guys there who were Three Stooges scholars, buying books on the comedy trio and having deep discussions on the pluses/minuses of Shemp versus Curly Joe.) We got along great – most people did with Harry. His thing was to crack me up while I was eating. He'd often talk about the various kinds of shits he was taking lately and was so graphic in his descriptions that at first everyone would be grossed out, but after awhile, laughing hysterically. He got me a few times, laughing so hard I couldn't finish eating. The guy was naturally funny. The odd thing? The dye shop had to be the worst job in the place. Harry would spend all day burning dried plastic off hot metallic rollers, some a foot long, others a few feet long and weighing tons. He'd stand there with a blowtorch and a putty knife, melting and scraping off burnt plastic with noxious fumes coming off as a result, then cleaning each roller with a mix of ammonia and acetone. A toxic, hot place to work. But Harry had a blast most days. Again, another sign to me that if you put your mind into your work and took pleasure in doing the job, you could do anything and still manage to be reasonably happy.

The few women in the place were usually middle-aged, hard as nails on the outside, but matronly once you talked to them. They had to be tough to put up with a room full of belching, farting guys talking sports and hunting all day. There was one girl, my age, and beautiful, who worked on the floor. She wouldn't give me the time of day. Blue eyes, long brown hair, a great body that was perfectly shaped in her white jumpsuit. The other guys said she wasn't married or dating. The other college guys came up zero with her, too, not sure if it was a college thing or she didn't want to deal with any guys in that place. She seemed out of place there, like a model who had wandered in for a Billy Joel video and was now held prisoner.

The few guys in the place around my age, in their early 20s, did tend to be standoffish with the college guys doing summer work. My quiet response was usually, I can't help that. Every older guy I worked with in the place told me he'd break my legs if he ever saw me come in there as a full-time worker. Not that it seemed like a bad place to me to work. They were coming at it from years of experience, while I was a novelty worker there for a few months in summer, not being exposed to the same pressures in work or life that they had going on. There was one college guy who did just that, said, I'm not going back to college in the fall, I like it here. A big guy, bigger than Ed. He thought he would be better off in a factory and was forcing himself to go to college for his parents' sake, who were non-too-pleased with his choice. In terms of factories, there were much worse ones to work in than that one.

I'll never forget at the end of the first day, after getting out of my uniform, standing there in my shorts and t-shirt. I was by the work clock, waiting for Dad, had punched out, was saying goodbye to the people I'd met that day as they left. As I bent over to untie my work shoes, I found that I couldn't. My stomach would cramp up each time. This was the first time I'd been on my feet for eight hours. When you go to school, you're sitting most of the day. The summer jobs I'd had before, all lawn mowing and landscaping, were a few intense hours of physical labor followed by immediate rest. This was eight hours of standing with two 15-minute breaks and a 30-minute lunch hour, but otherwise on my feet all day.

Dad and I would drive to and from work together in his shitty Dodge, and that's when we'd talk about work, the people I should befriend, those I should watch myself around. He was one of the "founding fathers" of the factory, so he knew it inside and out. I got to see a whole different side to him because of the summer job, and I liked it. I could see that he was well-respected at work, that he wasn't known as a shitbird or the type of pain-in-the-ass coworker I've since dealt with many times over. The guy who was quiet and tight-lipped around the house was gregarious at work in his own way. I knew his work ethic came from the Depression and fighting in World War II.

I got to see and feel what it was all about: the working-class. Honestly? It's not that much different from the white-collar world. I see it this way. In a factory, the worst things going are the drudgery and the boredom of doing what becomes a very basic job. (Believe me, most jobs in a factory are nowhere near as basic as you'd think, take years to perfect, but once you do, become dull.) Factor in dealing with deranged managerial types and never having any job security as low man on the totem pole in the corporate hierarchy (despite doing the work that must get done to produce goods). In an office, the worst things going are psychological warfare, hideous hunger games of status and one-upmanship, mental stress that's often far worse than anything you'd find in a factory, dealing with deranged managerial types and never having any job security no matter where you are on the corporate totem pole.

They both have their pluses and minuses. Having experienced both, I can see the one thing I miss about factory work is the sense of camaraderie: the feeling of being in something together, that you're not out to screw over your coworker, not because it doesn't get you anywhere, but simply because it's the wrong thing to do. In offices, there's far too much tension and class distinction to feel that close to too many coworkers. The thing about office work? Repeat after me: *more money.* That's pretty much it. There were a few lay-offs in Dad's tenure at the factory, but his seniority protected him from ever losing his job. I'm glad he had such a relatively good work life, and he was glad to have me there in his factory for a few summers, provided I was only visiting. He would have considered it defeat in some sense had I stayed. I would have, too. One of his finer accomplishments was watching his kids ascend to the middle class, even if he had no idea of the perils that awaited us!

1984: Born Again

In one of my classes during my sophomore year at Penn State, I sat behind a girl who caught my eye the moment I saw her. P was a real looker, probably still is: long, brown hair, warm eyes. What really struck me was how friendly she was, a sweet-natured, open individual. It didn't take me long to go crazy for her. In the process I found out she was the sister of a high-school classmate whom I liked but wasn't good friends with.

Unlike her brother, she had gone to Cardinal Brennan, and therefore inhabited that parallel universe in our towns. With P, it was taken a step further. Much to my chagrin, she was thinking about becoming a nun. Most people picture teenagers having sex from the age of 14 onward, but that didn't happen for me and P, considering she was on the verge of forfeiting sex all together in the service of the Lord. As we got to know each other, I also learned she was often depressed, with a surprisingly negative self-image. There were some good times, driving around that summer in the Yellow Hornet station wagon, listening to Springsteen's *Born in the USA* dubbed to cassette. The song "Bobby Jean" brings me right back to her and those times, kids driving around aimlessly, enjoying the moment and each other's company.

When I was at her house, her parents treated me like boyfriend material. In reality I was dealing with a young girl with a lot of craziness going on, much of it tied in with her strong sense of Catholicism. I suspect they were hoping I'd guide her into the boy/girl realm of things. But who knows. Like many homes in the Coal Region, the house was a papal shrine: pope and cardinal dolls, pictures of Jesus, numerous saints and popes all over the walls, enough crosses to guarantee safety from even far-sighted vampires. It was like going to church in a row house; I felt like kneeling and crossing myself every time I went through the front door.

My mother met her when I brought her around, and her immediate response was, "Now that's a beautiful girl." She was really impressed with P, as was everyone I knew who met her. The idea was stick with this one: if you're patient and things work out, you'll have a great woman on your hands and might even end up getting married.

One big roadblock was that a few months into this, I was ready for my junior year, i.e., moving from Schuylkill campus to the main Penn State campus, a huge transition for a kid who had never been away from home for more than a week. That summer was busy, between working in Dad's factory, trying to find a place to live, getting mentally prepared to be on my own for the first time and trying to keep this indefinable situation together with P.

I'll always remember that one odd night, a few days before moving, late August, sitting by my grandparents' graves in the cemetery, wondering what was going to happen with us. It stays in my mind mostly because I also had the first hemorrhoid of my life, a burning little knot above my asshole that was causing me much consternation, as I had no idea what it was.

I remember her assuring me that whatever strange thing we had going on wasn't going to stop, and that I could easily come home on weekends to see her. It was one of those nice, little moments where one person reassures another that all would not be lost due to a looming change. That it took a place on a clear, late-summer night, in a cemetery, only adds to the odd, touching quality of it.

That weekend I packed my meager belongings (most importantly, stereo, records and Radio Shack Nova 40 headphones ... this equipment would open the world for me in the next two years). Packing up, I realized Mom was in worse shape than I was. She looked like the Grim Reaper was coming to take me away to hell, as opposed to taking the next logical step in my life. Dad was fine. He laid $50 on me when he caught me outside loading up the station wagon. Mom made the mistake of trying to show me a map of how to get to State College, when I had already been there half a dozen times and knew the way. (The first time was my junior year of high school. Uncle Bill took me up for a Rutgers-Penn State game. Walking around the campus was incredible, a strong premonition.) Mom got hyperactive and strange upon departures. She opened up the atlas in front of me, and I snapped, "Mom, stop it. I know the way. You don't have to show me anything." She slammed the atlas shut and stormed into the cellar.

I had to go. Dad shook my hand and gave me advice on what to do in case the car broke down. It was overcast but not raining. In that moment I felt about as empty and afraid as a kid can get. I was leaving. Right now. Leaving home, possibly for good. I knew it had to happen. I didn't want to go, but I had to. Where's Mom? I'd had it. I was a bundle of nerves, wound up, and didn't feel like waiting around. I got in the car, turned the key and started driving.

The last thing I saw, looking in the rear-view mirror, was Mom, standing in the middle of our street, waving. She had run up from the basement when she heard me pulling out but was too late. That moment sticks with me now. I thought about driving back to say goodbye, but let it go.

I didn't weep as I left my hometown. That came a few towns later as I left Mount Carmel, when it sunk in that I was leaving home, alone in the world for the first time, which I've since come to realize is a wonderful, liberating feeling. I had no clue at the time. That feeling, as I recall, was confusing. Beat to shit, but knowing full well there was no turning back, and it had to be done.

As it turned out, that first year at the main campus was a blast. I found myself writing a weekly humor column for the newspaper, with a whole new stable of friends on the same wavelength. I found a very tolerable part-time gig in the German Department and kept a high GPA, despite much drinking and folly. No urge to screw around, as I was locked in on P in that way only love-struck teenagers can be. Believe me, opportunity knocked more than a few times! All the while, I was staying in touch with P and seeing her most weekends. Towards the end of that school year, in May, she had to come up to the campus herself as it was coming up on her turn to transfer in the fall, which had me elated.

I had noticed, especially when I got home that summer, she was even more troubled before regarding religion. I think she may have dumped the idea of becoming a nun all together, and was feeling a void or strong sense of guilt over it. Whatever it was, I could tell things were off in a way that had nothing to do with me. She seemed inconsolable.

That was a bad summer. The factory had an off year financially and dumped the summer college program, a cash cow for me the past two years. I tried my hand at two separate jobs, doing sales help at a commercial lumberyard and working midnight shift at a local lumberyard, but quit both within a week, the second after the first night. I can look back now and should have told myself, "Bite the bullet and do this shit for two months then go back to school." At the time, both jobs seemed unbearably ragged. The commercial place was run by two guys who made clear their disdain for college kids. My last day there, I noticed their toilet had clogged after taking a dump in it. I left it that way as a token of my gratitude. The second was a night-shift job where fellow employees, mostly guys I went to high school with, told me recurring stories of guys sawing off various body parts, with the hopeful rejoinder that if you put the severed fingers in a plastic bag on ice, they could still get you to the local hospital in time to have them re-attached.

I spent most of that summer watching MTV and killing time, while I sensed this thing with P was fading out due to her increasingly cloudy mood. One day after my birthday in June, she showed up at my house elated. We went out walking, and she had told me she met a new friend, E, who was part of a new church that had a wonderful message to tell regarding our lord and savior, Jesus Christ. Immediately, I could feel something was off. It was as if a car had shifted from reverse to third in terms of her mood, no transition whatsoever, an immediate decision to be overwhelmingly happy, which had me understandably suspicious.

P brought around her new friend E, and I knew things were going to devolve. E was a full-on, stereotypical Born Again: dumb as nails, disdainful, judgmental in a very bad, condescending way, and on a pendulum swing in life, going from one extreme to the other. She told me her story of Jesus saving her from drugs and that despicable way of life. Right then, I figured she'd be better off on drugs. The pendulum swing was a hallmark of more than a few Born Agains I met in the 80s: people who were on the verge of flushing their lives down the toilet due to some type of self-abuse, who suddenly had this magical transformation that made them full, whole, superior rays of light and happiness. I could tell P was overly impressed with E and her routine, when I could clearly see that E was a bullshit artist, not someone I would ever allow into my life, and very bad news for me. As it turned out, very bad news for everyone, as P's parents, still staunch Catholics, weren't having any of this Born Again nonsense.

P and I had always been honest with each other, and the following day I told her what I thought, that E didn't strike me as someone I wanted to be associated with, and that I thought the whole Born Again thing was a form of mental illness. P got offended, said I better get used to it, because E was like a big sister to her now, and that if I couldn't accept Jesus in the same way, there was no place for me in her life.

I'll give myself credit. Even with those odds against me, my immediate response was, "There's no place for me in your life." Not that I felt any need to define or stand up for whatever form of spirituality I endorsed. It was much more that I wholeheartedly rejected her form of spirituality and her new guide, who would have had a field day at the Salem witch trials. This news was like water off a duck's back to P, which unnerved me even more. There was nothing holy or human about how she was acting.

When I got back from that meeting, I told Mom, well, you won't be seeing P around here much anymore, and I told her why. She was disappointed and angry. Being a Protestant who had married into a family of Catholics, she knew well the sting of religious dogma and was as skeptical as I was. But she said, all for the best, think how much worse this would be if you'd gotten more involved and something like this had happened.

Of course, these things never stop on a dime. While I distanced myself from P, we stayed in touch, although I can't remember how. The killer for me was that when she came up to the main campus, she immediately found a Born-Again boyfriend and was hanging all over him the few times I saw her. Understand this was a woman who had previously been so uptight about physical contact that just to get her to hold hands was a major triumph. She finds Jesus, bam, next guy in line, provided he has the same rigid belief system, has this beautiful girl hanging all over him as if he was a rock star and she a groupie.

As those first few weeks at school moved on, I recognized how lucky I was to have removed myself from the situation, because whatever Born Again road she had gone down, she wasn't coming back any time soon. The first few weeks of that summer, I was sitting around waiting for her to come to her senses, to see through E's smoke screen, but it didn't happen.

I recall the last contact I had with her, late October my senior year of college. We sat on the main lawn of the campus, can't recall what we'd even talk about at that point as I had distanced myself. At one point, she recognized a fellow Born Again walking by on the other side of the lawn, told me to watch her stuff and ran over to celebrate His name and share good tidings.

While she was gone, I noticed she had a writing tablet and had been jotting something down. I couldn't help but look over to read it. It was a letter to E that read like something a Manson family member would write to Charlie. I can't recall exactly what, but along the lines of, "My life since accepting Christ, and you as my guide, has been nothing but profound joy and happiness, oh, thank you for saving me from eternal damnation." I can't recall the exact content, but the tone and word choice were very much along those lines. It was repetitious, too, the only message, with nothing genuinely personal noted.

I heaved a spiritual sigh and said to myself, "Thank you, Jesus, for removing me from this situation before I got too far in to leave of my own free volition." Because if I had become engaged or married to this woman, and something this bizarre and troubling had occurred, that would have been a much more painful ordeal. She came back and found me in a noticeably brighter mood as I had realized some endings made sense and were for the best. I bid farewell, and that's the last time I saw her. As I got up to leave, I felt so goddamned unencumbered that I nearly started skipping.

2004 Postscript: Blue Christmas

I took the bus home from New York a few days early that Christmas, for no other reason than I could. Late summer, Dad had been diagnosed with esophageal cancer in the fourth stage. All that year, he had been losing weight and looking good. After a few months, it became clear to Mom the reason for this was because Dad was having trouble swallowing food, and she finally hounded him into seeing a doctor.

Just before Christmas, Dad had been in the hospital about a week, after having a fitful December. He had been in for a few days, starting Thanksgiving afternoon. He nearly missed the dinner from being in bed, and I recalled feeling a sense of helplessness when I guided one of his arms into his flannel shirt, that was now three sizes too large. Things got a little better after that visit. He came back home for two weeks, then started struggling with what would eventually be identified as pneumonia. This came after a few horrible months of radiation treatments, and a failed attempt at chemo that had Mom convinced the doctors were trying to kill him.

I don't think anyone knew how to gauge the situation, doctors or family members. A lot of denial was going on.

As it was, I got off the bus and got myself to the hospital after some lunch. Seeing Dad in a hospital bed like that was shocking. He had lost about 100 lbs., was gaunt and thin in a very bad way, looked like he had aged 30 years since I last saw him a month earlier. He had on an oxygen mask and was watching the History Channel, about the only normal thing going on. He was coherent but was so weak that getting out of bed wasn't possible. I can tell you, seeing the man who brought me into the world and raised me in this sort of condition was a knockout punch to my senses. Numbness was the reaction, not sorrow or weeping; I didn't know what to make of it. If there's any emotion, it's anger at seeing someone I cared about so weakened, and I didn't know whom or what to get angry at.

We talked about the weather, Penn State football, how things were going in New York, etc. The usual stuff. Nothing dramatic. About the only dramatic thing was when I mentioned the bus ride back. He said, "You'll have to get the ticket that takes you straight by the house. I don't want your mother driving all the way up to Hazleton to get you." This was his way of saying he wasn't going to be able to do that anymore, a pleasant ritual for both of us over the past few years. We learned more about each other as adults in those half-hour car rides than we ever did as father and son.

I was there for an hour and figured I could do this every day while I was back there. Assuming this was a bout of pneumonia he was going to beat, I'd go back to New York two or three days after Christmas. I told Dad I'd be back tomorrow. He said, no, come back the day after, I think your mother and sister will be here a lot tomorrow, we'll have more time then. With that, I got up, and when I did, Dad stuck his left hand out and grabbed mine to shake hands.

Right there, he was saying goodbye, because we never shook hands. I gathered that he must have been worried about his situation if he was touching me like that. It unnerved me, but I didn't make a huge issue out of it and left. Not having any experience with a parent who was deathly ill, I had no idea how long he had left, whether or not this was a scenario that would play out many times over the next year. This was all new to me, and I didn't like it.

The next day passed, and nothing major happened. The major topic with Mom was how we were going to have Christmas Dinner with Dad in the hospital. The following day was one of those strange off-season days in December, in the mid-60s and drizzly. I decided to head down to see Dad that morning, then do some shopping. I got down there mid-morning to find his room dark, with the door halfway closed. Not sure what that meant, but I walked in anyway.

Dad was asleep, naked, with his sheets kicked down around his knees. Again, it was shocking to see him that thin. I pulled the covers back up over his chest, but made sure not to wake him. His breathing was labored, a raspy snoring, but I could tell by the rhythm that it was regular, sounded like he was in a deep sleep. My mind played a very bad trick on me: I thought Dad's eyes were open, and they were black slits. What it really was: he had lost so much weight that his eye lashes now looked much bigger than they had when his face was more full. I hung around a few minutes, realized there wasn't much to do there, used his bathroom, took one last look to make sure everything was still cool, then left. No nurses were around, and I didn't talk to anybody.

I went shopping at the Walmart in St. Clair, picked up some DVDs, drove home, about an hour after I had last seen Dad. It was drizzling. As I got out of the car, Sister K pulled by in her car with Mom in the passenger seat. Mom rolled down her window and said, "Your father died. We're going down there to take care of things."

The look on my face must have been something else. I couldn't believe it. A few seconds passed, as I was too bewildered to respond.

"I saw him sleeping about an hour ago," I finally said.

"Well, they called 15 minutes ago. It just happened. Do you want to follow us down?"

"No. I'll stay here in case anyone calls. Not much I can do anyway."

"All right. See you later."

So I went inside and chopped potatoes and celery for the turkey stuffing. Had to do something. This was the start of that period of shock between his passing and the wake. Those days floated by in a haze. Had some bad nightmares that first night, really horrible dreams about the black eyes. I tried to do normal things. I went out that night and had drinks with old friend George, who bought me a round when he heard the news. (He knew where I was at as both his parents had already passed on.)

Mom learned that Dad had woken up that morning, told the doctor he was going to die that day, asked if he could get an extra dose of morphine to get some sleep, and told him not to alert the family, because they'd been through enough. He took the back door, which was his way, not to be a burden, or the center of attention in any way. I don't think my life would be any better now if Dad had jolted awake while I was there and told me he was about to die. Gone is gone. Wherever you're going, no one is going with you. You're not going to jam revelations and finality into those last few minutes. Those left behind will deal with this the rest of their days, whatever does or doesn't happen.

Thank God for our relatives from Virginia, Aunt Ruth and her two sons, Randy and Jackie, who came up early to spend time with us. They always have a very relaxed, open demeanor, and the three of them coming up to comfort Mom was a tremendous boost, nudging all of us back to the impending reality of a wake and a funeral in short order.

I should also note how great everyone was in the neighborhood, although we had to deal with a constantly ringing phone. All the neighbors came by at some point to offer food and condolences. The night of his passing, someone must have walked through our kitchen door, left a case of Yuengling Black & Tan, and left, unannounced and uncredited.

(On the other hand, the crack team of physicians who had assembled to save Dad's life ... not one of them acknowledged his passing in any way. No cards. No follow-up calls. Nothing. The only person from the medical profession who reached out was our family dentist! The only note we received from the doctors was on the day we buried Dad: a bill from the radiologist. Mom tore it up and never paid it.)

I was expecting the wake to be a very bad time. It started out that way. They had Dad done up like The Scarlet Pimpernel. His face had way too much pancake make-up on it, and he looked deeply unnatural and off. I'd seen this before at other wakes and funerals, but it's jarring with a family member, to have his body on open display in a living room while people come by to pray and offer respects. If Dad had been at his own wake, he would have taken one look at himself, sighed, and left.

Once people started arriving, I felt a sense of purpose I hadn't in days, grateful and relieved to see friends of the family and relatives, even some strangers to me. That whole process had a healing quality to it. I felt like a lost kid before, but during the wake, I was grasping what it would mean to go on without Dad. I simply had to, and the best thing to do was absorb people's sympathy and keep moving forward.

The funeral was the exact opposite of the day he died: a bitter cold, windy, sunny day. Everything in stark clarity as opposed to that murky weather in which Dad passed. The weather suited the purpose of putting him in the ground. So many odd little moments that day. The absolute worst was having Mom and the rest of us kids gather at the funeral home for the closing of the casket. Frankly, I wish I could have avoided the situation, but it was tradition. We all stood there looking like we'd been shot, because we had in a sense. Before closing the casket, Mom let out a sob and touched Dad's face for the last time. Whatever weird shit I've gone through in my life, very few things are going to affect me as much as that moment. This was horrible to go through, but in that hard way death has, it was necessary. The priest had earlier said something to the effect of, "Living on after a loved one has passed is like walking alone through the desert." Truer words were never spoken, I thought. That's exactly how I felt those few days.

We then drove to the cemetery on the hill in our town and went through the funeral ceremony. The last time I had done this for a family member was with our grandmother over 20 years ago, a hot summer day. Back then, I had no concept of what was really going on, or how adversely affected my father and his siblings must have been.

Dad's funeral went off without any issues, then we all went to the awful Dutch Kitchen Diner for the post-funeral dinner. This is a minorly famous diner off Interstate 81 in Frackville that serves the worst food I've ever had. Really, I don't know who eats there regularly, but the place has been around for decades, so someone does. As with all bad places, I stuck with a burger and fries. Everyone ate, and talked, and then we all parted, a few of the relatives coming by the house to say goodbye. The sense of relief after all this, to clear everyone out of the house on a sunny, cold-as-hell winter's day and have silence, was palpable. It felt all right, the calm after a storm. Mom was devastated, we all felt like shit, but at least we were still around.

All these rituals, the wake, the funeral, the dinner, while I thought they were bullshit before, now made perfect sense. They were ceremonies allowing people, step by step, to put death into the context in which one could say goodbye, seek comfort, grasp the finality of seeing someone who is no longer there, close the lid, and put the box in the ground. A very hard, black-and-white proposition. But when you pass through each step, it guides you in the right direction, that a life has ended, as it must, and we move from one place to another, with the understanding that the coffin lowered into the ground is the fork in the road where the rest of us keep walking.

In some odd, comforting way, it felt like Dad was "around" after he died, more than when he was alive. That's because I was thinking about him all the time, carrying his memory in my bones, in my mind, in my voice, in my face, where people kept seeing him in me. I remembered the horror we felt in our early 20s to discover that we were "turning into our parents," as if this was a fate worse than death. Death has a funny way of recasting your fate. Now, the way his memory felt was like one of those sunny, windy days in early spring where cloud shadows sweep across the fields. I came to describe death as shadows, but not in a bad way. Look at the sidewalk on a sunny day. There's a shadow following you around. Sun goes down, shadow disappears. Then it comes back under the street light. This is how I live with memories of Dad now. Fading in and out, but always near.

Here's something I would do routinely while Dad was alive, but it takes on new meaning after his passing. As noted earlier, Brother J was the only one of us boys who took to Dad's mechanical lessons, usually delivered way too early on Saturday mornings for comfort. Whenever I see J working on a car, I approach him warily, stopping a few feet away while he grunts and grimaces away in his grease-covered overalls.

"Whatever you're doing," I say slowly, for emphasis, "you're doing it wrong."

I don't think Dad ever said that, but he was infamous for critiquing J when he undertook mechanical projects of his own. Nothing worse than bothering a man performing hard physical labor. Dad knew this as he would chafe at anyone talking to him while he was in the heat of battle with a faulty brake pedal. J knows I'm making fun of how Dad armchair quarterbacked his mechanical skills.

"That's the ticket," J responds, using one of Dad's favorite catch phrases, "I'm always wrong."

2013 Postscript: Another Blue Christmas

T.S. Eliot may have April down as the cruelest month, but given my track record, it's got to be December.

Mom had been cheating the grim reaper for a long time. Smoking since she was a teenager circa the late 1940s. Granted, not heavily, but for a smoker to breach into her 80s, this was good fortune. As it was, an aneurysm that she knew was coming took her down with only a few-minute warning. Luckily, this was at home with Brother J and Sister K right there to help her on the way out. She didn't know this was it, but surely must have pondered this as a dizzy spell came over her that morning. Sister K sensed the finality of what was happening, whispered her goodbyes, to which Mom snapped, "I'm still here!"

But not for long. Her final retort mirrored the sort of irritable jab I'd been giving her for years, when she was being too motherly, generally right before I was leaving for a bus to go back to New York. She'd try to pawn off free samples of cold medicine that she had picked up at The Dollar Store, or was still telling me about food in the refrigerator that I should know about. Feeling like a snotty, 15-year-old, I'd snap at her, not harshly, but a tone of mild annoyance in my voice. She'd say, "No need to get upset." Only adding to my guilt-ridden "I'm a dick" thought balloon.

A few minutes later, she'd give me a hug – a practice she began in earnest after Dad passed, making sure we touched one last time before I got on the bus. My trip at Thanksgiving was a perfectly normal visit with Mom in good health and spirits, only the usual aches and pains she always complained about. I'll see you again in about a month, I said, understanding that Thanksgiving was late this year and Christmas was right around the corner. In that moment, all was forgotten and forgiven, I was her wayward son, leaving again, but soon to return.

Too soon, only days later, this time with her in a coffin at the funeral parlor, rushing home in those cloudy days before the wake. As I learned with Dad's passing, a wake for someone that age is a good time, or as good a time as you're going to get in those few brutal days of assimilating the death of a parent. Mom's was no different, relatives and family friends showing up, paying respects, laughing over old memories and stories they had of Mom's generosity, her way with stray dogs and random people. Mom was like an open book who put everyone she met at ease, a talent I can tap into sometimes, but never as effortlessly as she did.

What really got me through was seeing my namesake, Uncle Bill from Point Pleasant, into his 90s, blind in both eyes but otherwise getting by physically. Due to his advanced years and need for assistance, I gather it hadn't made much sense to get a seeing-eye dog. As it turned out, my Cousin John, who moved back to Point Pleasant in the 90s, stepped up to serve as his eyes in public. If you've ever seen a boxer enter a ring at a large match, this was how John and Bill got around: John leading the way while Bill put his hands on John's shoulders and shuffled in place behind him, matching his steps. John would quietly announce, "slight incline on your left" or "three small steps coming up followed by a hard right."

I can't tell you how good it felt to sit and talk with him all those years on, with him still as sharp as ever beyond the blindness and old age. How good it made me feel to know I was named after him, and this guy was still around, not giving up despite taking an ass-kicking from life, as we all will if we hang around long enough. And of course, John, being a good son, stepping up and ensuring that his father could have some kind of life, honoring him on the other end for the years he raised him. You see these kind of things, it reminds you that our lives are filled with unassuming people doing selfless things as a matter of course with no reward, save the returning of a favor.

Afterwards, a lot of the relatives came back to the house. We had such a good time, having a few beers in the kitchen, laughing, warming our hands around that glow I'll feel the rest of my days when I remember her and what she meant to me and so many others.

Knowing she didn't suffer, like Dad did through months of radiation, went a long way towards easing that horrible pain of seeing one of your parents decimated by disease and harsh medical treatment.

As Uncle Bill got me through the wake, Uncle Bob got me through the post-funeral dinner, thankfully at the Mineshaft Café in Ashland as opposed to the Dutch Kitchen Diner. He was clearly devastated that his little sister had passed on. Seeing him work through his emotions gave me insight into how that next step will be. As blown out as I was, I could see that being able to handle a parent's death was one level, and dealing with the death of a sibling would be another. And hopefully not something I'd have to experience for a long time. It comforted both of us to talk about Mom and how they were raised, as I understood so little of that part of her life. It made me recognize that calm, warm sense of reasoning she had was something her parents must have taught her and Bob as kids. If it was any solace to Bob, all of us understood this about her and tried to emulate this quality as much as possible.

The strangest thing, and I wouldn't even call it the hardest, was seeing Mom's chair empty. This persistent reminder of an empty space. The first thing I did when I got home the evening after Mom died was get in her car so I could get some groceries for the next few days. I checked the trunk. Before I left after Thanksgiving, she had asked me to put a clear garbage bag of aluminum cans in there for her to donate to her friend from the animal shelter, who could sell the aluminum for scrap. Something she had done for years, the same way she held on to plastic bags from shopping excursions to give to the local Goodwill store.

Nothing in the trunk. Meaning she had gone out over the weekend and dropped them off. Her life had been normal right up to the very end. I sat down in the front seat and found her ghost again: the rear- and side-view mirrors turned down. When I repositioned them, it reminded me of when I left for college, and how I looked in the mirror and saw her run into the street to wave goodbye. Mom had her mirrors turned down so she wouldn't have to see cars behind her. She wasn't doing 20 mph on the road; she was doing the speed limit. From what I gather driving back there, doing the speed limit, even in a rural area like that, will generally find one or two angry drivers riding your ass, wondering why you're not doing 60 mph in a 45-mph zone.

It was quite an experience to take her grocery shopping in that car. She didn't believe in seat belts, the same idiotic way Dad didn't, and at that point in her life had a slight hunch to her shoulders. She hovered too close to the dashboard on the passenger side, but it made her seem like she was more attentive. She marveled that I could carry all the grocery bags out of the trunk in one trip. I gathered doing this was getting harder with each passing year, but it meant a lot to her that she could still do these things on her own.

On a trip a few years earlier when we were going down the candy aisle, she gazed over the small bags of individual chocolates. I could see all the Hershey bags were on sale and said, "Mom, I know you like a bargain, why not get a bag of Hershey Kisses?" She frowned at me, "After what they did to their workers when they moved their factories to Mexico? I'll never eat another piece of chocolate from Hershey again, those bums."

She meant it! Beyond that, every item she bought was measured against the item next to it on the shelf. If it was a cent or two cheaper, get the cheaper item. Donuts? Get the bag near or past expiration as it's marked down. Ditto, bread and ground beef, or any perishable item on the shelves. Keep the coupons handy, because a lot of them will be doubled at the register.

The hardest part of her death was acknowledging the absence of someone who would have given her life for mine. Two nights after the funeral, I found myself alone in the house, TV off, as I sat in her chair for a few minutes. This was strange for me as she *owned* that chair when she was alive; no one else ever sat there. Save for the cats who instinctively crawled on her lap to doze. (It's *my* chair now when I visit.) I had gone out shopping earlier to get out of the house and bought a Sharper Image harmonica at Boscovs. There was a display for peculiar little gifts next to the cash register; the harmonica was $5.00, so I figured why not. I pulled out that harmonica from the shopping bag and started blasting on it. Sister K's cats scattered. I loved the sound it made, how easy it felt, as though I was moments away from being able to play "Amazing Grace." (I still don't know how to play the damn thing.) After a few minutes of wheezing away, I started laughing at the absurdity of it. Mom would have found it funny, too.

I felt surrounded by her shadows. The weird tube socks that she'd cut the feet out of and use as wrist and elbow supports when her aches and pains acted up. I'd tell her,

Mom, you can buy Ace supports in the drug store that are made specifically for this reason and will last the rest of your days. I already knew her Depression-era answer: why spend money when I can make the same thing for free at home?

She still had the cheap windbreaker with my name emblazoned on the left breast that I gave her back in the 90s, from that lousy outdoor advertising company I worked at for a few years. The polyester pants that she'd wear until the elastic waistband frayed. The cheap sun visor she must have bought at a yard sale in the 80s. The cool keychain for her car with her name on it that one of us bought as a gift back in the 70s that I still touch every time I grab the keys for the car.

Old lady things. Later, I would wander through family pictures I had scanned into the laptop from previous visits. Mom teaching me how to write on our chalkboard before I even got into Kindergarten. (As a result, I would catch shit from grade school teachers for holding my pencil "wrong," not realizing I was holding it like a piece of chalk. I still do.) My favorite picture, Mom's high-school graduation photo, in which she looks stunning, where I can see vestiges of her face in mine. Mom smiling broadly that fateful Easter Sunday in 1972, still a knockout at 40.

It wasn't all good memories. I recalled an episode that still haunts me. This must have been around 1978, just as I was getting salty. Early summer. The Philadelphia Phillies were becoming a great team, with players like Steve Carlton and Mike Schmidt hitting their stride. Mom knew how much I loved the team, and while she was out shopping one day, came across a Phillies t-shirt that she thought I would love. A white t-shirt, with that big fat 70s Phillies "P" in the middle, with the word Philadelphia on top in red letters, and Phillies on the bottom. A basic look that she knew suited my taste.

She brought it home for me, apropos of nothing. Not my birthday, hadn't done anything to merit her surprising me with a gift. The kind of thing a good mother would do for her son. She came through the door as I was lazing on the couch, watching TV. I got a surprise for you, she said, and pulled out the t-shirt, smiling. I took one look at the shirt and blurted out, "I'm not going to wear that."

The look on her face crumbled as if I had shot her through the heart. It wasn't hurt. It was hurt and rage. That she took the time and money to think about me, and like the spoiled brat I could be at times, it didn't register. Along with the lack of manners to not graciously accept a gift. She dropped the shirt on the floor, shook her head, tears welling up in her eyes, and walked away.

I picked up the shirt a few minutes later, after pretending it wasn't even there. It suddenly occurred to me that I liked it. I really liked it. Sure enough, I'd wear that shirt constantly, until I out-grew it a few years later. I never apologized to her for the way I had acted. Place the episode in context. I was too young to drive, so that meant I had to tag along with Mom when she went to the mall. Kids at that age tend to be resentful that they're still dependent on their parents. I'd make sure when we were in the mall that we weren't walking together, lest one of my equally emotionally-stunted friends saw us, and what would they think of me walking with my Mom. I was willing my parents *not* to exist because doing so acknowledged that I was still a child.

Fast forward to a memory that had nothing to with Mom directly, April 2006, walking down the main drag in my neighborhood in Astoria, New York on a Saturday morning. I saw three people walking ahead of me: a mother and her two sons, who looked to be roughly 10 and 15 years of age. The 10-year-old was skipping and holding his mother's hand as they walked. Both of them looked over-joyed to be with each other. The 15-year-old walked a dozen feet in front of them, sullen, wearing his standard-issue hooded zipper sweatshirt, turning around every now and then to make sure they were still there.   He looked like he wanted to be anywhere but there.

I remembered how both kids felt, at different points in my childhood. Mom was still very much alive in 2006, so I adopted a scolding tone in the imaginary lecture I had prepared for the 15-year-old, knowing that saying anything to him would be a waste of time. After December 2013, I could tell him with all certainty, one day you will turn around and not see anyone behind you to feel embarrassed over, or run towards when you realize what a fool you've been.

About the Author

William S. Repsher grew up in a small town in northeast Pennsylvania and has lived in New York City since 1987. If you've made it this far and still haven't concluded that he's an imbecile, let this picture serve as the last nail in the coffin.